THE CAMBRIDGE COMPANION TO BRITISH LITERATURE OF THE 1930s

The 1930s is frequently seen as a unique moment in British literary history, a decade where writing was shaped by an intense series of political events, aesthetic debates, and emerging literary networks. Yet what is contained under the rubric of 1930s writing has been the subject of competing claims, and therefore this *Companion* offers the reader an incisive survey covering the decade's literature and its status in critical debates. Across the chapters, sustained attention is given to writers of growing scholarly interest, to pivotal authors of the period, such as Auden, Orwell, and Woolf, to the development of key literary forms and themes, and to the relationship between this literature and the decade's pressing social and political contexts. Through this, the reader will gain new insight into 1930s literary history, and an understanding of many of the critical debates that have marked the study of this unique literary era.

JAMES SMITH is a Reader in English Studies at Durham University. His most recent book was *British Writers and MI5 Surveillance, 1930–1960* (Cambridge, 2013). He has published widely on other aspects of 1930s literature and culture, such as on the censorship of 1930s film societies, and on government surveillance of radical literary magazines during the decade.

A complete list of books in this series is at the back of this book.

THE CAMBRIDGE COMPANION TO BRITISH LITERATURE OF THE 1930s

EDITED BY

JAMES SMITH
University of Durham

CAMBRIDGE
UNIVERSITY PRESS

CAMBRIDGE
UNIVERSITY PRESS

University Printing House, Cambridge CB2 8BS, United Kingdom

One Liberty Plaza, 20th Floor, New York, NY 10006, USA

477 Williamstown Road, Port Melbourne, VIC 3207, Australia

314–321, 3rd Floor, Plot 3, Splendor Forum, Jasola District Centre,
New Delhi – 110025, India

79 Anson Road, #06–04/06, Singapore 079906

Cambridge University Press is part of the University of Cambridge.

It furthers the University's mission by disseminating knowledge in the pursuit of
education, learning, and research at the highest international levels of excellence.

www.cambridge.org
Information on this title: www.cambridge.org/9781108481083
DOI: 10.1017/9781108646345

First published 2019

Printed in the United Kingdom by TJ International Ltd. Padstow Cornwall

A catalogue record for this publication is available from the British Library.

Library of Congress Cataloging-in-Publication Data
NAMES: Smith, James, 1981– editor.
TITLE: The Cambridge companion to British literature of the 1930s / edited by James Smith.
OTHER TITLES: Cambridge companions to literature.
DESCRIPTION: New York : Cambridge University Press, 2019. | SERIES: Cambridge
companions to literature | Includes index.
IDENTIFIERS: LCCN 2019028688 (print) | LCCN 2019028689 (ebook) | ISBN 9781108481083
(hardback) | ISBN 9781108646345 (epub)
SUBJECTS: LCSH: English literature – 20th century – History and criticism.
CLASSIFICATION: LCC PR471 .C34 2019 (print) | LCC PR471 (ebook) | DDC 820.9/00912–dc23
LC record available at https://lccn.loc.gov/2019028688
LC ebook record available at https://lccn.loc.gov/2019028689

ISBN 978-1-108-48108-3 Hardback
ISBN 978-1-108-70379-6 Paperback

Contents

Notes on Contributors

KRISTIN BLUEMEL is Professor of English and Wayne D. McMurray Chair in the Humanities at Monmouth University. She is author of books and articles on modernist and intermodernist writers and artists, including Dorothy Richardson, Stevie Smith, George Orwell, and Gwen Raverat, and co-editor of *Rural Modernity in Britain: A Critical Intervention* (2018). She recently brought back into print an edition of *Blitz Writing* by Inez Holden (2019).

JOHN CONNOR is Lecturer of Literature and Politics at King's College London. He is finishing a book manuscript on the mid-century historical novel and researching a second project on the second-world reception of British Communist, proletarian, and anti-colonial writing. His work has appeared or is forthcoming in the *Journal of Modern Literature, Modernist Cultures, The Review of English Studies*, and in several edited collections, including *A History of 1930s British Literature*.

BENJAMIN KOHLMANN teaches English literature at Hamburg University. He is the author of *Committed Styles: Modernism, Politics, and Left-Wing Literature in the 1930s* (2014) and of *Speculative States: British Literature, Institutionality, and Reform* (forthcoming). With Matthew Taunton, he has co-edited *A History of 1930s British Literature* (2019).

PHYLLIS LASSNER is Professor Emerita in The Crown Center for Jewish and Israel Studies, Gender Studies, and Writing Program at Northwestern University. In addition to essays on interwar women writers and on Holocaust representation in literature and film, her publications include two books on Elizabeth Bowen, *British Women Writers of World War II, Colonial Strangers: Women Writing the End of the British Empire*, and *Anglo-Jewish Women Writing the Holocaust*. Her most recent book is *Espionage and Exile: Fascism and Anti-Fascism in British Spy Fiction and Film* (2016).

She was the recipient of the International Diamond Jubilee Fellowship at Southampton University. Forthcoming essays concern Holocaust refugee art, Polish post-Holocaust film, and British Holocaust theatre. She serves on the Advisory Board of the Space Between Society as well as the Education and Outreach Committee of the Illinois Holocaust Museum.

ISOBEL MADDISON is a Fellow of Lucy Cavendish College, University of Cambridge, where she is a College Lecturer and the Director of Studies in English. She works primarily on female modernism and on the connections between modernism and popular fiction. She also has interests in women's writings of the Great War. Isobel has published on the work of Dorothy Richardson and Katherine Mansfield, and is the author of *Elizabeth von Arnim: Beyond the German Garden* (2013) plus several essays on this writer. Since 2015, Isobel has been President of the International Elizabeth von Arnim Society.

MARINA MACKAY is Associate Professor of English and Tutorial Fellow of St Peter's College, University of Oxford. Her books include *Modernism and World War II* (2007), *The Cambridge Introduction to the Novel* (2010), and *Ian Watt: The Novel and the Wartime Critic* (2018).

PETER MARKS is Professor of English at the University of Sydney. His books include *George Orwell the Essayist: Literature, Politics and the Periodical Culture* (2011), *Imagining Surveillance: Eutopian and Dystopian Literature and Film* (2015), and *British Literature of the 1990s: Endings and Beginnings* (2018).

TYRUS MILLER is Dean of the School of Humanities and Professor of Art History and English at the University of California, Irvine. He is author of *Late Modernism: Politics, Fiction, and the Arts Between the World Wars* (1999), *Singular Examples: Artistic Politics and the Neo-Avant-Garde* (2009), *Time Images: Alternative Temporalities in 20th-Century Theory, History, and Art* (2009), and *Modernism and the Frankfurt School* (2014). He is the editor of *Given World and Time: Temporalities in Context* (2008) and *A Cambridge Companion to Wyndham Lewis* (2016). He is the translator/editor of György Lukács, *The Culture of People's Democracy: Hungarian Essays on Literature, Art, and Democratic Transition* (2012) and series co-editor of Brill's *Lukács Library* series.

JANET MONTEFIORE is Professor Emerita of the University of Kent. Her books include *Feminism and Poetry* (1987, 1992, 2004), *Men and Women*

Writers of the 1930s (1996), and *Rudyard Kipling* (2007). She is editor of the *Kipling Journal* and Chair of the Sylvia Townsend Warner Society.

GLYN SALTON-COX is Associate Professor of English and Affiliate of Feminist Studies and History at the University of California, Santa Barbara. He is the author of *Queer Communism and the Ministry of Love: Sexual Revolution in British Writing of the 1930s* (2018), and his work has also appeared in *Modern Language Quarterly*, *Critical Quarterly*, *Comparative Literature*, *Keywords: A Journal of Cultural Materialism*, and *Twentieth-Century Communism*. He is currently working on a monograph on the cultural history of the lumpenproletariat.

JAMES SMITH is Reader in English Studies at Durham University. His most recent book was *British Writers and MI5 Surveillance, 1930–1960* (2013). He has published on various other aspects of 1930s literature and culture, such as on the censorship of 1930s film societies and on government surveillance of radical literary magazines during the decade.

MIA SPIRO is Lecturer in Jewish Studies at the School of Critical Studies, University of Glasgow. She is the author of *Anti-Nazi Modernism: The Challenges of Resistance in 1930s Fiction* (2013) and has published articles on Jewish literature, Holocaust narratives, and the representation of Jews in the years leading up to the Second World War.

JUDY SUH is an Associate Professor in the English Department at Duquesne University. Her research interests include modern British fiction, travel literature, war literature, postcolonial literature, and British film. Her book *Fascism and Anti-Fascism in Twentieth-Century British Fiction* (2009) focusses on extremist politics and British modernist, middlebrow, and popular literature. She has published articles and chapters on Isabella Bird, Jean Rhys, D. H. Lawrence, Christopher Isherwood, Virginia Woolf, Agatha Christie, and others, and is currently working on a book manuscript on war, race, and politics in modern British travel narratives.

CLAIRE WARDEN is Senior Lecturer in English and Drama at Loughborough University. Her research interests include modernism, performance practice, and physical culture. In addition to numerous articles and chapters, she is the author of three monographs: *British Avant-Garde Theatre* (2012), *Modernist and Avant-Garde Performance: An Introduction* (2015), and the 2016 British Academy–funded *Migrating*

Modernist Performance: British Theatrical Travels through Russia, as well as co-editor of *Performance and Professional Wrestling* (2016).

TIM YOUNGS is Professor of English and Travel Studies at Nottingham Trent University. He is the author or editor of several books, including *The Cambridge Introduction to Travel Writing* (2013) and *The Cambridge History of Travel Writing* (co-edited with Nandini Das, 2019). He is founding editor of the journal *Studies in Travel Writing*.

Introduction

James Smith

On first glance, British literature of the 1930s offers a natural subject for a dedicated *Cambridge Companion*. As critics have often remarked, few other decades seem to claim such a compelling status as a distinct literary-historical era, with a series of political events, aesthetic debates, and emerging literary networks providing an identity that goes beyond the normal convenience of decade-based periodisation and into 'one of literary history's most stable and flourishing concepts'.[1] With just a slight nudging of the boundaries, the 1930s is often characterised as running from 1929 until 1939, from the stock market crash of 1929 until the arrival of the Second World War, with September 1939 marking an end to the epoch as the world entered a cataclysmic new phase.[2] Between these acute flashpoints came a climate of social and ideological tensions. Capitalism and the old order were, for many, at the point of collapse, making sections of the intelligentsia restless for alternatives. Events such as the rise of Nazism and fascism, the outbreak of the Spanish Civil War, and the instigation of the Popular Front of anti-fascist activism added urgency to these debates. Consequently, much of the literature composed in the period engaged with distinctive ideas and concerns, such as how writing could best grapple with these new social issues, whether writing should be propaganda or art, and whether an author could remain detached or needed to commit to a firm political cause. A wave of new authors rose to prominence on the back of such impetus and a new constellation of literary publications, cultural associations, and literary movements took shape. Even authors who had established their reputations in previous eras were drawn into these concerns, as they joined debates about the appropriate roles of literature and art, or were forced to confront their own social and political views under the darkening shadows of the approaching war.

Yet, if this above narrative provides a convenient framework for analysis, and if library shelves provide various books attesting to the 1930s as a well-established concern, this can also obscure the extent to which the decade resists attempts to too-neatly tie down its parameters and preoccupations in a single survey. For what is contained under the rubric of 1930s writing has proved to be a contested concept, the subject of revisions and competing claims, as various 'myths, counter-myths, and [. . .] "intermyths"' were constructed and then assailed over the past eighty years.[3] Such debates were begun by key cultural actors in the decade, in manifestos and publications that sought polemically to seize the central literary ground for certain writers or types of art, and were consolidated in many of the memoirs and essays that followed the decade's end, hindsight allowing authors and observers to privilege certain themes in their retrospective gaze.[4] George Orwell's 1940 essay 'Inside the Whale', for example, crafted a powerful yet contentious case for the politics and preoccupations of the decade's literature – a case that, as the various engagements with Orwell in this present volume attest, continues to provoke heated debate to this day. And across the latter half of the twentieth century, academic critics followed suit, as the 1930s consolidated its identity as a distinct field, along with the reputations of certain authors and movements who became focal points of study.

Perhaps most influential in shaping later perceptions of the 1930s as a field of literary-historical study was Samuel Hynes's account, *The Auden Generation: Literature and Politics in England in the 1930s* (1976). In this landmark work, the 1930s was framed as the realm of a specific generation: the young writers born after 1900, predominantly English and middle class, displaying some degree of continuity across their consciousness and types of art, and with W. H. Auden at the heart.[5] The importance of Hynes's work was immense, eloquently advocating the value of this as a literary-historical moment and setting out many of the themes and lines of analysis that continue to influence the field to this day. But this book was still only a partial view, with the organisation around Auden and his networks obscuring the wider range of authors and modes at play. Consequently, in the decades that followed, the revision and reconsideration of what made up 'literature of the 1930s' continued in various critical waves. If listing just a few central markers of these debates, they might include Valentine Cunningham's *British Writers of the Thirties* (1988), a monumental work that greatly expanded the decade's literary frame, and Janet Montefiore's *Men and Women Writers of the 1930s: The Dangerous Flood of History* (1996) and Jane Dowson's anthology *Women's Poetry of the 1930s* (1996), works that asserted the importance of the many women writers who had been missing from earlier accounts. Others, such as Andy Croft's *Red Letter Days: British Fiction in the 1930s* (1990), provided crucial attention to the left-wing literary climate that had otherwise been overshadowed by critical focus on the Auden group. And, as has been suggested,[6] the titles of many of the essay collections dedicated to the era – John Lucas's *The 1930s: A Challenge to Orthodoxy* (1978), Steven Matthews and Keith Williams's *Rewriting the Thirties: Modernism and After* (1997), Patrick Quinn's *Recharting the Thirties* (1996), Antony Shuttleworth's *And in Our Time: Vision, Revision, and British Writing of the 1930s* (2003) – give the sense of a general and continued flux of scholarship: challenging, rewriting, recharting, and revisioning a constant critical preoccupation as competing versions of the decade were mapped out.

As the structure of this *Companion* attests, many of these once-pioneering positions have now become the norm: women writers, for example, no longer occupy a separate terrain and are instead integral parts of the literary spectrum addressed. But this expansion of the literary history of the 1930s is still a process in action, spurred by a range of new scholarship and new interdisciplinary approaches that continues to re-evaluate the 1930s on other vectors. Perhaps most notable is how developments in the field of modernist studies have changed the way the literary history of the 1930s is conceived. For much of the twentieth century, the 1930s had an awkward position in the overarching categories used by critics to periodise the modern period. It came after the peak of the 'high' modernism of the opening decades of the twentieth century, with authors such as T. S. Eliot and James Joyce having already released many of their most influential works in the early 1920s. Yet it was not generally of the ironic 'postmodernist' sensibility that came to categorise the post-war literary fields. And, as Benjamin Kohlmann's chapter in this volume explores at greater length, the frequent turn towards overt politics in 1930s writing grated against the politics and practices of much academic literary criticism of the twentieth century, which privileged characteristics such as detachment, ambiguity, and indeterminacy as the most rewarding literary traits for close reading and scrutiny.

Consequently, this awkwardness sometimes led to critical marginalisation or neglect: as one study assessed in 2003, looking back at the status of 1930s writing in the wake of poststructuralist literary theory, 'Though the debates arising from various strands of theory had considerable impact on the kinds of texts studied at undergraduate level, there was no obvious or compelling place for the thirties in the new English.'[7] However, in the past twenty years or so, with the expansion and recalibration of twentieth-century periodisation under the rubric of the 'new modernist studies', the 1930s now provides a major focal point for this field of research, with critical concepts such as late modernism, intermodernism, or 'the first media age' all treating the 1930s as a crucial part of the modern literary terrain rather than some sort of outlier.[8] Of course, the expanding concept of modernism is only one context of the current research on the 1930s: continued interdisciplinary work in media history and cultural history, the recovery of neglected or overlooked authors, developing understandings of political subjectivity and identity, the study of middlebrow and popular forms, and the expansion of postcolonial perspectives are just some of the other aspects of modern literary scholarship which are greatly expanding the figures and themes now understood as part of the literary history of 1930s Britain.

It is at this junction that this *Companion* is located, bringing together a team of international scholars to explore the literature of this decade in light of these scholarly concerns. Sustained attention is given to the writers most frequently anthologised as '1930s writers', but the *Companion* also casts a wider net, with chapters analysing the development of key literary forms and modes as well as the relationship between literature and the decade's pressing social and political themes. This informs the way the chapters have been structured. The *Companion* opens with a sequence of chapters addressing how the major literary genres evolved across the decade, before later chapters expand out into analysis of broader contexts and themes. As noted, in many literary-historical accounts, poetry has been considered the decade's most significant literary form, as exemplified by the achievements of W. H. Auden and his circle. In the opening chapter, Janet Montefiore uses the influential anthology, Robin Skelton's *Poetry of the Thirties* (1964), as a pivot for reflecting upon the shifting perceptions of the decade's poetry, assessing the status of those canonised by inclusion in such anthologies as well as the importance of other poets whose significance has only more recently been recognised. For Montefiore, the works of Auden, Stephen Spender, Cecil Day-Lewis, and Louis MacNeice continue to form the core of the decade's poetry, as their best writing still stands as a powerful 'creative response to the moment of the Depression, the rise of fascism and of the Popular Front, and the imminence of the Second World War'. But this chapter also balances their work against that of figures such as Nancy Cunard, Naomi Mitchison, and Stevie Smith, as well as the 1930s work of the major poets of the older generation such as T. S. Eliot and David Jones. What Montefiore's chapter therefore conveys is not a dismissal of the Skelton-era canon but instead a demonstration of how expanding perspectives have allowed the contribution of other poets to the decade's most pressing debates to be more clearly seen.

Given the prominence of 1930s poetry in many literary histories of the era, the novel risks being a secondary focus for critics, but, as Marina MacKay's chapter on the 1930s novel notes, 'the literary novel in the 1930s no longer suffers from this kind of neglect, even if some individual writers do'. As MacKay shows, the 1930s novels of Graham Greene, Evelyn Waugh, and Christopher Isherwood attest to the literary energy of 'canonical' authors. Equally, the novels of Lewis Grassic Gibbon and Naomi Mitchison made major contributions to the Scottish literary renaissance, and Elizabeth Bowen, Stevie Smith, Jean Rhys, Rosamond Lehmann, and Patrick Hamilton are a further range of important novelists writing in the 1930s who have increasingly come to scholarly attention. Across this diverse span of authors, MacKay detects certain core tendencies that might be taken as characteristic of these 1930s novels. For one, there is a blurring of cultural modes: 'the "literary novel" of the 1930s routinely overlaps with a range of forms, including the novel of intrigue, memoir, satire, dystopian fiction, historical fiction, and the fable.' And underpinning this impulse is a political and social consciousness, with MacKay finding 'few corners in the 1930s novel into which the threat of violent upheaval does not intrude' – a lingering sense of 'self-destruction' giving the literary novels of this decade a distinctive, if unsettling, edge.

If poetry has overshadowed the novel in critical accounts of the 1930s, then drama is often relegated to a distant third place (if indeed achieving a place at all), with conventional British theatre historiography typically viewing the 1930s as a conservative era with little of the interest offered by the new wave of the 1950s. Claire Warden's chapter, through mapping the range of dramatic activity, challenges this omission, assessing that, while drama lacks 'a connecting through-line' for easy critical assessment, the 1930s saw a variety of theatrical innovations in 'terms of mode, genre, site, technique, and personnel'. In this reading, the 1930s stage becomes an important site for three core developments in British theatre history. It was the site of 'a small, turbulent, but fruitfully fertile experimental theatre scene' in which developments such as Expressionism gained some foothold in British theatre practice, most significantly in the work of Auden and Isherwood. It was also an era which saw important innovations in performance as a political form, with organisations such as the Workers' Theatre Movement and Unity Theatre 'creating theatre that challenged typical political and theatrical orthodoxy'. And drama remained one of the most significant cultural modes turned to by the public amidst the darkening social and political climate, with 'amusing or diverting theatricals (detective stories or historical dramas, for example) remain[ing] the most popular forms of performance', with figures such as Noël Coward at the peak of their success, and with radio drama increasingly providing a significant new outlet for plays. What emerges from this chapter is therefore a renewed sense of the importance of drama as cultural terrain in the 1930s itself and the decade's role as an incubator for many of the key debates that would come into fuller focus in later eras of modern theatre history.

The next sequence of chapters focusses on the wider contexts of literary markets and aesthetic debates. As Peter Marks's chapter on publishing and periodicals makes clear, the 1930s was a particularly disruptive decade for the economics of literary publishing: by the end of the decade, many major venues had undergone transformations or had simply ceased to exist. Yet it was also the era of some of the most profound moments in modern publishing. The decade's vibrant periodical culture saw the founding of literary-critical ventures such as F. R. Leavis's *Scrutiny* and the continued operations of T. S. Eliot's *The Criterion* – periodicals which indelibly changed modern perceptions of literature and criticism. The 1930s was also the site of key moments in modern left-wing literary publishing, such as the operations of *Left Review* and the Left Book Club, and of pioneering feminist venues such as *Time and Tide*. The book trade also responded to the times, from the evolving work of 'high' cultural venues such as the Hogarth Press to perhaps the most enduring development, the launch of Penguin Books, whose price and format fundamentally transformed the economics of publishing and accessibility of literature for a wide audience. While the restrictions of the Second World War curtailed much of this activity, it did not erase the achievements of the 'boom time' of the 1930s, which achieved an impact that continued long after the decade's close.

As has already become clear from the above account, the 1930s presents slippery territory for many traditional literary hierarchies. It is no surprise, then, that the 1930s was a key moment in the 'battle of the brows' and has consequently become a significant site for new scholarship on middlebrow and popular writing. As Isobel Maddison's chapter analyses, 1930s literature faced a range of cultural upheavals and challenges. Cinema attendance continued to grow exponentially, buoyed by the rise of the 'talkie' film, with the medium now providing a popular and affordable form of entertainment and attracting 'audiences novelists could only dream of'. The decade also saw a growth in affordable lending libraries and a desire by many readers for lighter, escapist material to offset the foreboding political and economic climate. Consequently, the literary marketplace saw a 'proliferation of novels written predominantly for a wide readership, particularly of middle-class women'. This boom in commercial fiction generated profound 'anxieties about cultural authority' in intellectual circles, with critics often disparaging the work of middlebrow authors, which, as Maddison shows, has led to the undervaluing of successful and widely read 1930s writers such as Elizabeth von Arnim and Rosamond Lehmann. And, beyond the 'middlebrow', Maddison's chapter also examines the crucial contributions of the 1930s to popular fiction and culture, such as its role in the so-called golden age of detective fiction, as well as being a crucial moment in the development of the espionage fiction genre – all evidence of the extent to which the 1930s was the site of a vibrant fiction-writing scene that has too often been excluded from 'highbrow' literary-historical accounts.

On the other hand, as Tyrus Miller's chapter on 1930s modernism makes clear, this developing literary climate did not simply supplant the prior generation of the avant-garde, no matter how much new authors and networks clamoured for prominence. As Miller puts it, 'it was not as if, on the final day of 1929, the key representatives of high modernism had simply vaporised', with writers such as Woolf, Wyndham Lewis, and Eliot continuing to publish significant work, showing how this supposedly residual movement continued to develop across the decade and interact with the British literary scene. More broadly, Miller also sees the 1930s as a site in which modernism's impulses evolved in other ways: in many of the 'mixed mode texts' that were written and published in the decade by authors such as Eliot and Auden, and in the forms of visionary and surrealist poetics developed by a range of authors such as Herbert Read, Humphrey Jennings, Len Lye, Charles Madge, David Gascoyne, Dylan Thomas, George Barker, and Hugh Sykes Davies. Miller's chapter therefore pulls apart the modernist/anti-modernist divide that has often been used by 1930s writers and later critics as ways to separate the decade from earlier phases of literature, showing the complex ways in which the 1930s and modernism were unavoidably intertwined.

The next group of chapters considers the role literature played at the intersection of the decade's social and political tensions. Of course, debate over the political identity of writers has always been a key 1930s theme: the famous pamphlet *Authors Take Sides on the Spanish War* (1937) made very public demands for authors to specify where they stood on issues such as fascism and the Spanish Civil War. But, while such overt declarations of left-versus-right political affiliations are well noted, the politics of 1930s writing continues to be contentious terrain, both in terms of how it relates to the ideologies of left-wing movements and parties and, more recently, regarding how class-based political identity intersects with other sites such as ethnicity, gender, and sexuality. John Connor's chapter, on communist and working-class writing, analyses the much-debated nature of the influence that communism had upon the literary movements of the time. Connor is clear about the influence the Soviet Union–led Communist International had upon British culture: '1930s Britain found itself a node in a global movement of proletarian and revolutionary writers that took inspiration, and sometimes instruction, from Moscow.' Yet the lines of influence that Connor finds here are complex. Early in the decade, Britain's radical 'culture flourished rather in spite of than because of the [British Communist] Party', with a variety of writers attempting to develop new forms and creative networks at a point where supporting such ventures was not a Party priority. As the decade progressed, the loosening of official positions on art and the rise of the Popular Front saw an 'easing off' in 'the revolutionary rhetoric' and instead a focus on 'the defence of culture and civil liberties', and an increasing number of middle-class authors aligned themselves with the Party. Importantly, Connor's chapter also provides attention to a range of 'worker-writers' who did not operate in the typical networks of communist or radical culture. Such writers offered 'no vanguard sensibility' and there was 'no political didacticism or narrative arc of insurgency' to be found in their work. Yet their writing was nonetheless an important part of the decade's production of proletarian art, 'demand[ing] recognition and cultural justice for their works and days', and Connor shows how this writing played a significant role in the decade itself and established many of the parameters for more inclusive social realist cultural representations that would come to the fore in post-war culture.

While the mandate of this volume is '*British*' writing, there is an acute consciousness that this is a contested term, and a sequence of chapters in the *Companion* question how 1930s literature dealt with issues of place, nation, and Britain's role in the global order. Britain in the 1930s was a nation near the peak of its reach as an imperial power, albeit one now tipping into the downward slope of decline, with the colonies and dominions demanding autonomy and independence, and the intelligentsia in Britain and abroad increasingly challenging the legitimacy of such a system – a process that Judy Suh's chapter on Empire charts out. While acknowledging that much of the popular culture of the decade presented a jingoistic glorification of this imperial ideology, Suh contends that the cracks in this edifice were increasingly evident in other aspects of the decade's cultural work. Suh locates this challenge across three main literary trajectories. Key British writers increasingly reflected upon the Empire in their writing, with authors such as Woolf creating 'a significant field for anti-imperial thinking in Britain' and activists such as Nancy Cunard overtly linking this to a critique of racial politics at home. Equally, Suh examines writers such as Jean Rhys, Rumer Godden, and George Orwell, individuals who were 'born into colonial governing-class families in the Caribbean, India, and Burma', a perspective that allowed them to cast a critical perspective over the colonial structures while also at times showing 'a deep ambivalence towards anti-colonial revolts that they had witnessed in the past and undoubtedly expected in the future'. Finally, the literature of the decade included the powerful voices of émigré writers such as Mulk Raj Anand and C. L. R. James, as well as the Anglo-Irish Olivia Manning and her work on the Anglo-Irish War – all figures who contributed 'proto-revolution[ary]' perspectives on colonised cultures to the heart of the 1930s British literary scene.

Tim Youngs's chapter detects a similar impulse behind much of the decade's proliferation of travel writing, which provided a major literary mode for 're-examinations of Britain's place in the world', spurred by 'conflicts abroad, uncertainty about one's position in the world, [and] dangerous inequalities at home'. As Youngs notes, the 1930s is 'remarkable' for the extent and sophistication of its travel writing. It saw landmark travel books published such as Robert Byron's *The Road to Oxiana* (1937), as well as experiments with the mode by established authors such as Auden and Isherwood, with these perspectives often spurred by the growing technology and infrastructure of the 'petrol age'. International travel narratives, while often overtly occupied with documenting an author's journey to wars and frontiers, also became sites for exploring inward-facing quests, whether Graham Greene's journeys to discover what 'home society has repressed in its members', or Freya Stark's positioning of herself as 'someone operating between cultures' when exploring the Middle East. And, when narratives focussed upon travel within Britain itself, some of these became powerful works of social critique, with the accounts of Orwell and J. B. Priestley allowing the authors to 'speak truth to power, exposing inequality, injustice, and poverty'. As Youngs's chapter highlights, such writing was not merely significant for the range of social and political themes it addressed but for the ways these narratives offered a major experimental mode of literary expression, providing 'a formal innovation and a critical seriousness about contexts, perspectives, and methods rarely seen since'.

This *Companion* also seeks to address some of the assumptions behind the 'British' national category. For British is too often assumed to be synonymous with English, and particularly with England's south-eastern 'golden triangle' of Oxford–Cambridge–London that so often dominates literary maps. While this is a concern manifested across several chapters, it takes the forefront in Kristin Bluemel's chapter, which analyses how the decade saw a distinct, important movement of literary works dealing with regional and rural concerns. As Bluemel notes, the 1930s saw the growth of the 'cult of the countryside' in literature, travel books, and periodicals, but her focus is not on this homogenised and sanitised '1930s print culture fixated on thatched roofs, village greens, and hedgerows'. It is, rather, on the regional rural novels of H. E. Bates, Winifred Holtby, Richard Llewellyn, and Lewis Grassic Gibbon – authors who offered 'powerful cultural and aesthetic work' that contested 'the south-east England rural ideal'. Linking these distinct literary works – which focus on rural regions of the Midlands, Yorkshire, Wales, and Scotland – are concerns such as the rural worker and an aesthetic in which 'land instead of landscape [is] the focus of our gaze'. Bluemel's chapter therefore not only inscribes these authors and locations as significant manifestation of the British literary culture of the era but suggests that this work is the beginning of a new critical process and that 'new attention to non-metropolitan arts and places' challenges us to 'redefine the history of 1930s literature itself'.

Glyn Salton-Cox's chapter addresses the contribution of the decade to modern queer literary history, seeing the decade as in many ways 'foundational for twentieth-century queer literature, politics, and culture in Britain'. Considering the role of well-known authors and reintegrating neglected writers into such debates, Salton-Cox resists frameworks that simply relegate 1930s literature to a narrative of 'the closet and repression' that is incomparable with open political action and instead provides a far more nuanced account of the complex negotiations at work. Certainly, much of this queer culture was developed 'under conditions of censorship, repression, and vilification'. This includes the impact of obscenity trials, the 'privatising sense of sexual radicalism' exhibited by the works of several Bloomsbury authors, and a post-1930s legacy in which certain queer authors were privileged due to their new-found image of 'respectable' homosexuality. But as Salton-Cox's analysis shows, this is not the full span. Authors such as Auden displayed 'homosexual desire relatively openly' in aspects of their work and, in locations such as Weimar Germany, there was a convergence of sexual and political radicalism that profoundly influenced figures such as Isherwood. This queerness also influenced the literature of the decade in other ways, such as the collaborative modes of Auden and Isherwood or Ackland and Warner, and the focus on gender performance in the dystopian work of Katharine Burdekin, showing the ways the 1930s serves as a crucial staging post in the history of modern queer literature.

And, of course, one of the distinctive tensions is how to relate the literature of the decade to the politics and crisis created by war and the rise of the far right. Phyllis Lassner's chapter examines the position of the 1930s as an era between wars, in which memories and legacies of the First World War became entwined with growing foreboding about the outbreak of a new war. As Lassner shows, although separated from the 1914–18 conflict by more than a decade, the 1930s was a 'posttraumatic' era where many of the traumas of the war were only just beginning to be articulated in writing, for 'a decade had to pass before the experiences of the First World War would crystallise into writing that mediated between the immediacy and self-questioning memory of men's posttraumatic ambivalence'. Consequently, the 1930s was shaped by a new wave of war memoirs – in many cases from combatants but in other cases also from authors such as Vera Brittain, whose *Testament of Youth* (1933) provided the decade 'a feminist pacifist war chronicle that inserted a woman's experience and voice into a genre that had been dominated by men's perspectives'. This presence 'shadowed debates' as the posttraumatic literary climate increasingly grappled with the prospect of further conflicts and a new world war. Lassner includes in this analysis works such as Orwell's treatment of the Spanish Civil War and also 'a succession of dystopias' such as Naomi Mitchison's *We Have Been Warned*, political fables and surrealist spy fiction by authors such as Rex Warner and Stevie Smith, and public debates by Rebecca West, Phyllis Bottome, Storm Jameson, and Rose Macaulay. Lassner's chapter therefore shows the intricate and varied ways literature of the 1930s contested issues around war, appeasement, and pacifism, as well as how authors manifested their concerns about whether British democratic institutions and beliefs were strong enough to prevail.

Mia Spiro's chapter then examines perhaps the most defining, but fraught, political debate that echoed within 1930s literature – that of the role of the writer as an activist against the rising threat of fascism.

As Spiro emphasises, the 'question for many politically concerned writers of the 1930s [...] was not *whether* their writing could effect change in the tumultuous political climate but *how*'. But Spiro also crucially here shows the dynamics of this debate as it was enacted by writers. As it is contended, 'British writers were far more perceptive of political and social theories regarding fascism, and far more concerned with the nuances of international politics', than simplistic 'for-or-against' divisions suggest: writers had different motivations for their political activity, different fears about the threats posed by fascism, and different understandings of what constituted fascism itself. While some British writers and intellectuals did initially flirt with far-right movements, Spiro's chapter explores the many others who, across a diverse range of literary modes, strove 'to prod the public out of their complacency', including the writing of Woolf and Isherwood, the involvement of writers in activist organisations such as PEN (now known as PEN International), literary engagements with the threats of anti-Semitism, and the variety of writers who travelled abroad to support or serve in Spain during the civil war. Even with the onset of the Second World War and the despondency of some authors over fascism's march, many other authors were motivated to set their sights on a new phase of work, 'contributing to the war effort against the Nazis' or using their writing to lead 'debates about the radical impact of the war on British society'.

   Benjamin Kohlmann provides the final chapter in this volume and looks back at the status of the 1930s in critical discourse, examining the ways this decade has been shaped and analysed by the writers of the era and subsequent scholars. Across this critical discourse, Kohlmann identifies certain 'master narratives' in play – such as the idea that the dominant force behind 1930s writing was a form of politicised anti-modernism or that this writing can be generally characterised, by the end of the decade, by its failure and disillusionment – and tracks how the result has often been conflicting versions of 'partisan history' offered by writers and scholars. As Kohlmann argues, such views of the 1930s as a self-contained 'literary-historical anomaly' have had significant consequences for literary history, such as hardening ideas that literature and politics are antithetical (a view of particular consequence as anti-communism took force in the Cold War). Even recent attempts to expand conceptions of the decade have not wholly solved these limitations: while certain authors and works are now privileged within the canon of the new modernist studies, this still serves to isolate the extensive range of creative outputs from the decade that resist any form of modernist categorisation. In response, Kohlmann considers new ways to periodise the decade that move beyond these frames, arguing that we should see the 1930s as 'a historical moment whose hopes and anxieties are intimately connected to our own present' – a broadening that not only offers a reconsideration of the 1930s as a literary-historical era itself but prompts us also to 'interrogate conventional assumptions about the politics of writing'.

Kohlmann's call here links to an emerging tendency in scholarship towards seeing the decade in a 'long 1930s' frame, an analysis that is less concerned with a fixed ten-year period and a predetermined range of '1930s themes' and more interested in the place of the decade as a 'pivot' for a wider range of concerns. In doing so, this view of a 'long 1930s' is held to be 'a way to address two interlocking problems: the limitations of a reified and ossified critical canon of 1930s writings and the failure of literary criticism to understand the complex politics of interwar culture, especially as they continue in the Second World War and shape its aftermath'.[9] While this *Companion* has not been designed or structured directly on these assumptions, it is nonetheless evident that these are critical concerns that many of the chapters in this volume generally share; and therefore this *Companion* might be seen as contributing towards this new phase of scholarship that seeks to expand the canonical, cultural, and political parameters we understand the 1930s as operating within.

What also stands out, when looking across the varied chapters of this *Companion*, is the extent to which they demonstrate how scholarship on the 1930s has undergone a rejuvenation, as the tensions and preoccupations of the Cold War fade and a new generation of scholarship moves beyond many of the well-worn debates. As critics such as Andy Croft warned, for many years it was all too easy to frame the 1930s as an era of intellectual dishonesty or failure, crowned by endless repetition of Auden's description of the 1930s as the 'low dishonest decade'.[10] Certainly, many chapters still note a sense of foreboding in the literature of the era, as well as the many moments of acute crisis and debate – but they also show how writers were engaged in active responses to various unique social and political tensions, not some universal folly that invalidates politics as a literary concern. As MacNeice (cited in Kohlmann's chapter) aptly reflected: 'We may not have done all we could in the Thirties, but we did do something.' Taken together, these chapters show the extent to which the literature of the 1930s created this writing of energy, innovation, and lasting value.

Notes

1. Valentine Cunningham, *British Writers of the Thirties* (Oxford: Oxford University Press, 1988), p. 14. For analysis of the 'self-contained' status of the decade, see also Rod Mengham, 'The Thirties: Politics, Authority, Perspective', in *The Cambridge History of Twentieth-Century Literature*, ed. by Laura Marcus and Peter Nicholls (Cambridge: Cambridge University Press, 2004), pp. 359–78.

2. See Cunningham, *British Writers of the Thirties*, pp. 14–16, for discussion of the shifting boundaries of the decade.

3. Patrick Deane, 'Introduction', in *History in Our Hands: A Critical Anthology of Writings on Literature, Culture and Politics from the 1930s*, ed. by Patrick Deane (London: Leicester University Press, 1998), pp. 1–15 (p. 13). For a wider analysis of literary-political myths surrounding the 1930s, see Adrian Caesar, *Dividing Lines: Poetry, Class, and Ideology in the 1930s* (Manchester: Manchester University Press, 1991).

4. See Janet Montefiore, *Men and Women Writers of the 1930s: The Dangerous Flood of History* (London: Routledge, 1996), pp. 11–19, for further analysis of how this 'rhetoric of memory' (p. 12) has shaped subsequent perceptions of the decade.

5. This framework is set out in Samuel Hynes, *The Auden Generation: Literature and Politics in England in the 1930s* (London: Bodley Head, 1976), pp. 9–14.

6. See Benjamin Kohlmann, *Committed Styles: Modernism, Politics, and Left-wing Literature in the 1930s* (Oxford: Oxford University Press, 2014), pp. 199–200.

7. Mary Grover and Chris Hopkins, 'Introduction', *Working Papers on the Web*, 6 (2003). https://extra.shu.ac.uk/wpw/thirties/.

8. For an article that has assumed the status of this field's manifesto, see Douglas Mao and Rebecca L. Walkowitz, 'The New Modernist Studies', *PMLA*, 123.3 (2008), 737–48. Major scholarship that introduced concepts of late modernism includes Tyrus Miller, *Late Modernism: Politics, Fiction, and Arts between the World Wars* (Berkeley and Los Angeles: University of California Press, 1999), and Jed Esty, *A Shrinking Island: Modernism and National Culture in England* (Princeton: Princeton University Press, 2004). Critics have further refined understandings of late modernism in response to the era of the Second World War: see, for example, Marina MacKay, *Modernism and World War II* (Cambridge: Cambridge University Press, 2007), and Steve Ellis, *British Writers and the Approach of World War II* (Cambridge: Cambridge University Press, 2015). For intermodernism, see *Intermodernism: Literary Culture in Mid-Twentieth-Century Britain*, ed. by Kristin Bluemel (Edinburgh: Edinburgh University Press, 2009). David Trotter, *Literature in the First Media Age: Britain between the Wars* (Cambridge, MA: Harvard University Press, 2013), provides a major account of the relationship of this era's literature to developments within media and technological history.

9. Leo Mellor and Glyn Salton-Cox, 'Introduction', *Critical Quarterly*, 57.3 (2015), 1–9 (p. 7). See also *A History of 1930s British Literature*, ed. by Benjamin Kohlmann and Matthew Taunton (Cambridge: Cambridge University Press, 2019), where the editors advance a detailed account of their own 'long 1930s' approach. In a parallel vein, the recently released *Cambridge Companion to American Literature of the 1930s*, ed. by William Solomon (Cambridge: Cambridge University Press, 2018), approaches this 'as a period during which political and literary ambition combined to produce an enduringly meaningful set of cultural artifacts' (p. 6).

10. Andy Croft, *Red Letter Days: British Fiction in the 1930s* (London: Lawrence and Wishart, 1990), pp. 15–30.

CHAPTER I

Poetry

Janet Montefiore

For most twenty-first-century readers, the starting place for studying the poetry of the 1930s is Robin Skelton's much-reprinted 1964 anthology *Poetry of the Thirties*. More influential even than Samuel Hynes's book *The Auden Generation* (1976), it established the 1930s English canon as the poems of upper-middle-class educated men born between 1902 and 1916, a generation cut off from traditional certainties by the Great War in which they were too young to fight. Consciously departing from the patriotism and rural imagery of Georgian poetry, these men admired T. S. Eliot's *The Waste Land* (1922) but refused the modernist decentring of the post-Romantic subjective 'I'. Skelton's anthology is a treasure trove of otherwise out-of-print works, including poems repudiated by Auden (who allowed them to appear on the condition that Skelton 'make it clear that "Mr W. H. Auden considers these five poems to be trash which he is ashamed to have written"'),[1] Spender's early poems celebrating political revolution and sexual liberation through images of modern technology, all of MacNeice's foreboding 1930 lyrics (except his 'Epilogue' to *Letters from Iceland* with its famous conclusion 'Still I drink your health before / The gun-butt raps upon the door'),[2] and much astonishingly powerful surrealist and dream poetry from Dylan Thomas and Hugh Sykes Davies. He included more poems by Auden (thirteen poems), Spender (twelve), and MacNeice (thirteen) than any other, though Dylan Thomas and Day-Lewis (nine each) and Empson and Gascoyne (eight each) are not far behind, followed by Bernard Spencer, Francis Scarfe, Kenneth Allott, Geoffrey Parsons, Geoffrey Grigson, and other lesser-known figures. All except Day-Lewis appeared regularly in Grigson's magazine *New Verse* (1933–9), while Dylan Thomas and Davies also published in Roger Roughton's *Contemporary Poetry and Prose* (1936–7). This anthology has an unusual coherence: its political tone is Marxist or more generally left-wing and almost always hostile to bourgeois certainties, and the same topics, imagery, and rhetoric of modernity recur in many poems, thanks mainly to the influence of Auden.

This definition of 1930s poetry can obviously be criticised for its narrowness. Even in his own terms, Skelton fudged a little: some of his chosen poems by Spender and Empson date from the late 1920s, and others by Auden and Spender were not collected until Auden's *Another Time* (1940) and Spender's *The Still Centre* (1939). Of course, neither Auden nor Spender stopped writing poetry in 1940, though they did change the way they wrote. After leaving for the USA in 1939, Auden repudiated what his editor Mendelson called his 'public role as court poet to the left', insisting that 'poetry makes nothing happen',[3] and Spender never, after 1940, equalled either the excitement of his 1930s poems or their fertility: two collections, *Poems* (1933) and *The Still Centre*, the book-length poem *Vienna* (1934), and the verse play *Trial of a Judge* (1938). Nor were Auden, Spender, and the men of *New Verse* the only poets responding to contemporary history during the 1930s. Older poets published major work, notably T. S. Eliot's 'Burnt Norton' (1936), Herbert Read's *The End of a War* (1933), and David Jones's *In Parenthesis* (1937). And, as I have pointed out elsewhere,[4] Skelton's version of the 1930s left out virtually all women: of the twenty poets later anthologised by Jane Dowson in *Women's Poetry of the 1930s* (1996), he included only Anne Ridler. Valentine Ackland (b. 1906), Kathleen Raine (b. 1908), E. J. Scovell (b. 1907), and Stevie Smith (b. 1902) would all have met his age requirements but not Naomi Mitchison, Nancy Cunard, and Sylvia Townsend Warner, all active poets in the 1930s but born before 1900. Taking this work into account, the poetry of the 1930s can, as I argue in the 'Women Poets' section in this chapter, be defined in very different terms from the familiar 'Auden Group' and their followers.

That said, it is impossible to ignore the young left-wing political poets, not only because, as George Orwell contemptuously wrote in 'Inside the Whale' (1940), 'Auden, Spender & Co.' dominated literary fashion,[5] but because, for all the notorious cliquishness and misogyny with which later critics, including myself, have taxed them,[6] the best of their work has worn well as a creative response to the moment of the Depression, the rise of fascism and of the Popular Front, and the imminence of the Second World War.

The Auden Group

One landmark publication of these poets was Michael Roberts's anthology *New Signatures* (1932), featuring poems by Auden, Spender, Day-Lewis,

and Empson. Roberts's introduction argued that, because industrialism
has made traditional rural imagery obsolete for English poets and, even
more seriously, because of 'the effect of pure science in undermining our
absolute beliefs', recent English poetry has mostly been either bad conventional verse or 'esoteric work which was frivolously decorative or elabo-
rately erudite'. The latter category obviously alludes to two famous poems
published in 1922, Edith Sitwell's *Façade* ('frivolous') and T. S. Eliot's *The
Waste Land* ('erudite'). Auden and Day-Lewis, in contrast, wrote
approachable poetry which did not ignore the challenges of modernism
and 'in which imagery taken from contemporary life consistently appeared
as the natural and spontaneous expression of the poet's thought and
feeling'. The poets' impersonality came 'not from extreme detachment
but from solidarity with others', as in Spender's poem 'The Funeral' (1932),
of which Roberts cautiously approved: 'Poetry is here turned to propaganda, but it is propaganda for a theory of life which may release the poet's
energies for the writing of pure poetry as well as provide him with
standards which may make simple and direct satire possible again.'[7] It
remains unclear, however, whether poetry is already coming from such
political inspiration or will be written only in the future, when a full
humanity is available to all.

New Signatures helped to launch the 'Auden Group'. That term was
resisted by its members but Auden, Spender, and Day-Lewis were so
closely linked as friends and colleagues that they do invite the label.
They and MacNeice all first met as Oxford undergraduates between 1925
and 1928; Auden and Day-Lewis co-edited the 1927 anthology *Oxford
Poetry* and Spender began printing a selection of Auden's poems in 1928
(it was completed by a commercial printer). Day-Lewis was the dedicatee
of Auden's first collection *Poems* (1930) and Spender of his second book
The Orators (1932), the first of whose six 'Odes' looks at the prospects for
'Wystan, Stephen, Christopher [Isherwood], all of you'.[8] Day-Lewis's *The
Magnetic Mountain* (1933) directly apostrophises 'Wystan, lone flyer, bird-
man, my bully boy!' and his *A Hope for Poetry* (1934) argues for Auden and
Spender as key figures for the rebirth of poetic energy.[9] Auden, the pre-
eminent poet of the 1930s, called himself in one poem the 'son of a nurse
and doctor, loaned a dream'[10] and, following this lineage, wrote as
a diagnostician combining the insights of Freud and Marx on the contradictions of capitalism. His brilliantly lively and often parodic idioms can
leave their reader uncertain whether the speaker is a healer or himself
diseased. He experimented endlessly with forms. *Poems* (1930) includes
blank verse with hints of Old English alliterative metre, Owenesque half-

rhymed couplets, free-rhyming Skeltonic dimeters, tetrameter couplets, and songs. *The Orators* opens with a speech followed by prose poems, riddles modelled on the Old English *Exeter Book*, a fictional 'Journal of an Airman', a sestina, a parody Litany, and six Odes to the poet's friends. The metrically more regular poems of his *Look, Stranger!* (1936) use every kind of lyric stanza; in *The Dog Beneath the Skin* (1935), cabaret songs alternate with the panoramas of alliterative, unrhymed choruses; *Another Time* (1940) contains ballads, songs, 'Spain 1937' in a stanza invented by the poet, and the 'Elegy to Sigmund Freud' in syllabics. The travel book *Letters from Iceland* (1937), written with MacNeice, contains Auden's long conversational 'Letter to Lord Byron', which light-heartedly summarises recent English social and cultural history, and the poets' 'Last Will and Testament' in *terza rima*. In *Journey to a War* (1939), written with Christopher Isherwood, Auden's meditative Rilkean sonnets entitled 'In Time of War' set the contemporary conflict in China within long perspectives from humanity's past from the discovery of language onwards.

Except in his love poems, Auden's stance is impersonal. The penultimate item of his *Poems* begins with the imperative 'Consider this and in our time / As the hawk sees it or the helmeted airman', cutting from this timeless yet modern aerial view to a discarded cigarette 'smouldering on a border' at a garden party of the rich and powerful and a sporting party 'dangerous, easy, in furs, in uniform', their feelings 'supplied [. . .] by an efficient band' broadcast elsewhere to countrymen in the 'stormy fens'. These ominous glimpses of glamour, social division, and trouble brewing preface a challenge to a 'supreme Antagonist' who bedevils the English by creating division through repression in the mind and social inequality, and whose 'admirers' in a stagnant country, now in the ascendant, will bring down themselves and the people to 'immeasurable neurotic dread'.[11] The collection's closing 'Sir, no man's enemy' (a poem later repudiated by Auden) more hopefully implores a severe yet benign life force to rebuild English political and psychic structures and 'look shining at / New styles of architecture, a change of heart'.[12] The poems of *Look, Stranger!* are more directly political, aware of the threat to European liberal democracy and the urgency of choosing right in a time of 'crisis and dismay' but a little more hopeful. The 'Prologue' (1932), prophesying the advent of social revolution, imagines England seen from a height, a 'reef [. . .] between all Europe and the exile-crowded sea' (Yeats's 'mackerel-crowded sea' becoming an ocean of the dispossessed), soon to be the target of irresistible change. In 'A Summer Night' (1934), the moon looks from the 'European sky' onto growing violence in the east, forecasting 'the

crumpling flood' of a violent revolution – and, more tentatively, the rebirth
of a just society where grace and kindness will no longer be conditioned by
social privilege. Despite the bouncy satire of 'A Communist to Others'
(1932), Auden was never a propagandist. The Marxism of 'To a Writer on
His Birthday' (1935) lies not so much in its aspiration to 'Make action
urgent and its nature clear' as its final vision of the 'dangerous flood / Of
history, that never sleeps or dies, / And, held one moment, burns the
hand' – which is moving precisely because of its political uncertainty.[13]
Similarly, Auden's slightly later 'Spain 1937' (1937), notoriously and ten-
dentiously attacked by Orwell, has been well described by Frank Kermode
as 'not a marching song or a recruiting poster; it is an attempt to express
what it feels like to confront a great historical crisis'.[14]

The world of dream – or more often of nightmare – is never far away in
Auden's 1930s poems. Always aware of 'the heart's invisible furies',[15] Auden
invented a public poetry which still has power to move and excite, out of
the edgy relationship between an overtly subjective dream world and the
threatening external history of reactionary England and fascist-dominated
Europe, which his poetry seeks to grasp and explain. His rhetoric articulated the relationship between an isolated individual and the political crises
which he (always he) perceives, fears, desires, and suffers, though mostly
indirectly, but which he does not control and hardly even influences.
Giving brilliant, haunting words to the plight of the liberal bourgeois,
Auden powerfully influenced contemporaries, like Spender ('Who live
under the shadow of a war / What can I do that matters?') and Kenneth
Allott ('From this wet island of birds and chimneys / Who can watch
suffering Europe and not be angry?').[16] Empson's send-up 'Just a Smack at
Auden' (1937), with its justified mockery of the homosocial in-group tone
of many Auden poems, is also a backhanded tribute to Auden's prophecies
of coming disaster, a perception Empson himself evoked in the terrifying
repetitions of his villanelle 'Missing Dates' (1940) and its refrain 'The waste
remains, the waste remains and kills'.[17]

Spender wrote in retrospect that: 'To be modern meant in the thirties to
interpret the poet's individual experience of lived history in the light of
some kind of Marxist analysis.'[18] His 1930s poetry is far more personal than
Auden's, more overtly revolutionary, and more interested in contemporary
technology, most famously in 'The Express', 'The Pylons', and 'The
Landscape near an Aerodrome' (all 1932). Poems like 'Oh Young Men'
(1931) and 'Not palaces, an era's crown' (1933) urge their readers, invariably
imagined as 'young men', to reject outdated convention and privilege, to
'advance to rebuild [...] advance to rebel' ('Oh Young Men'), and to

repossess their own bodies, 'Touch, love, all senses' under the slogan 'Death to the killers, bringing light to life' ('Not palaces'). 'The Funeral' imagines a future utopia where workers of the 'World State' joyously celebrate the completed life of one who 'excelled all others in making driving-belts' as 'one cog in a golden and singing hive'. 'Not palaces' likewise invokes the 'architectural gold-leaved flower / From people ordered like a single mind'. His best-known poem 'I think continually of those who were truly great' (1933) rewrites post-war elegies by imagining its classless heroes as fighters for freedom and liberation, 'the desires falling across their bodies like blossoms [. . .] those who in their lives fought for life'. Here nationalist rhetoric and patriotic crowds are transformed into harmless images from the natural world, where true heroes are 'fêted by the *waving* grass / And [. . .] the *streamers* of white cloud' (italics mine).[19]

A similar rhetoric of political revolution imagined as bodily liberation can be seen in Rex Warner's communist-inspired 'Hymn' (1933), which follows Spender in equating revolution with physical love: 'All flesh is a flag and a secret code. [. . .] But they shall love instead their friends and their wives, / owning their bodies at last, things which they have sold.'[20] Charles Madge's 'Instructions' (1933) imagines how, 'after the revolution [. . .] we shall see all things new / Not as a craze or a surprise, but hard, naked, true'.[21] Also influential was Spender's fascination with electricity, in the eroticised body drinking 'energy' 'As from the electric charge of a battery' in 'Not palaces', and most famously in 'The Pylons' (which got the Auden group tagged as 'the pylon poets') where the grotesquely feminised giant iron shapes carry their charged lines 'like whips of anger'. Spender's vision of the pylons as forerunners of utopian skyscraper cities could almost pass as Futurist until the poem's final iambic pentameter, 'Where often clouds shall lean their swan-white neck', which recuperates modernity into traditional romance.[22] Similarly, Cecil Day-Lewis, in 'From Feathers to Iron' (1931), invokes power technology as a fertility symbol ('Look there, gasometer rises, / And here bough swells to bud') and, in 'The Magnetic Mountain', invokes a 'new world' of communism as both mine and machinery: 'in the rich veins / Are tools, dynamos, bridges, towers, / Your tractors and your travelling-cranes'.[23]

These poems are full of urban landscapes, often desolate. The characteristic scenery of Auden's poems is a post-industrial England of disused railways, power stations 'deserted, since they drew the boiler fires', and stagnant 'silted harbours, derelict works [. . .] strangled orchards, and the silent comb / Where dogs have worried'.[24] Geoffrey Grigson finds evil lurking in 'The urinals, the henbane heap, / The oil patches of the lorry yard'. Spender's

'Landscape near an Aerodrome' is diseased, with 'chimneys like lank black
fingers [. . .] and squat buildings' behind trees 'like women's faces / Shattered
by grief', all dominated by the tyranny of religion, 'the church blocking the
sun'.[25] Louis MacNeice's 'Birmingham' (1934) has suburban roads that are
bordered by 'half-timbered houses with lips pressed / So tightly and eyes
staring at the traffic through bleary haws', connoting a narrow feminine
domesticity. The aesthete poet may enjoy watching 'the trams like vast
sarcophagi move / Into the sky, plum after sunset, merging to duck's egg,
barred with mauve' but against these bright colours stand 'the factory
chimneys on sullen sentry'.[26] The poets are alert to the misery of poverty-
stricken lives: in 'Carol' (1935), Day-Lewis warns that 'When baby is hungry /
'Tis best not to wake', and Spender's 'An Elementary School Class Room in
a Slum' (1939) foresees the children's future 'painted with a fog / A narrow
street sealed in with a lead sky, / Far far from rivers, capes, and stars of
words'.[27] Love poems are haunted by impending catastrophe: for John
Cornford about to face battle in 1936, love is 'the shadow that chills my
view' and, in Dylan Thomas's 'The force that through the green fuse drives
the flower' (1934), the power of eros brings death to the 'lover's tomb'. Auden
and MacNeice were both master-poets of the poignant, threatened moment:
in MacNeice's beautiful 'The Sunlight on the Garden' (1938) and 'Meeting
Point' (1939), and in Auden's foreboding 'Lay Your Sleeping Head' (1937) in
which the cost of the lovers' joy will be paid in betrayal.[28] And, in Auden's
'Easily, my dear, you move, easily your head' (1936), the beloved is threatened, not only by marching mobs 'five feet, six feet, seven feet high' and
their dictators but by his own narcissism and potential for corruption.[29]

   The nearest thing to a manifesto produced by any of the 'Auden Group'
is Day-Lewis's short book *A Hope for Poetry* (1934). (The title of Spender's
essay 'Poetry and Revolution' in Roberts's overtly left-wing *New Country*
(1933) may look like a manifesto but insists on a liberal humanist line: 'good
artists [. . .] should not be led astray into practical politics. Art can make
clear to the practical revolutionaries the historic issues which are in the
deepest sense political.')[30] Day-Lewis argues that the new poetry of the
post-war writers, notably Auden and Spender, marks a creative departure
from the alienations of modernity. 'Post-war poetry was born amongst the
ruins', in a world 'inimical apparently both to poetry and to the social
ideals which living poets affirm', and its 'immediate ancestors are Hopkins,
Owen and Eliot'. 'Ancestors' – or, more prosaically, inspirational masters –
are vital to the modern poet who has been cut off from the past by the
trauma of the Great War and the innovations of modernism. His chosen
forebears are thus 'not merely the geographers but [. . .] the creators of his

poetical world'. Hopkins is a 'true revolutionary poet' who reforged 'inherited forms of language, fusing them into new possibilities', Owen is a 'true revolutionary' in his war poems, 'opening up new fields of sensitiveness for his successors', while Eliot's *The Waste Land* is important as a 'social document' that, by communicating the 'nervous exhaustion, the mental disintegration' of educated people after the war, 'enlarged our conception of the field of poetic activity'.[31] For Day-Lewis, the new poetry used the techniques and language of modernism while repudiating Eliot's quietism. Or, as Spender's 1975 retrospect would later put it, 'what the modernists had done was to present us with a medium in which it was possible for us to write about modern life, say whatever we chose, without taking thought as to whether language and form were "poetic"'.[32]

Women Poets

Women, as I argued in the chapter on women poets in *Men and Women Writers of the 1930s* and as Jane Dowson showed in her anthology *Women's Poetry of the 1930s*, wrote poems responding to the political crises of the period.[33] Part IV of *Poetry of the Thirties*, 'And I Remember Spain', has most of the canonical Spanish Civil War classics (except for Edgell Rickword's 1938 satire 'To the Wife of a Non-Interventionist Statesman', presumably because Rickword, born 1898, was too old to qualify for inclusion).[34] There are Auden's meditations on the Spanish Civil War as the moment of crisis on which hangs the fate of Europe in 'Spain 1937'. There is also the volunteer soldier John Cornford's 'Letter from Aragon' (1936), his love poem 'Heart of the Heartless World' (1936), and his contemplation of the coming battle in 'Full Moon at Tierz' (1936), a work which ponders the coming crisis when 'our decisive hold is lost or won' and sets personal anxieties like the 'loneliness that claws my guts' against his communist commitment.[35] MacNeice remembers visiting Spain just before the war began as a careless tourist, seeing the 'mob in flower' outside a church but unaware that Spain would shortly mean 'our grief, our aspirations', and Spender writes of war victims like the 'so young and so silly' boy dead under a tree in 'Ultima Ratio Regum' (1939), or the suffering entrenched soldiers of 'Two Armies' (1939).[36] The section could equally have included 'To Eat To-Day' (1938) by Nancy Cunard (director of the questionnaire *Authors Take Sides on the Spanish War* (1937)), a poem about Italian pilots carelessly tossing their bomb ('bloody sandwich it's made down there') on a Barcelona family

and a treasured half-pint of oil,[37] or works by Warner, who visited
Spain in 1936 and 1937 and 'wrote as much as anybody did about the
war'.[38] Like Spender's, her poems are those of a visitor and often about
places ('Benicasim' (1938), 'Waiting at Cerbere' (1939)) but less personal and more passionately partisan. Whereas Spender's 'Port Bou'
(1939) describes an encounter with smiling militiamen carrying 'rusty
carbines' and the poet's own unheroic terror when the Republican
firing practice starts up, Warner's poem of the same title invokes 'the
fire that quenched / the fire on this hearth, that brought / down these
walls', to 'strengthen the resolved fury / of those who fight for Spain'.[39]
And an account of the queer poetry of the 1930s ought certainly to pay
attention to *Whether a Dove or Seagull* (1933) by Warner and her lover
Valentine Ackland, alongside the love poems of Auden and Spender
(see Glyn Salton-Cox's chapter in this volume for further discussion of
the decade's queer literature).

    Naomi Mitchison, another under-read 1930s poet, writes as a woman
and feminist as well as a socialist. She attacks the 'Young men, haters of
women' in the poem 'New Verse' in their own rhetoric of new technology
('To us the dams and pylons, the fields plowed with tractors, [...] The
pressing and battering of the half-formed idea, / To us in silent creation'),
and celebrates the joys of sexual liberation in 'The Midsummer Apple Tree'
(1933): 'Comrade, comrade, come away [...] What we want we both shall
get'.[40] Her long poem *The Alban Goes Out*, published as a pamphlet in
1939, praises the skill and co-operation of working fishermen. Her 1940
'Clemency Ealasaid', mourning the death of her newborn daughter at the
time of Europe's disintegration into total war, can be read alongside Louis
MacNeice's scrutiny of himself and his failed marriage at the time of the
Munich crisis in *Autumn Journal* (1939). Samuel Hynes wrote that
MacNeice showed 'how the present forced him to judge the past; how
the public world invaded private life, and how private losses coloured his
attitude towards public crises' in his rendering of 'that insistent thirties
theme, the interpenetration of public and private worlds'.[41] These remarks
could apply equally to Mitchison's more direct, intimate meditation:

> My breasts tingle and stab with milk that no one wants,
· Surplus as American wheat, surplus and senseless. [...]
> If my baby had been starved by England, would I ever forgive?
> Roll up the map of Europe.[42]

    Stevie Smith was, in the 1930s, better known for her *Novel on Yellow
Paper* (1936) than for the poems she began publishing from 1935, collected

in *A Good Time Was Had By All* (1937) and *Tender Only To One* (1938). Thanks to the increased attention paid since 1980 to women poets, her poetry is today more noticed by critics than that of Day-Lewis and even Spender. Her 1930s poems already manifest her characteristic preoccupations with storytelling, addressing major questions like the nature of heroism in 'Alfred the Great' (1937) and the existence – or not – of God, as in 'Mother, among the dustbins' (1938), where the mother's sceptical 'Man is most frivolous when he pronounces' is rejected by the child: 'Can you question the folly of man in the creation of God? Who are you?'[43] Also present are her characteristically deceptive simplicity, rapid shifts of tone and register, and broken rhythms. Jane Dowson argues that Stevie Smith's 'opposition to institutionalised uniformity, her intolerance of social injustice and her sensitivity to the ill-treatment of artists [. . .] put her firmly within the conventional boundaries of Thirties poets',[44] and yet her quirky ironies, alternating flippancy with melancholy, her individualism, and her rule-breaking all put her outside them. Her four-line 'Alfred the Great' about a working man who 'keeps a wife and seven children on £2 10/ Paid weekly', yet who 'never has abandoned hope',[45] upsets expectations by playfully identifying the legendary Saxon king with a working man, using the ceremonial language of 'Honour and magnify this man' for the humdrum bathos of a family and weekly wage. The poem and its sketch of Alfred in his back garden standing in front of a washing line make him both type and individual like other characters from Smith's poems such as 'Little Master Home-From-School' (1938), who had 'a father for a fool' coming innocently home to a house of tragedy, and the selfish unfaithful husband 'Major Macroo' (1937), who ruthlessly exploits his doting neglected wife: 'And she could lump it and that was that.'[46] Stevie Smith's feminism and her radicalism in 'Private Means is Dead' is implied in these poems' mockery of the ruling sex and class but, as one would expect from a writer whose first publication was entitled *Novel on Yellow Paper: or, Work it Out For Yourself*, it is not spelled out. I have suggested elsewhere that Stevie Smith is in some ways close to Auden's 1930s poetry in her semi-parodic allusions to literature, popular music, and especially to Anglican hymns and liturgy; in her ironic rendering of middle-class English idioms; and in the black humour of her narrative poems, as in 'The Murderer' (1938) whose story is not unlike Auden's ballad 'Victor'.[47] But against these similarities must be set Stevie Smith's deliberately irregular metres, her cutting in the manner of Edith Sitwell (the bête noire of the 1930s male poets)[48] from incantation to doggerel in poems like 'The Bereaved Swan' (1937) ('Wan / Swan / On the lake / Like a cake / Of soap') which hovers between irony and melancholy in its own stylised world.[49] Stevie Smith never sounds like anyone but herself.

Long Poems

The 1930s is also a period of long poems, beginning with Auden's brilliant four-part *The Orators*, whose multiple voices both diagnose and manifest the sickness of the bourgeois Englishman's psyche. One might also add the verse plays of the 1930s, such as Auden's *The Dance of Death* (1933) and three more plays written with Isherwood, *The Dog Beneath the Skin* (1935), *The Ascent of F6* (1936), and *On the Frontier* (1938); Louis MacNeice's *Out of the Picture* (1937); Spender's *Trial of a Judge* (1938);[50] and Eliot's *Murder in the Cathedral* (1935) and *The Family Reunion* (1939). But I do not discuss them here because, although some of their poetry is fine, notably the songs by Auden and his choruses for *Dog Beneath the Skin*, and the choruses of the Women of Canterbury in Eliot's *Murder in the Cathedral*, they belong more to the story of theatre than of poetry and are addressed elsewhere in this volume. Spender's *Vienna* (1934), T. S. Eliot's 'Burnt Norton' (1936), and Louis MacNeice's *Autumn Journal* (1939) all seek in different ways to comprehend the present moment within a much wider context, while David Jones's *In Parenthesis* (1937) seeks to do something similar for the 'moment' of the Battle of the Somme. The poems by Eliot and David Jones present obvious problems of periodisation. 'Burnt Norton' is the first of the *Four Quartets* which Eliot completed with 'Little Gidding' in 1942, while *In Parenthesis* recreates the private soldiers' experience of trench warfare twenty years earlier, using the modernist techniques of Eliot's *The Waste Land* such as fragmentation, layering of voices, and collaging demotic speech and lines from popular songs with bits of pre-Reformation poetry, Malory's *Morte D'Arthur*, medieval Welsh epic battles, and myths of sacrifice. 'At no time', Jones wrote in his preface, 'did one so much live with a consciousness of the past, the very remote, and the more immediate and trivial past, both superficially and more subtly', with an awareness of the endless variety of British histories and cultures and beneath these 'the Celtic cycle that lies, a subterranean influence as a deep water troubling, under every tump in this Island'.[51] As with Virginia Woolf's *Between the Acts* (1941), where a rural pageant of English history is played in the shadows of the imminent Second World War and of the forgotten darkness 'before roads were made, or houses',[52] Jones's title *In Parenthesis* brackets the moment of modern war (the shells, Verey lights, and uniforms) with medieval epic: 'When they put up a flare, he saw many

men's accoutrements medleyed and strewn up so down and service jackets
[. . .]. It fared under him as the earth had quaked – and the nose-cap pared
his heel leather.' Jones further invokes the world of Christian liturgy and of
myth during the slaughter in Mametz Wood, whose numinous glamour
becomes a source of irony: 'and a Golden Bough for / Johnny and Jack /
and blasted oaks for Jerry / and shrapnel the swift Jupiter for each expectant
tree'.[53] This modernism is, like Eliot's, less interested in contemporary
history than in the intersection of the temporal experience of modern war
with the timeless world of myth, and yet the bombs, shells, and gas masks
are made more vividly present by Jones collaging them with the archaic
'accoutrements' of medieval romance.

Other long poems address contemporary history directly. Stephen
Spender's *Vienna* was written after Spender visited the city in the spring
of 1934, after the failed Viennese coup by Social Democrats was brutally
suppressed by the right-wing nationalist *Heimwehr* movement. Its leader
Dollfuss was himself assassinated by an Austrian Nazi later that summer,
not before about two thousand socialists had been killed by shelling and
bullets or executed. Ambitious but never much admired, *Vienna* is difficult
to read because it assumes that the reader already knows the recent history
which is refracted through the poet's baffled, indignant meditations. These
are sometimes vivid:

> Ministerial lips smile, but what's transparent
> As thin glass is their transparent smile
> Over thin lips: the glass is dashed down suddenly
> And murder glares.

But the lines can also be clotted, as in 'A thousand faces, like the death
sphinx paw / Murmuring on million desert'. There is anger, regret, yearning for a 'stranger' to arrive and destroy the tyrant, and mourning for 'the
death of heroes', and an ending that zigzags obscurely between the poet's
own complicated emotional life and a perilous Europe where the just are
driven underground, 'building insect cells / Beneath the monstrous shell of
ruins'.[54]

More successful and better remembered is Louis MacNeice's *Autumn
Journal*. In twenty-four numbered sections, beginning in the late summer
of 1938, it records the Munich crisis, the last days of the Spanish Republic
(MacNeice visited Barcelona in December 1938), and ends with the sands
of the year running out into the coming war. It is written in a flexible yet
roughly regular conversational form which seems to have been invented by
the poet. MacNeice's perceptions, regrets, apprehensions, and frequent

arguments with himself are rendered as continuous unmarked quatrains of long four-stress lines with unrhymed dissyllabic endings, alternating with short three-stress ones with monosyllabic rhymes. Using this form for a partly meditative, partly up-to-the-minute 'journal' carries some risk of monotony, which MacNeice avoids partly by reining in his own discursiveness with regular strong rhymes, partly by playing variations on his basic form, and most of all by the poem's range of subject, especially in the first fifteen sections (the last third of *Autumn Journal* is noticeably duller). MacNeice moves light-footed from the 'conferences, adjournments, ultimatums' of the Munich crisis (Part VII) and his anxious apprehensions as 'Hitler yells on the wireless, / The night is damp and still' while soldiers cut down trees in the park for a gun-emplacement, to memories of his marital idyll in Birmingham unaffected by the 1930s slump when 'sun shone easy, sun shone hard / On quickly dropping pear-tree blossom' and 'We slept in linen, we cooked with wine' while others queued at the Labour Exchange (Part VIII).[55] There are memories of the poet's schooldays and of undergraduate brilliance ('And it really was very attractive to be able to talk about tables / And to ask if the table *is*': Part XIII), and sardonic meditations on MacNeice's work as a university lecturer and on the value (or not) of the classical studies he teaches. There is a section on his own love–hate relationship with Ireland whose beauty fills him with nostalgia but whose Free State he dismisses as 'A cart that is drawn by somebody else's horse / And carrying goods to somebody else's market' (Part XVI).[56] He also writes regretfully and affectionately about his failed marriage (he doesn't mention being a father, though his son was born in 1935). But most of all, MacNeice returns to his own powerlessness as a liberal intellectual in a dark time. Despite his generous desire for social justice and admiration for 'the stubborn heirs of freedom / Whose matter-of-fact faith and courage shame / Our niggling equivocations' (Part XXIII), all the poet himself does, unforgettably, is to think while he watches the world slide to catastrophe:

> Johnny Walker moves his
>   Legs like a cretin over Trafalgar Square.
> And in the Corner House the carpet-sweepers
>   Advance between the tables after crumbs
> Inexorably, like a tank battalion
>   In answer to the drums. (Part V)[57]

To end by discussing this poem at length may suggest that *Autumn Journal* is *the* exemplary poetry book of the 1930s. That would be misleading, for no single book or poem can be that; even as a poem about the end of the 1930s, this one has rivals in Auden's 'September 1, 1939' and Mitchison's 'Clemency Ealasaid'. What gives the poetry of the 1930s its lasting interest is the quality, liveliness, and, above all, the sheer variety of poems responding to the difficult history of this decade.

Notes

1. *Poetry of the Thirties*, ed. by Robin Skelton (Harmondsworth: Penguin, 1964), p. 41. The five poems repudiated by Auden are his 'Sir, no man's enemy', 'A Communist to Others', 'To a Writer on His Birthday', 'Spain 1937', and 'September 1 1939'.
2. Louis MacNeice, 'Epilogue', in *Letters from Iceland* (London: Faber & Faber, 1937), p. 241.
3. W. H. Auden, *The English Auden: Poems, Essays & Dramatic Writings, 1927-1939*, ed. by Edward Mendelson (London: Faber & Faber, 1977), pp. xix, 242.
4. See Janet Montefiore, *Men and Women Writers of the 1930s: The Dangerous Flood of History* (London: Routledge, 1996), pp. 1–2, and chap. 4.
5. George Orwell, 'Inside the Whale', in *The Collected Essays, Journalism and Letters: Volume One*, ed. by Sonia Orwell and Ian Angus (London: Secker and Warburg, 1968), p. 512.
6. See, for example, Valentine Cunningham, *British Writers of the Thirties* (Oxford: Oxford University Press, 1988), especially chaps 2 and 5; and Montefiore, *Men and Women Writers*, chap. 3.
7. Michael Roberts, preface to *New Signatures* (London: Hogarth Press, 1932), pp. 9, 11, 15, 19.
8. Auden, 'The Orators', in *The English Auden*, p. 94.
9. Cecil Day-Lewis, 'The Magnetic Mountain', in *Collected Poems, 1929–1933* (London: Hogarth Press, 1935), p. 29. For a detailed account of mutual dedications, see Cunningham, *British Writers of the Thirties*, pp. 136–7.
10. Auden, 'The earth turns over', in *The English Auden*, p. 145 (Some editions give the last word as 'room').
11. Auden, 'Consider this', in *The English Auden*, pp. 46–7. My reading of 'Consider this' draws on *W. H. Auden: A Commentary* by John Fuller (London: Faber & Faber, 2007), pp. 74–5.
12. Auden, 'Sir, no man's enemy', in *The English Auden*, p. 36.
13. Auden, 'Prologue', 'A Summer Night', and 'To a Writer on His Birthday', in *The English Auden*, pp. 118, 136–8, 157.
14. Frank Kermode, *History and Value* (Oxford: Clarendon Press, 1988), p. 78. On Orwell and 'Spain', see also Montefiore, *Men and Women Writers*, pp. 12–16.
15. Auden, 'The Capital', in *The English Auden*, p. 236.
16. Stephen Spender, 'Who live under the shadow of war', in *New Signatures*, p. 91; Kenneth Allott, 'From this wet island', in *Collected Poems* (London: Secker & Warburg, 1975), p. 43.

17. William Empson, 'Just a Smack at Auden', and 'Missing Dates', in *Poetry of the Thirties*, pp. 64, 73.
18. Stephen Spender, 'Background to the Thirties', in *The Thirties and After* (London: Fontana, 1978), p. 25.
19. Spender, 'Oh young men' and 'The funeral', in *New Signatures*, pp. 86, 95; 'Not palaces, an era's crown', in *Selected Poems* (London: Faber, 1940), p. 26; 'I think continually', in *New Signatures*, p. 89.
20. Rex Warner, 'Hymn', in *Poetry of the Thirties*, p. 59.
21. Charles Madge, 'Instructions', in *Poetry of the Thirties*, pp. 83–4.
22. Spender, 'The Pylons', in *Poetry of the Thirties*, p. 100.
23. Cecil Day-Lewis, 'From Feathers to Iron, 14', in *Poetry of the Thirties*, p. 101; 'The Magnetic Mountain', in *Collected Poems 1929–33*, p. 46.
24. Auden, 'Get there if you can' and 'Consider this', *The English Auden*, pp. 48, 47.
25. Geoffrey Grigson, 'Three Evils' (1936), in *Poetry of the Thirties*, p. 223; Spender, 'Landscape near an Aerodrome', in *Poetry of the Thirties*, pp. 82–3.
26. MacNeice, 'Birmingham', in *Poetry of the Thirties*, pp. 80–1.
27. Day-Lewis, 'Carol', and Spender, 'An Elementary Classroom in a Slum', in *Poetry of the Thirties*, pp. 113, 51.
28. John Cornford, 'To Margot Heinemann'; Dylan Thomas, 'The force that through the green fuse'; MacNeice, 'Meeting Point' and 'The Sunlight on the Garden'; Auden 'Lay your sleeping head, my love', in *Poetry of the Thirties*, pp. 146, 228, 192, 273, 191.
29. Auden, 'Easily you move', in *The English Auden*, pp. 152–4.
30. Stephen Spender, 'Poetry and Revolution', in *The Thirties and After*, pp. 48–53 (p. 52).
31. Cecil Day Lewis, *A Hope for Poetry* (Oxford: Basil Blackwell, 1936), pp. 2, 40, 2, 5, 12, 17, 23.
32. Spender, 'Background to the Thirties', in *The Thirties and After*, p. 26.
33. See Janet Montefiore, *Men and Women Writers*; and *Women's Poetry of the 1930s*, ed. by Jane Dowson (London: Routledge, 1996).
34. For a close reading of this poem, see Janet Montefiore, 'Edgell Rickword: An Exchange with Alan Munton', in *Arguments of Heart and Mind: Selected Essays 1977–2000* (Manchester: Manchester University Press, 2002), pp. 97–111.
35. Cornford, 'Full Moon at Tierz', in *Poetry of the Thirties*, pp. 137, 138.
36. MacNeice, 'Autumn Journal, VI', and Spender, 'Ultima Ratio Regum', in *Poetry of the Thirties*, pp. 162, 163, 149.
37. Nancy Cunard, 'To Eat To-Day', in *The Penguin Book of Spanish Civil War Verse*, ed. by Valentine Cunningham (Harmondsworth: Penguin, 1980), pp. 169–70.
38. Valentine Cunningham, *Spanish Front: Writers on the Spanish Civil War* (Oxford: Oxford University Press, 1986), p. xxxii.
39. Sylvia Townsend Warner, 'Port Bou', in *Women's Poetry of the 1930s*, p. 154; Spender, 'Port Bou', in *Poetry of the Thirties*, pp. 146–8.

40. Naomi Mitchison, 'New Verse', in Jill Benton, *Naomi Mitchison: A Biography* (London: Pandora, 1990), p. 90; 'The Midsummer Apple Tree', in *Women's Poetry of the 1930s*, p. 79.

41. Samuel Hynes, *The Auden Generation* (London: Faber, 1976), p. 368.

42. Naomi Mitchison, 'Clemency Ealasaid'. This was written in 1940 and first published as epigraph to *The Bull Calves* (London: Jonathan Cape, 1947).

43. Stevie Smith, 'Mother, Among the Dustbins', *Tender Only To One* (London: Jonathan Cape, 1938), p. 32.

44. Dowson, *Women's Poetry of the 1930s*, p. 140.

45. Stevie Smith, 'Alfred the Great', in *A Good Time Was Had By All* (London: Jonathan Cape, 1937), p. 14.

46. Stevie Smith, 'A Father For A Fool', in *Tender Only To One*, p. 26; 'Major Macroo', in *A Good Time*, p. 78.

47. Montefiore, *Men and Women Writers*, pp. 131–2.

48. For a discussion of the *New Verse* poets' vendetta against Edith Sitwell, see Robin Skelton's introduction to *Poetry of the Thirties*, pp. 28–30.

49. Stevie Smith, 'The Bereaved Swan', in *A Good Time*, p. 41. For detailed commentary on the stylistic effects of 'Major Macroo' and 'The Bereaved Swan', see Montefiore, *Men and Women Writers*, pp. 129–31.

50. For a discussion of these plays by Auden, Isherwood, Spender, and MacNeice and the way they represent women, see chap. 3 in Montefiore, *Men and Women Writers*, pp. 84–94.

51. David Jones, *In Parenthesis* (London: Faber, 1963), p. xi.

52. Virginia Woolf, *Between the Acts* (London: Hogarth Press, 1941), p. 158.

53. Jones, *In Parenthesis*, pp. 180, 178.

54. Stephen Spender, *Vienna* (London: Faber, 1934), pp. 21, 25, 39, 42–3.

55. Louis MacNeice, *Autumn Journal* (London: Faber, 1939), pp. 30–1, 34.

56. MacNeice, *Autumn Journal*, pp. 51, 63.

57. MacNeice, *Autumn Journal*, pp. 92, 23.

CHAPTER 2

The Literary Novel

Marina MacKay

'It is not an exaggeration to say that for most people "a book" means a novel.'[1] So wrote Q. D. Leavis in her pioneering *Fiction and the Reading Public* (1932), reflecting on the supremacy of the novel in an era when universal literacy had created what she called an 'inveterate general reading habit' among the British.[2] Yet the novel of Leavis's own decade would be so comprehensively overshadowed by poetry in the course of the following half-century that it was still the case in the late 1980s that Valentine Cunningham could write in his landmark survey of the period that 'when we think of literature in the 1930s our current orthodoxies usually have us thinking first of poets'.[3] As a consequence of newer critical developments ranging from the recovery of women's writing across the interwar period to the chronological encroachments of modernist studies into the middle of the century, the literary novel in the 1930s no longer suffers from this kind of neglect, even if some individual writers do.

The 1930s Canon

There are, to be sure, 1930s novelists whose canonical standing is virtually self-evident. The prolific Graham Greene, for example, published no fewer than six major novels in the 1930s: *Stamboul Train* (1932), *It's a Battlefield* (1934), *England Made Me* (1935), *A Gun for Sale* (1936), *Brighton Rock* (1938), and *The Confidential Agent* (1939). Although *Brighton Rock* remains the most durably canonical of these early works, perhaps because it is the novel in which Greene's appetite for what might otherwise be considered sub-literary melodramatic plots is most obviously legitimised by the much further-reaching questions he asks there about the nature of good and evil, the characteristic outlines of a Greene novel are clear from the first. *Stamboul Train* is set on the Orient Express with a large cast of characters from which emerges as the central figure an exiled communist revolutionary returning to his native Balkans in pursuit of his own martyrdom;

Dr Czinner is the prototype of all those haunted, shabby, quixotic men who will populate Greene's subsequent fiction. At one late point in the novel, a group gathers in a compartment of the train and a character announces that 'We really have here the elements of a most interesting discussion; the doctor, the clergyman, and the writer', to which the martyred communist Dr Czinner asks if he has 'not left out the penitent'.[4] Many of the preoccupations of Greene's later novels are named here in embryonic form: reflections on the role of the writer, on the diagnostic and the diseased, and on religious consciousness in its most lacerating forms.

Stamboul Train may seem an unlikely text with which to begin a chapter on the literary novel in the 1930s – when Greene retrospectively came up with the distinction between 'novels' and 'entertainments', inevitably problematic categorisations that he eventually stopped using, *Stamboul Train* was subjected to a downgrade: not a literary novel at all, then.[5] In reality, and as will become clear in what follows, the implicitly sui generis 'literary novel' of the 1930s routinely overlaps with a range of forms, including the novel of intrigue, memoir, satire, dystopian fiction, historical fiction, and the fable. More importantly, though, *Stamboul Train* can be taken as typical not only of Greene's fiction but of the fiction of its decade more broadly because, by its very nature, as a novel set on a transcontinental train, it reflects so explicitly on the newly threatening ambiguities of place and nation that will give so sinister an edge to the period's fiction. 'How old-fashioned you are with your frontiers and your patriotism', Dr Czinner announces, in a line that could come from any number of this decade's novels: 'The aeroplane doesn't know a frontier; even your financiers don't recognize frontiers.'[6]

Christopher Isherwood, to take another of the un-controversially canonical novelists of the 1930s, also writes of dissolved borders and itinerant figures in *Mr Norris Changes Trains* (1935), which opens with a chance meeting on a train as it crosses a continental frontier, and, more hauntingly, in his hybrid novel/memoir/story collection *Goodbye to Berlin* (1939). In this classic work about an expatriate Englishman watching the rise of Nazism from what are cast as (in all senses) the queer perspectives of the Berlin demi-monde, everything, in the end, depends upon who gets to leave Germany in time and who doesn't. Displacement and deracination in this iconic 1930s work can mean anything from literary exile to forced flight, and if anything really marks the tonal difference between the English novelistic canons of the 1920s and 1930s, it is the extent to which the modernist cosmopolitanism attendant upon having a fundamentally unshaken sense of Britain as the centre of the world gives way to a pervasive sense of dispossession and instability across Britain and the European continent as a whole.

Late Modernism

Among the interwar novelists whose reputations have deservedly benefitted from the turn to later and second-generation modernisms, the Anglo-Irish Elizabeth Bowen wrote of many different forms of homelessness in her fiction of the 1930s. Indeed, it seems darkly symbolic of the development of her work that she ended the 1920s with a literal image of people de-housed by violence, when, in the final scene of her novel *The Last September* (1929), Republican insurgents burn down Danielstown, the Irish country house in which the novel is set. The unwelcoming foreign house in the title of Bowen's *The House in Paris* (1935) serves as a kind of postal sorting office for unwanted children en route between one unreal home and another. Children like them are 'people's belongings', thinks the orphaned Henrietta at the prospect of illegitimate Leopold being reclaimed from adoptive parents by his birth mother, and a language of half-hearted or doubtful ownership pervades the novel.[7] Leopold's adoption in infancy is characterised as his having 'left [. . .] with the Americans' baggage', and, when his birth mother's husband retrieves Leopold, in what the novel implies is sadistic marital punishment for her ancient infidelity, helpless Leopold imagines the act as the 'theft of his own body'.[8] Portia Quayne in *The Death of the Heart* (1938) is another of Bowen's socially embarrassing homeless children, the offspring of an affair in her father's late midlife that broke up his first marriage. On the death of her parents, Portia comes to live with her older half-brother Thomas and his wife Anna. As a result of her shamed parents' exile, Portia has grown up in cheap hotels on the continent, and her father's dying wish that Thomas and Anna Quayne give Portia a home in order that she get her first chance to experience '*normal, cheerful* family life' is both legalistically observed and rendered poisonously ironic by the adult characters involved (the satirical emphasis on 'normal' and 'cheerful' is her sister-in-law Anna's).[9]

There are certainly continuities between the fiction of the 1920s and 1930s. In his contemporary *Enemies of Promise* (1938), Bowen's friend Cyril Connolly noted with approval the continuing influence of E. M. Forster on the decade's prose fiction (including Bowen's own); but another earlier writer whose work quietly resonates in the work of 1930s novelists like Bowen is the late short story writer Katherine Mansfield – at least as much so as the expected Virginia Woolf.[10] Cunningham considers Rosamond Lehmann among the most gifted women novelists of her time and 'inexplicably ignored in all the standard accounts' of 1930s literature, and it is surely not tendentious to wonder how far this long-standing neglect follows from the gendered nature of her concerns, which are very Mansfield-like in their small scale.[11] Lehmann's psychologically penetrating and often funny coming-of-age novel *Invitation to the Waltz* (1932) reads much like an elaboration of Katherine Mansfield's 'Her First Ball' (1921), a story with which it shares not only its entire plot – an upper-middle-class young woman going to her first ball experiences the flux of disappointments and exhilarations that follow from the gap between expectations and outcomes – but its gently ironic perspective on the naivety of the heroine, as well as on the absurdities of the people she encounters. And so, for example, Lehmann's adolescent Olivia Curtis meets for the first time at the ball a masculine type unknown to her but implicitly known all too well to the adult reader: taking at his own evaluation the rather 1930s-sounding neurotic young poet Peter Jenkin and his efforts to be shockingly modern ('Of course she's had a very unsatisfactory sex-life', he says of his mother), Olivia is naive enough to be somewhat impressed by his predictable discursive manoeuvres ('Such a totally fresh point of view', Olivia innocently marvels, 'so disquieting and subversive').[12]

Lehmann's following novel, *The Weather in the Streets* (1936), sees an older, married Olivia, now separated from her husband, embarking upon a destructive affair with Rollo Spencer; now himself also married, the young Rollo was a fleeting but charismatic figure at the ball in the earlier novel where he meets for the first time both Olivia and the woman he marries. *The Weather in the Streets* is vastly more sober in mood than the novel upon which it builds – notwithstanding another very 1930s in-joke against neurotic young poets, when the illicit couple sign themselves 'Mr. and Mrs. Spender, London' in a hotel register while on a dirty weekend.[13] In the course of this increasingly unhappy affair, Olivia falls pregnant, leading to the protracted horrors of an illegal abortion and the return of her lover to his wife.

Lehmann was by no means the only woman novelist to approach in a frank way the costs of women's new – if highly relative and uneven, it goes without saying – sexual freedom in a culture in which the economic and social power of men remained unchanged. Here, a good example would be the slightly older Jean Rhys, who drew on her own past experience of financial dependency upon deeply unreliable men to create her three un-consoling but strikingly atmospheric novels of consciousness about displaced women on their uppers in 1930s London and Paris. In *After Leaving Mr Mackenzie* (1931), ageing Julia Martin is reaching the end of her precarious career as a mistress in Paris (it is in fact Mr Mackenzie who has left her, although the title implies that it was the other way round – a gutsiness or self-delusion worthy of Julia herself); in *Voyage in the Dark* (1934), West Indian chorus-girl-turned-kept-woman Anna Morgan is almost killed by the abortion that marks the last of her more hopeful love affairs; *Good Morning, Midnight* (1939) finds bereaved Englishwoman Sasha Jansen drinking in Paris to forget her many losses.

These examples obviously give an incomplete picture of 1930s fiction by women as largely psychological and private portraits, although Rhys in particular anticipates the kind of inwardness George Orwell would describe in 1940 when he wrote of late modernist fiction as written from 'inside the whale'.[14] Here, with a mixture of approbation and regret, he noticed a turning away from politics among some of the decade's best novelists. But sometimes what reads initially as psychological fiction about the emotional lives of women registers more overtly public anxieties. Stevie Smith's eccentric *Novel on Yellow Paper* (1936) recounts from the perspective of the simultaneously flighty and worldly Pompey Casmilus a series of unsatisfactory relationships (and she simply *cannot* marry dull Freddy): 'For this book is the talking voice that runs on, and the thoughts come, the way I said, and the people come too, and come and go, to illustrate the thoughts, to point the moral, to adorn the tale.'[15] But then cosmopolitan Pompey visits her beloved Germany, and her thoughts take a sharply political turn when she contemplates 'that hateful feeling I had over there, and how it was a whole race was gone run mad':

> But oh now well, then he said, what the Russians did to the German prisoners on the Russian front that, like that is too bad to be set down, but No, Germans could not bear to see, even to see such cruelty, they could not bear it, they would be mad.
>
> But then see what they did this time to the Jews and the Communists, and later than this right nowadays to the Jews and the Communists, in the latrines, and the cruel beating and holding down and beating, and enjoying it for the cruelty.
>
> Oh how deeply neurotic the German people is, and how weak, and how they are giving themselves up to this sort of cruelty and viciousness, how Hitler cleared up the vice that was so in Berlin, in every postal district some new vice, how Hitler cleared that up all. And now look how it runs with the uniforms and the swastikas. And how many

uniforms, how many swastikas, how many deaths and maimings, and hateful dark cellars and lavatories. Ah how decadent, how evil is Germany to-day.[16]

In *Over the Frontier* (1938), Pompey finds herself in Germany again – and finds herself in a different kind of novel as well: a parody of espionage fiction rendered deeply unfunny by Pompey's explicit reflections on the allure of the dehumanising cruelty and violence upon which this type of fiction depends. Smith's 1930s novels are novels of consciousness at the end of an intellectual line that runs from *Tristram Shandy* to Woolf, and although the associative narrative drifting between the trivial and the appalling that ensues as a result can feel (at least in retrospect) uncomfortable in its whimsy, where Smith's novels speak of their own period especially it is in how completely they insist upon the infiltration of the public world into private consciousness.

Historical Fictions

Commenting on Georg Lukács's *The Historical Novel* – which was itself a product of the mid-to-late 1930s, although not published until much later – Perry Anderson describes the historical novel as 'the most consistently political' among all the forms of prose fiction.[17] It is not surprising, then, to find that historical fiction was one of the major literary modes of a thoroughly unsettled decade, nor should it be surprising to find that women novelists were among its most ambitious practitioners, as Janet Montefiore demonstrated in her influential revisionist study *Men and Women Writers of the 1930s*.[18] In Sylvia Townsend Warner's *Summer Will Show* (1936), an Englishwoman in Paris finds herself caught up in the February Revolution of 1848; *After the Death of Don Juan* (1938), written against the background of the Spanish Civil War, is set in a grotesquely caste-divided late eighteenth-century Spain. Without being capriciously anachronistic or allegorically topical, these novels allow the anxieties of their decade to resonate quite clearly, as when, for example, Warner includes in *Summer will Show* – published in the year after the enactment of the Nuremberg race laws – a long and harrowing account of a Lithuanian pogrom that the heroine's Jewish lover Minna only barely survived as a child.

The crises of the 1930s are more overtly the lens through which the distant past is viewed in the historical fiction of the Scottish socialist writer and activist Naomi Mitchison. *The Corn King and the Spring Queen* (1931) is set on the shores of the Black Sea two thousand years ago and reads at times as much like a fantasy novel as a work of historical fiction, a blurring of history and myth not unusual in the work of her generation of Scottish novelists (the fiction of the nationalist Neil Gunn offers many examples of this mode). However, for Mitchison writing sixty years later, this novel was historical in two important senses, as she argued that it was both based on her long-standing interest in classical antiquity and shaped by her anxieties about the period in which she was writing:

> [M]y account of what was happening in Sparta or Athens or even Egypt is all based on real history, but the view was moulded by what I – and many another person – was thinking in the Europe of those days, with Mussolini and his fascists in Italy and already the shadow of Hitler in Germany. If I was writing this book now I might treat my characters and my story differently.[19]

The effects of present conditions are even more visible in her later historical novel *The Blood of the Martyrs* (1939), set during the axiomatically brutal first-century persecution of the early Christians – whom the novel's Romans routinely refer to as 'Jews', in a historically unproblematic and yet, at this date, powerfully loaded phrasing. Their persecutor Nero is presented here as a Hitler-like figure whose cult of personality has been created to mask the social and economic fragility of his empire; thus, for example, characters at a dinner party discuss politics in first-century Rome in ways that would serve equally well for the Germany of Mitchison's time: 'What about the finances?' asks one man. 'I'm not sure that's going so nicely. Here in Rome, half the citizens are on the dole. And I'd like to know just how the Exchequer are paying for these pageants and parades and cardboard imitations of the Olympic Games that are got up to keep their minds off reality!'[20]

Another of the major novelists of the interwar Scottish literary renaissance, Lewis Grassic Gibbon turned to very recent history in his masterpiece *Sunset Song* (1932), one of the most formally experimental working-class novels of the 1930s (and discussed further by Bluemel's chapter in this volume), although relatively little read outside of its native country. Although the novel's characters cannot know it, their way of life in a farming community in the north-east of Scotland is going to be brought to a violent end by the coming of the First World War and the deaths that follow. In another example of the melding of myth and history, the ancient past of the land saturates the pre-war present of Gibbon's last rural representatives, as when the heroine Chris Guthrie either sees or dreams the ghost of a dead Roman soldier in his ancient Caledonian exile, or meditates upon the prehistoric standing stones that seem to promise some form of continuity amidst historical flux (in the novel's devastating final scene, the central stone is transformed into a war memorial to the men of the village who have been killed in France). Under his real name, James Leslie Mitchell, Gibbon published a more conventional type of historical novel the following year. *Spartacus* (1933) is an account of the famous slave rebellion from the perspective of a literate slave and sexually exploited eunuch who joins the rebels. As with Gibbon's treatment of the Great War in *Sunset Song*, this is very emphatically the fictional counterpart of recounting history from below – which was, instructively enough, a historiographical concept first articulated as such (*'histoire vue d'en bas'*) in the 1930s by the *Annales* historian Lucien Febvre.

A more middle-class perspective on recent British history can be found in the family saga. The year 1932 saw the awarding of the Nobel Prize for Literature to John Galsworthy, author of the best-known iteration of this kind of fiction earlier in the century, *The Forsyte Saga* (1922). The long-range family novel took many forms through the 1930s, ranging from the populist and sentimental to the politically confrontational and formally innovative. It is difficult to think of Virginia Woolf's synchronic *The Waves* as a novel of the 1930s, although it was published in the autumn of 1931, but *The Years* (1937) is more characteristic of the decade, following as it does the generations of the Pargiter family through a series of scenes set at moments from the 1880s through the late 1930s. It is not especially surprising that *The Years* proved to be one of Woolf's most immediately saleable novels; an appetite for the domestic perspective on the nation's modern history had been confirmed at the start of the decade by the extraordinary success of Noël Coward's immensely successful play *Cavalcade*, which opened in 1931 and became an Academy Award–winning film in 1933. Coward's plot follows the upper-middle-class Marryot family through the turning points and cataclysms of the century's opening decades, intertwining the history of the household with that of the nation through snapshots of the Boer War and the death of Queen Victoria, the loss of the *Titanic*, and the Great War and its Armistice. Rather appropriately, one of the best-known lyrics from *Cavalcade* is 'Twentieth-Century Blues', since what modern history typically amounts to in these long-range works is a mixture of social emancipation and a series of devastating losses.

Speculative Fictions

While some novelists were looking backwards in an effort to work out how the British had arrived where they were, others were looking far forward, and it was no less a reflection of the unsettled political conditions of the

decade that pseudo-futuristic dystopian fiction was another common form
taken by the 1930s novel. To begin with the most famous among them,
Aldous Huxley had already acquired a fashionable reputation by the
middle of the 1920s, but his most-read work remains *Brave New World*
(1932). 'Standard men and women; in uniform batches' are the key to
'social stability' for the architects of the new world order, and this was
famously a decade in which social stability was sorely wanting.[21] *Brave New
World* is also, of course, a comic novel at the same time as an attack on the
culturally homogenising and emotionally anaesthetic forces of interwar
consumerism and rather savours the absurdity of what it is meant to be
denouncing – notwithstanding world leader Mustapha Mond's contention
that 'you've got to stick to one set of postulates. You can't play Electro-
magnetic Golf according to the rules of Centrifugal Bumble-puppy.'[22] If
Huxley's later influence went in one direction towards the 1940s Orwell of
Nineteen Eighty-Four (1949), it went in another towards Evelyn Waugh –
who would end up rewriting *Brave New World* as 'Love Among the Ruins'
(1953) as a bilious broadside against the post-war welfare state he despised.
Meanwhile, back in the 1930s, Waugh produced four satirical novels – *Vile
Bodies* (1930), *Black Mischief* (1932), *A Handful of Dust* (1934), and *Scoop*
(1938) – and ended the decade with the symptomatically titled *Work
Suspended* (written 1939). Huxley's streamlined luxury future finds contemporary expression in the schematic but often very funny conflicts
between the old world and the new in these novels; we might think, for
example, of interior designer Mrs Beaver's depredations in *A Handful of
Dust* on the literal fabric of English heritage, with her plans for 'white
chromium plating' redesigns of rooms in Victorian Gothic manors, and
the division of London townhouses into minuscule flats with 'every transatlantic refinement'.[23] In more direct homage to Huxley, perhaps, the
earlier *Vile Bodies* announces itself as a novel of 'the near future, when
existing social tendencies have become more marked' and presents a febrile
and funny – and perhaps in this respect inadvertently far-sighted – account
of a hyper-mediated society in which the media shape reality rather than
report upon it.[24]

Also evidencing a debt to *Brave New World*, but from a completely
different political perspective from that of the conservative Waugh, the
Marxist Patrick Hamilton's dystopian satire *Impromptu in Moribundia*
(1939) sees the main character travel to a distant planet only to find there
a grotesque exaggeration of life in middle-class Britain (the joke is that the
narrator doesn't recognise it). More characteristic of Hamilton's usual style
and interests are the three short novels collected as *Twenty Thousand Streets*

Under the Sky (1935) – largely realist stories of boozing and bad faith, anticipating Hamilton's best fiction in the 1940s – but *Impromptu in Moribundia* is historically telling in its despairing denunciation of English culture:

> I saw cupidity, ignorance, complacence, meanness, ugliness, short-sightedness, cowardice, credulity, hysteria and, when the occasion called for it, [. . .] cruelty and blood-thirstiness. I saw the shrewd and despicable cash basis underlying that idiotic patriotism, and a deathly hatred and fear of innovation, of an overturning of their system, behind all their nauseatingly idealistic postures and utterances.[25]

If this final rant recalls – albeit, I think, without the authorial irony – poor Gulliver's traumatised tirade against human corruption after his stint with the Houyhnhnms, another important inspiration for the novel is the H. G. Wells of *The Time Machine* (1895), although Hamilton's fantastical feat of engineering offers a journey through space rather than time. Wells himself is among the oldest of the many living novelists at whom the novel directs its scattershot fire; Hamilton's oddly assembled hit list of writers in this novel includes figures with as little in common with each other as John Buchan, Siegfried Sassoon, James Joyce – and an unspecified Sitwell sibling. This is a usefully eccentric cross-section of British literary culture insofar as it reminds us of the limits of our traditional generational historiography of the 1930s, which has always placed disproportionate emphasis on the writers born around the middle of the century's first decade. (It is primarily under the more recently formulated rubric of 'late modernism' that the importance of older writers to the literature of the 1930s has been foregrounded, in work by critics such as Tyrus Miller, Jed Esty, and John Whittier-Ferguson.)[26]

'He turns out books almost weekly' is Hamilton's scornful verdict on the writer 'Sllew' – as in Samuel Butler's Victorian dystopia *Erewhon*, names are merely reversed here.[27] As Steve Ellis has pointed out in his study of British literary culture in the late 1930s, Wells's many influential contributions to the political debates of this period have largely been forgotten, and, as Ellis goes on to show, Wells was an extremely public and prolific figure as the Second World War arrived.[28] Among his large body of work from this period, Wells's moderately futuristic novel *The Holy Terror* (1939) is particularly interesting in its political insecurities because, on the one hand, it essentially advances an authoritarian global order as a response to the perceived failures of national versions of sovereign democracy (in keeping with Wells's long-standing views about the need for a one-world government) and, on the other hand, is sharply attuned to the notorious reversibility of utopia and dystopia in all totalitarian contexts.

Needless to say, there were many real-world totalitarian dystopias in Europe by this stage, and Rex Warner's allegorical *The Professor* (1938) outlines and prefigures the catastrophic fates of the central European states. The spring of 1938 saw the annexation of Austria, and, most controversially, in the autumn of that year the model post-1918 democracy of Czechoslovakia was abandoned by its British and French allies for the sake of what finally amounted to only another eleven months of uneasy peace ('serving C.S. on the altar & bidding it commit suicide', as Woolf wrote in her diary that week).[29] Warner's short novel recounts the final week in the life of a liberal democrat whose educated humanism proves no match for the violent and irrational forces of political reaction. A classicist like Warner himself, the professor is 'a man quite unfitted for power', 'rich in the culture of many languages and times, but for his own time [. . .] most inapt':

> He believed against all the evidence, scholar though he was, not only in the existence but in the efficacy of a power more human, liberal, and kindly than an organization of metal. He believed not simply in the utility but in the over-riding or pervasive power of the disinterested reason.[30]

As these schematic distinctions suggest, this is obviously a less private allegory than Warner's first novel *The Wild Goose Chase* (1937), although it shares its precursor's somewhat surrealistic flavour. The same is true of Edward Upward's hallucinatory novella *Journey to the Border* (1938), in which a private tutor to an upper-middle-class English family experiences a political awakening at a racecourse populated by mysterious fascists. In keeping with Upward's own political beliefs, the tutor comes to believe that his only escape from psychological disintegration is to become a communist (or, as the Party is cast here, to join the Internationalist Movement for Working-Class Power) – although, as Benjamin Kohlmann has pointed out, the actual ending of the novel seems strangely conditional and irresolute for a writer who retained his communist certainties long after contemporaries had abandoned theirs.[31]

Writing late in 1939, Julian Symons named Warner's and Upward's novels as evidence of the prevalence of the fable in recent fiction, yet suggested that the fables themselves were not to be taken seriously but constitute merely 'a kind of joking framework' put around stories that are intended to serve 'commonsense, practical ends'.[32] But not all of the decade's dystopian novels had this quality of fable to start with. In her novel *In the Second Year* (1936), by contrast, Storm Jameson's long-standing commitment to realist narrative, circumstantial and expansive, comes into its own to suggest the perverse ordinariness of life in the fascist Britain where the novel is set. The novel is 'disturbingly vivid', to borrow Elizabeth Maslen's description, but this is not because it is as lurid or melodramatic as the material would suggest but precisely because it is not.[33] Maslen quotes a contemporary critic who remarked that Jameson's 'gentlemanly and urbane' fascist England is one in which '[a]trocious things are done with perfect manners'.[34]

Spectres of Catastrophe

By the second half of the decade, then, narratives of the future have none of the freewheeling absurdity of a *Brave New World*. In Orwell's *Coming Up For Air* (1939), insurance salesman George Bowling finds himself haunted by 'this kind of prophetic feeling that [. . .] war's just round the corner, and that war's the end of all things'.[35] This coming war of Bowling's and Orwell's imagination looks a great deal like the perpetual state of war in *Nineteen Eighty-Four*:

> I can hear the air-raid sirens blowing and the loudspeakers bellowing that our glorious troops have taken a hundred thousand prisoners. I can see a top-floor-back in Birmingham and a child of five howling and howling for a bit of bread. And suddenly the mother can't stand it any longer [. . .] because there isn't any bread and isn't going to be any bread. I see it all. I see the posters and the food-queues, and the castor oil and the rubber truncheons and the machine-guns squirting out of bedroom windows.[36]

In response to the feeling of protracted catastrophe, Bowling spends the few pounds he has recently won on the horses on a sentimental journey to the Thames Valley of his childhood – now obliterated by suburbanisation and the growth of light industry. 'England gets squalider and squalider', announces Olivia Curtis in Lehmann's *The Weather in the Streets*, looking through the car window at the suburbanisation of rural England: 'So disgraced, so ignoble, so smug and pretentious [. . .] and nobody minds enough to stop it.'[37] Anticipating the pervasive apprehension in Orwell's novel that there is a curious continuity between recent national transformations and the destructive future, there ensues in Lehmann's novel an oddly telling slide from the burgeoning of the bungalow to the imminence of bombing: 'Personally I subscribe to the Society for the Preservation of Rural England', says Olivia's respondent, and he elaborates his point with what seems to be, but implicitly is not, an unrelated point:

'And furthermore [. . .] I'm all for the League of Nations. But if people want war they'll have war.'[38]

'Well, it's like this war that's coming . . .' begins Father Rothschild in Waugh's *Vile Bodies*, again as if out of the blue: '*What war?*' asks the hapless Prime Minister: 'No one has said anything to me about a war.'[39] In Waugh's friend Henry Green's *Party Going* (1939), commuters stuck by bad weather on a London railway platform on their way home from their office jobs are suddenly 'targets for a bomb'.[40] Christopher Isherwood looks at the ugly ornaments on his Berlin landlady's writing desk as liable to be 'melted down for munitions in a war'.[41] There are few corners in the 1930s novel into which the threat of violent upheaval does not intrude.[42] There are fewer novels still in which that upheaval would not be felt, on some level, as some kind of a comeuppance for a national culture that its own fiction casts as intent upon self-destruction. To return, finally, to Greene, a character at the end of his 1936 thriller *A Gun for Sale* makes this point most bluntly: 'perhaps even if she had been able to save the country from a war, it wouldn't have been worth the saving'.[43] No wonder, then, that, when Greene looked back on the squalor of the 1930s from the perspective of the Second World War, he found that '[t]he world we lived in could not have ended any other way'.[44]

Notes

1. Q. D. Leavis, *Fiction and the Reading Public* (London: Chatto & Windus, 1939), p. 6.
2. Ibid., 4.
3. Valentine Cunningham, *British Writers of the Thirties* (Oxford: Oxford University Press, 1988), p. 23.
4. Graham Greene, *Stamboul Train* (London: Vintage, 2001), p. 106.
5. Bernard Bergonzi, *A Study in Greene: Graham Greene and the Art of the Novel* (Oxford: Oxford University Press, 2006), p. 61.
6. Greene, *Stamboul Train*, p. 149.
7. Elizabeth Bowen, *The House in Paris* (London: Vintage, 1998), pp. 52–3.
8. Ibid., pp. 215, 233.
9. Elizabeth Bowen, *The Death of the Heart* (New York: Anchor, 2000), p. 13.
10. Cyril Connolly, *Enemies of Promise* (Chicago: University of Chicago Press, 2008), p. 27.
11. Cunningham, *British Writers of the Thirties*, p. 26.
12. Rosamond Lehmann, *Invitation to the Waltz* (London: Virago, 1981), pp. 192, 197.
13. Rosamond Lehmann, *The Weather in the Streets* (London: Virago, 1981), p. 171.

14. George Orwell, 'Inside the Whale', *in The Collected Essays, Journalism and Letters: Volume One*, ed. by Sonia Orwell and Ian Angus (London: Secker and Warburg, 1968), pp. 493–527.

15. Stevie Smith, *Novel on Yellow Paper* (London: Virago, 2015), p. 25.

16. Ibid, pp. 76, 77.

17. Perry Anderson, 'From Progress to Catastrophe', *London Review of Books*, 33.15 (28 July 2011), p. 24.

18. Janet Montefiore, *Men and Women Writers of the 1930s: The Dangerous Flood of History* (London: Routledge, 1996), pp. 142–77.

19. Naomi Michison, 'Introduction', *The Corn King and the Spring Queen* (Edinburgh: Canongate, 1990), p. x.

20. Naomi Mitchison, *The Blood of the Martyrs* (Edinburgh: Canongate, 1988), pp. 20–1.

21. Aldous Huxley, *Brave New World* (New York: Perennial Classics, 1998), p. 7.

22. Ibid., p. 236.

23. Evelyn Waugh, *A Handful of Dust* (Boston: Little, Brown, 1962), pp. 106, 53.

24. Evelyn Waugh, 'Author's Note', *Vile Bodies* (Boston: Back Bay, 1999), n.p.

25. Patrick Hamilton, *Impromptu in Moribundia* (London: Constable, 1939), p. 284.

26. Tyrus Miller, *Late Modernism: Politics, Fiction, and the Arts Between the World Wars* (Berkeley: University of California Press, 1999); Jed Esty, *A Shrinking Island: Modernism and National Culture in England* (Princeton: Princeton University Press, 2004); John Whittier-Ferguson, *Mortality and Form in Late Modernist Literature* (Cambridge: Cambridge University Press, 2014).

27. Hamilton, *Impromptu in Moribundia*, p. 249.

28. Steve Ellis, *British Writers and the Approach of World War II* (Cambridge: Cambridge University Press, 2015), pp. 109–46.

29. Virginia Woolf, *The Diary of Virginia Woolf, Volume Five: 1936–1941*, ed. by Anne Olivier Bell and Andrew McNeillie (San Diego: Harcourt Brace, 1984), p. 173.

30. Rex Warner, *The Professor* (London: Faber, 2008), p. 7.

31. Benjamin Kohlmann, *Committed Styles: Modernism, Politics, and Left-Wing Literature in the 1930s* (Oxford: Oxford University Press, 2014), p. 193.

32. Julian Symons, 'A London Letter: The Wartime Literary Situation', *The Kenyon Review*, 2.2 (Spring 1940), p. 254.

33. Elizabeth Maslen, 'A Cassandra with Clout: Storm Jameson, Little Englander and Good European', in *Intermodernism: Literary Culture in Mid-Twentieth-Century Britain*, ed. by Kristen Bluemel (Edinburgh: Edinburgh University Press, 2009), p. 25.

34. Philip Henderson, quoted in Maslen, 'A Cassandra with Clout', p. 26.

35. George Orwell, *Coming Up For Air* (San Diego: Harcourt, 1950), p. 29.

36. Ibid., pp. 30–1.

37. Lehmann, *The Weather in the Streets*, p. 25.

38. Ibid.

39. Waugh, *Vile Bodies*, p. 184.
40. Henry Green, *Party Going*, in *Living, Loving, Party Going* (London: Penguin, 1993), p. 483.
41. Christopher Isherwood, *Goodbye to Berlin*, in *The Berlin Novels* (London: Vintage, 1999), p. 244.
42. This infiltration of global violence into ordinary private life continues into the next decade, Thomas Davis suggests in his wide-ranging discussion of literary responses to the perceived crises of individual and national sovereignty represented by the Second World War and decolonisation. Davis argues that modernist techniques more usually associated with the 1920s were repurposed in Britain in order to register world-systemic distress through representations of ostensibly everyday life. Thomas S. Davis, *The Extinct Scene: Late Modernism and Everyday Life* (New York: Columbia University Press, 2015).
43. Graham Greene, *A Gun for Sale* (London: Vintage, 2005), p. 179.
44. Graham Greene, 'At Home', *Collected Essays* (London: Vintage, 2014), p. 334.

CHAPTER 3

Drama

Claire Warden*

In 1938, Stephen Spender imagined a 'revolution in the ideas of drama',[1] a theatre that could both deal with the complex socio-politics of the decade and take on new aesthetic challenges. The trouble, of course, was what this drama might look like in practice. In fact, in addressing the multifarious artistic and political disputes of this period, drama in the 1930s resists easy critical definition, residing in a liminal sense betwixt and between positions, terminology, and aesthetics. It can be read as highbrow, lowbrow, or middlebrow, with many individual examples flitting between these permeable categories. It appeared at both ends of the political spectrum, used as a weapon in the class struggle or as an upholder of the establishment; however, oftentimes it seemed to ignore these tensions occurring beyond the theatre walls. It was occasionally experimental, playing with language, set, or characterisation. Yet, in other cases, it simply continued traditions begun in the nineteenth century or even earlier. Even 'drama' as a concept was a site of contest, distinct and yet connected to equally fluid terms such as 'theatre', 'performance', and 'play'. This describes drama in general, of course, but these issues became particularly germane in the 1930s, a decade defined, after all, by conflict and unrest, the rise of new technology, economic downturn, and oppositional politics. This expansiveness is both a blessing and a curse for a chapter like this. It means it is difficult to develop a connecting through-line, and yet also leads to variety in terms of mode, genre, site, technique, and personnel. Maggie Gale accurately suggests that 'British drama underwent significant transformation during the inter-war period',[2] but it remains difficult to really explain the true nature of this transformation. This chapter aims to negotiate some of the awkward political and aesthetic issues that both engendered and complicated these on-stage innovations, considering performances in three overlapping sections: the experimental, the political, and the entertaining.

---

* With thanks to Ben Harker for his insightful comments and suggestions.

Experimental Aesthetics from the Continent: Expressionism in British Theatre

British theatre historiographies often present the 1930s as a decade of didactic political plays and/or entertaining farces, spectacles, or thrillers that provided some escape from the turbulent politics. While Continental European theatre exhibited some of the artistic techniques and perspectives of movements such as futurism, dada, and surrealism, British theatre seemed to remain proudly remote. But to leave it there is to neglect the histories of a small, turbulent, but fruitfully fertile experimental theatre scene that appeared in Britain during the 1930s, particularly engaging with the methods and aesthetics of expressionism. Expressionism appeared on the international stage before the First World War as an often violent and ecstatic response to the twentieth century: Oskar Kokoschka's 1909 *Murderer Hope of Womankind* is a landmark example of this new form. Expressionism disrupted established ways of creating theatre, rejecting the linearity and characterisation of naturalism or the well-made play, and the escapist amusements of music hall and variety. It remained a fertile movement throughout the 1920s, using fragmented narratives in episodes or pictures, harking back to the religious *Stationendrama*. Expressionism fosters an energetic stage environment engendered both by actors' heightened emotion (performances often contain ecstatic or painful screaming, the *Schrei*) and by scenographic elements reflecting the isolated protagonist's inner turmoil. Expressionism has been accused of being apolitical but, in the 1930s, appeared at both ends of the polarised political spectrum; whether didactic or not, expressionism maintained a 'faith in the power of rhetoric to reach beyond the theatrical frame and directly influence the ethical, social and political behavior of audiences'.[3] While predominantly a German movement, examples can be found in other parts of the world including Ireland (Sean O'Casey, who spent much of the 1930s in London) and the USA in the work of Eugene O'Neill, Sophie Treadwell, and Elmer Rice.

By the 1930s, expressionism had long since disappeared in Germany, not least because of the Nazi crackdown on experimental art. In a British context, companies did produce expressionist plays during the 1920s – Newcastle's People's Theatre's version of *Masses Man* (1925–6) and the Independent Labour Party's production of *The Machine Wreckers* in 1923 (both Ernst Toller) are two examples. Experimental theatre spaces certainly introduced British audiences to the wondrous complexities of expressionism throughout the 1920s and early 1930s: examples include Peter Godfrey at the Gate, Terence Gray at the Festival (Cambridge), Nigel Playfair at the Lyric, and André van Gyseghem at the Embassy. Despite their diversity, these figures and theatres have something in common: by the mid-1930s, all had suffered traumatic rupture. After producing plays by O'Neill and Toller, Gray left the Festival in 1933, bequeathing it to Joseph Macleod and then to Tyrone Guthrie who both aimed for a more conservative aesthetic because, in Guthrie's words, 'we felt that Cambridge had already had a good dose of *avant-garde* theatre'.[4] Under severe financial pressure, Playfair departed the Lyric in 1932 complaining that no new plays were being written. Godfrey, exhausted from years of producing plays by Nikolai Evreinov and Gerhart Hauptmann, amongst others, sold his Gate Theatre to Norman Marshall in 1934, while van Gyseghem left the Embassy in the same year, fatigued by the need to produce plays, such as Hans Chlumberg's *Miracle at Verdun*, in short two-week periods. Evidence here would initially suggest that the 1930s was a decidedly less fertile decade for experimental work as practitioners abandoned the avant-garde in favour of the commercial, popular, and decidedly less 'foreign'.

As Playfair lamented, few new experimental plays seemed to appear on the British stage in the 1930s. Newly available books such as Léon Moussinac's *The New Movement in Theatre*, which appeared in Britain in 1931, gave British theatres the opportunity to understand expressionism, and other movements, in performance. But new experimental writing was rare. Velona Pilcher, though American, co-founded the Gate Theatre Studio and her expressionist play *The Searcher*, finally produced as part of a variety evening at the Grafton Theatre, London, in 1930, was a notable exception. Like many of Toller's plays, *The Searcher* focusses on soldiers and nurses during war, and, in a typically expressionist description, was referred to as 'dramatisation of an unresolved neurosis [. . .] with the true quality of all nightmares'.[5] But, by and large, expressionism was regarded as a mode to be imported through the plays of Toller, O'Casey, and O'Neill, rather than as a catalyst for new work.

There were some other exceptions to this rule, however. J. B. Priestley, for example, who wrote *Dangerous Corner* (1932) and *Time and the Conways* (1937) during this period, also penned *Johnson Over Jordan* (1939), a play which resonated with both the interestingly complex narrative style of his so-called time plays and the linguistic vibrancy of continental expressionism. Indeed, responding to Basil Dean's version of *Johnson Over Jordan*, prominent theatre critic James Agate referred to it as an 'old fashioned piece [. . .] our author has gone back to the Expressionism of the nineteen-twenties [. . .] dead almost before it was alive'.[6] Dean employed designers

Edward Carrick (Edward Gordon Craig's son) and Elizabeth Haffenden to create the set and masks respectively, both of which reflected a frightening expressionist-style dystopia. As with many of the performances described in this chapter, Dean's *Johnson Over Jordan* was less than successful, deemed an indecipherable throwback to a vanished German experiment; *The Times'* reviewer sums up the general response to Dean's production:

> No one but a fool would venture to say of it briefly either that it is good or that it is bad, for it is a struggling, courageous play, an experiment exciting even in its failures.[7]

The notion of brave failure defines much of the theatre of this period.

Priestley was not alone in his dynamic, though flawed, expressionist experiment. Christopher Isherwood and W. H. Auden began collaborating on a series of plays in the 1920s. This partnership culminated in their three best-known works: *The Dog Beneath the Skin* (1935), *Ascent of F6* (1936), and *On the Frontier* (1938). Reflecting on the absence of Britain from typical narratives of modernist performance, Christopher Innes refers to the 'expressionistic experiments of O'Casey, Auden and Isherwood' as rather baulking the trend.[8] While, I suggest, Britain had a decidedly more active and vibrant avant-garde theatre scene in the early decades of the twentieth century than might be initially imagined, Auden and Isherwood's plays do stand out as rare examples of British 1930s expressionism. All three plays have political intentions, with Sir Francis Crewe confronting the self-righteous hypocrisy of Pressan Ambo's middle classes (*The Dog Beneath the Skin*), the *Ascent of F6* critiquing patriotic propaganda, and *On the Frontier* theatricalising conflict and dictatorship. All three also exhibit a degree of experimentalism, such as *Ascent of F6*'s representative figures Mr and Mrs A, *Dogskin*'s masking, and *On the Frontier*'s innovative bipartite set.

Often these plays, alongside works such as *Trial of a Judge* by Stephen Spender (1938) and T. S. Eliot's *Sweeney Agonistes* (1932), are described as 'poetic drama', works written in (at times) obscure poetic verse that, some critics have argued, represent a highbrow approach to theatrical writing. This categorisation, however, as Olga Taxidou recognises, is potentially awkward as 'the poetic legacy is sometimes used to justify the "unperformability" of the Anglophone dramas'.[9] It is easy to presume that poetic drama was part of an elitist strategy. However, in his 1938 *The Future of English Poetic Drama*, Auden actually claims that 'poetry is a medium which expresses the collective and universal feeling'.[10] Eliot's ecclesiastical verse drama *Murder in the Cathedral*, produced in Canterbury in 1935 and at the Mercury Theatre in 1935, provides an example here. Poetically dramatising the assassination of twelfth-century Archbishop of Canterbury Thomas Becket, *Murder in the Cathedral* initially appears to be far removed from the tense politics of the 1930s. However, the murderous Second Knight's affirmation that 'unhappily, there are times when violence is the only way in which social justice can be secured'[11] can be clearly read alongside the growing threat of fascism; indeed, producer Ashley Dukes referred to the Knights as 'all perfect Nazis'.[12] To regard poetic drama as, first and foremost, a linguistic or exclusively highbrow experiment disconnected from the socio-political context is then, as Sarah Bay-Cheng and Barbara Cole note in *Poets at Play*, decidedly problematic as, in reality, 'poetic drama attempts to resolve the basic division between poetry as literature and theater as performance'.[13] Auden and Isherwood's plays, for example, are tricky to perform. There are almost unworkable episodes such as Act II, Scene 5 of *The Dog Beneath the Skin* in which Alan's feet talk to each other, a section the published play suggests 'should probably be cut' in performance.[14] However these plays also contain a good deal of potential for on-stage reworkings. One particular 1930s theatre collective understood this: Rupert Doone's Group Theatre.

Doone founded Group Theatre in 1932 and, as well as including writers like Auden, Isherwood, Eliot, Spender, and Louis MacNeice, also employed the services of artist Robert Medley and composer Benjamin Britten, amongst others. Its key contributors were largely leftist in outlook and all directly opposed fascism in the late 1930s. Group adopted methods from pioneering contemporary international practitioners such as the Ballets Russes, Jacques Copeau, Jean Cocteau, and Kurt Jooss, amongst others, but its members were also interested in older theatre history, producing Mystery Plays and harlequinades. It had an established connection with Nugent Monck's Elizabethan-style Maddermarket Theatre, Norwich, which, by 1933, had produced Shakespeare's entire canon of plays.[15] (In fact, the 1930s marked a significant decade for the way Shakespeare's plays were performed and a number of innovative renderings appeared, including Robert Atkins's blank space restaging of *Henry V* in a boxing ring in Blackfriars Road (1938) and Russian émigré Theodore Komisarjevsky's productions in Stratford (1932–9), which played with the theatricality and artificiality of the stage and gave him the reputation of '*enfant terrible* and foe to the traditional').[16]

Group's leader Doone trained as a dancer and briefly performed with the Sergei Diaghilev's Ballets Russes. As leader of Group, Doone promoted a Wagnerian *Gesamtkunstwerk* (that is a form of Total Theatre that synthesised the various arts on the stage) or, perhaps more accurately, a Diaghilevian 'theatrical collage'.[17] By way of example, take Auden's *The Dance of Death*. Performed first at the Westminster Theatre in 1934 and later alongside Eliot's *Sweeney Agonistes*, *The Dance of Death* was, in a sense, a political play, narrating the decline of the British middle classes. Auden presented this theme by mixing old (the ancient figure of Death) and new (contemporary dance from Jooss and elements from Cocteau's 1917 *Parade*).[18] It concludes with the rather comical entrance of Karl Marx. Auden maintained that this play was intended 'for acting not reading', that its narrative and intention could only be really understood through embodied interpretation.[19] Poetic drama like *The Dance of Death* is not, then (appropriating Martin Puchner's useful term), 'anti-theatrical' but rather actually understood best through performance.[20] In fact, Auden wrote *The Dance of Death* in response to Doone's request for a ballet scenario. Doone danced the part of Death using acrobatics and fragmented gestures (à la Ballets Russes), wearing a sun mask designed by artist Henry Moore; he described the production as a 'political ballet-charade'.[21] However, strangely, given its experimental aesthetics, critics largely evaluated *The Dance of Death* in narrow political terms, with Ivor Brown sarcastically suggesting 'a good dose of doctrine was had by all'.[22]

'All you can hear/Is politics, politics everywhere'

Theatre has inherently political elements: its liveness, its ability to bring people together, its 'capacity to pretend' and 'propose alternative realities'.[23] These characteristics also mean that theatre can be read as potentially dangerous. In response, plays of the 1930s still came under the jurisdiction of the Lord Chamberlain who actively censored the theatre until 1968. Some productions, like Gray's version of Sergei Tretiakov's *Roar China!* (1931), were prevented entirely; the Lord Chamberlain regarded foreign works, created without British restrictions, with particular suspicion.[24] Gray fought hard against theatre censorship throughout the late 1920s and early 1930s and his decision to abandon the Festival was partly due to the frustrations he felt about, in his words, 'this Nursery Governess of ours'.[25] The changing political context of the 1930s made a significant difference to the Censor's decisions. For example, he initially refused a licence for *On the Frontier*, stating that 'at such a time as this the best interests of the country are served by avoiding any unnecessary exasperation to the leaders of the German people – even if this entails a certain muzzling of contemporary playwrights'.[26] A licence was eventually granted subject to changes in the script; even the word 'leader' was removed as being too closely associated with Hitler.[27] While Nazi characters were not entirely absent from the stage, pressure from the German Embassy and changing British political positions (from condemnation to appeasement) certainly meant that even ambiguous allusions to contemporary German politics proved problematic. Other moral, sexual, and religious concerns also drew the attention of the Censor. Partly to get around his heavy pencil, many of the groups discussed in this chapter (including the Gate, the Embassy, and the Arts Theatre) were actually paid subscription clubs rather than public theatre companies. This organisational decision had a number of benefits: plays were not subject to the same limitations, companies could partly withdraw from the commercialism of popular theatre, and directors could stage productions of particular interest to subscribers so could more easily consider foreign or challenging plays.[28] This gave these groups far greater economic and aesthetic freedom so that, as one example, Godfrey could stage O'Neill's banned play *Desire Under the Elms* at the Gate in 1931.

In addition to the coercion of the Censor, theatre experienced other commercial and aesthetic pressures as radio and cinema began to usurp its position as the premiere popular art.[29] While radio threatened the theatre (and, as dramatised in both *Ascent of F6* and *On the Frontier*, was often regarded as a suspect instrument of propaganda), it also furthered drama's cause. Val Gielgud, Productions Editor of BBC Drama during the 1930s, was described as operating a 'national theatre of the air' and, by the end of the Second World War, the BBC produced some four hundred plays every year.[30] Cinema, too, put considerable pressure on live performance: by 1937, confirms Andrew Davies, twenty million Britons attended five thousand cinemas each week.[31]

Responding to the pressures from the Censor and the rise of new technologies, political groups seemed unsure as to the best way of creating theatre that might impact, and even revolutionise, society. Consequently, throughout the 1930s, unions and political collectives often ignored theatre, regarding it, at times, as unimportant and, at others, as irritatingly obscure and avant-garde. One exception was the commissioning by the Trade Union Congress (TUC) of Miles Malleson's *Six Men of Dorset* (1934). Malleson's play dramatises the story of the Tolpuddle Martyrs, a group of agricultural workers transported to a penal colony for setting up a friendly society in the nineteenth century. The events marked a seminal moment in the history of British trade unionism and led to a vital, transformative victory for workers' rights. While Malleson's play is historical in focus, he includes particular challenges to the contemporary audience; in the final scene, leader George Loveless recites his poem but concludes saying 'But I be tired . . . Now it's for them that come after', a clear encouragement to the 1930s audience.[32] The 1937 production in Wolverhampton starred Sybil Thorndike and Lewis Casson, two stalwarts of theatre of the 1930s, associated with both successful West End productions and smaller leftist groups. It is particularly notable that Malleson uses a distinct Dorset dialect in *Six Men of Dorset*; indeed, a number of plays were written and produced in this decade that challenged the dominance of Received Pronunciation on the stage. Robert McLellan's comedy *Toom Byres* (produced at Curtain, Glasgow in 1936), for example, begins with Jeanie saying 'Dear me, is't yersell, Miss Peggy? My hairt gied sic a ding. It's sic an eldritch, eerie nicht.'[33] The dialect reflects the Scottish Borders' setting. In addition, Vance Marshall's *A. R. P.* (1938) used cockney accents to narrate an everyday family's response to the war preparations,[34] while the performers of small political theatre groups were simply encouraged to use their own accents without affectation or 'faux luvviness'.

Many of these groups, brought together in 1928 by Tom Thomas and his collective the Hackney People's Players under the banner of the Workers' Theatre Movement (WTM), produced declamatory agitprop plays as well as versions of Continental European works by Toller and Karel Čapek, amongst others. A self-proclaimed 'expression of the workers' struggle in dramatic form',[35] the WTM, in Ness Edwards's terms in his influential *The Workers' Theatre* (1930), aimed to 'organize the working class for the conquest of power'.[36] The WTM wanted to significantly transform the balance of society. What sort of theatre, its members wondered, could be most politically effective in this new age of fascist expansionism? Was agitprop really the most successful method? Soviet Russia was turning to socialist realism: could its linear narratives, realistic dialogue, rounded characters and unwaveringly positive endings work in a British context? How could political theatre also be artistically exciting? Should political theatre look like George Bernard Shaw's witty anti-war 'political extravaganza' *Geneva* (1938), which he updated to reflect changing circumstances?[37] Or perhaps like Montagu Slater's *Stay Down Miner*, produced by Left Theatre in 1936, which cast and recast the audience as blacklegs and Court jurors?[38] The WTM and related organisations responded to these questions by performing short political sketches and humorous satires in non-traditional spaces such as working men's clubs, village halls, or even outside factories or on town hall steps. The Popular Front's post-1936 strategy of political pageant (using hundreds of performers, songs, and iconographic spectacle) to counteract the advancement of fascism would also prove most effective.[39] (Pageantry, an ancient British tradition, is not, of course, an inherently leftist political form. In the 1930s, it was reworked not only by the Popular Front but also by poet-playwrights such as Eliot whose fundraiser pageant *The Rock* (1934) narrated the building of a church.)

By the mid-1930s, the WTM had disintegrated, shaken by aesthetic and political disagreements. Unity Theatre, a new initially amateur Britain-wide collective, rose from WTM's ashes and set out to investigate the problematic relationship between politics and theatre. Unity's collaboration with Group Theatre, however, illustrates the challenge of resolving these anxieties. Group performed Spender's anti-fascist play *Trial of a Judge* at Unity Theatre's home (Goldington Street) in 1938 with stage décor by artist John Piper. This expressionistic play with emblematic characters tells the tale of the Judge who fights back against fascist powers by standing up for the family of a murdered Jewish man. Eventually he is imprisoned and sentenced to death. Politically this play chimed with both the humanist principles of Group and the more radical politics of Unity. While the revolutionary figures die, the finale is not entirely without hope; indeed, in a direct nod to the audience, character Third Red confirms (mirroring Loveless's final encouragement in *Six Men of Dorset*), 'No, honour forgets / Our minds, rejects our bodies, rises / In other bodies and wears better days'.[40] However, the collaborative experiment was hampered by tensions. Many Unity members objected to the obtuse language, vaguely symbolist design, and bleak ending. Indeed, there were reports of heckling from spectators.[41] For many audience members, the experimental approach and rather gloomy conclusion diluted its radical message. Unity's more successful productions tended to be less obscure or open to interpretation. Counteracting the hazy symbolism of *Trial of a Judge*, its version of American Clifford Odets's *Waiting for Lefty* (1936–7) proved to be a lucrative production financially and in terms of bringing in new theatre-makers (such as director John Allen).[42] Its 1938 production of Nikolai Pogodin's *Aristocrats* was equally successful, using innovative projection to liven up this socialist realist play.

Unity also pioneered the living newspaper form, a method of creating political work that was already popular overseas, particularly in America where the Federal Theatre Project presented plays about electricity ownership, poverty, and sexually transmitted diseases.[43] Unity's living newspapers worked in a similar way to print newspapers by providing information and telling stories. But, rather than simply present facts, they looked to dramatise current issues in entertaining and engaging ways. Scripts were often generated collectively and the makers chose themes local or at least relevant to their audiences. The living newspaper's rapid cinematic montage structure partly moved away from both the lengthy linear narratives of realism and the (sometimes) drab didacticism of agitprop. Unity produced living newspapers throughout the mid-twentieth century, including several towards the end of the 1930s, dealing with contemporary issues at home (the 1938 *Busmen* focussed on the real 1937 Coronation bus strike) and abroad (*Crisis* in the same year discussed the Nazi search for *lebensraum* and was performed on the eve of Chamberlain's visit to Munich after being written in the previous seventy-two hours).[44] Other companies also saw the benefit of the living newspaper model, including Joan Littlewood and Ewan MacColl's Theatre Union, whose 1940 *Last Edition* reflected back on the 1930s with its European fascist expansionism and local unemployment.[45]

Unity developed a reputation for creating theatre that challenged typical political and theatrical orthodoxy. In the 1930s, this included Ben Bengal's *Plant in the Sun* (1938), starring African-American actor, singer, and activist Paul Robeson. Robeson had already performed in a number of British productions during the 1920s and 1930s, including *Othello* at the Savoy in 1930. Politically, Robeson felt a real affinity with Unity's aims and turned down more lucrative roles in order to perform in Herbert Marshall's version of this realist play about strikers in New York. *Plant in the Sun* marked a major success for Unity, both aesthetically (it used neon signs and groundbreaking lighting effects) and in terms of coverage: it won significant awards, encouraged new members to join, and received unanimously positive reviews.[46] Notwithstanding Robeson's star quality, this was definitely a collective enterprise; the *Guardian* reviewer even noted that Robeson, despite tremendous stage presence, 'properly maintained his anonymity, keeping the balance with his thoroughly capable colleagues'.[47] This determined sense of communality stood in stark contrast to the more star-focussed approach of the West End theatres.

Escaping the 1930s? Entertainment and the Theatre

In the mid-1930s, Walter Greenwood wrote a new play with Ronald Gow based on his successful novel. *Love on the Dole*, a study of Salford working-class communities, appeared first at the Manchester Repertory Theatre in February 1934 and later transferred to the Garrick (London, 1935). It was one of the surprise successes of the decade; despite its regional, working-class Northern focus, after its London run *Love on the Dole* even appeared as a popular film. In it Salford is dramatised as a polluted space of unemployment, illness, and conflict. In contrast to this demoralising urban environment, Greenwood also depicts various forms of escapism. While the central romantic couple (Larry and Sally) enjoys hillwalking, many of the escapist pleasures – gin drinking, gambling, soldiering, and eventually, in Sally's case, prostitution – are far less healthy. Sally's determined proclamation, 'aren't we all dead, all of us in Hanky Park',[48] sums up the distressing sense of entrapment felt by Salford's inhabitants, whose only pleasures seem to make them ill, poor, traumatised, or morally suspect, at least in the eyes of their gossiping neighbours.

In an era of political uncertainty, economic downturns, and conflict, many searched for the temporary distractions dramatised in *Love on the Dole*. While British 1930s drama had moments of experimentation and political engagement, amusing or diverting theatricals (detective stories or historical dramas, for example) remained the most popular forms of performance, although, as with all theatre, they came under significant pressure from the cinema. To present this thorny relationship between entertainment and experimentation (in terms of either politics or aesthetics) in such a diametrical way is, of course, to do a profound disservice to both. Auden understood music hall as the 'most living drama of to-day',[49] as did Bertolt Brecht, one of the mid-twentieth century's most important and prolific playwrights and theatre-makers. While Brecht despised drama that compelled audiences into a sort of trance, his theatre, from the Charlie Chaplin–influenced comedians to the use of satirical song, illustrated his interest in popular forms. Brecht's influence on Britain was felt more acutely later in the century with plays by Howard Brenton and Caryl Churchill that, in Janelle Reinelt's terms, exhibit a 'British Epic Theater'.[50] But Brecht plays did appear on the British stage far earlier, in productions such as *Anna Anna* (*The Seven Deadly Sins of the Bourgeoisie*), which brought Lotte Lenya to the British theatre (Savoy 1933), and Unity's version of *Senora Carrar's Rifles* (1938). Brecht grasped the potential of the music hall (or, from the German tradition, cabaret), suggesting that cabaret music exhibits the gestic, that is the combination of gesture and expression, so key to his epic theatre model. While escapist music hall and variety might appear to be dramatic traditions in conflict with engaged political drama, actually there is a good deal of overlap between them. How an audience might be entertained remained a driving force for 1930s theatre-makers regardless of their political allegiances or intentions.

In 1935, songwriter and matinee idol Ivor Novello took over the Theatre Royal, Drury Lane, and produced six musical shows. His 1935 musical play *Glamorous Night* at Drury Lane was one of the most successful theatrical events of the 1930s, building on the achievements of Noël Coward's *Cavalcade* some four years earlier.[51] Sketch/song revues also appeared at the Gate and Little Theatres to great success.[52] The most popular and abiding plays from the 1930s also provided leisurely distractions for their audiences. Coward, for instance, wrote a number of new plays in this decade, including *Private Lives* (1930, starring Laurence Olivier) and *Tonight at 8.30* (Phoenix 1936), which, in revue structure, juxtaposed comedies such as *Red Peppers* with tragedies, albeit suffused with Coward's customary wit, like *The Astonished Heart*. 'On the whole', suggests Frances Gray, 'the theatre that Coward worked in was geared to reassurance', bringing comfort, entertainment, and diversion.[53] However, during the 1930s, Coward also wrote a number of plays challenging his reputation as doyen of British establishment comedy, including the darkly comedic *Design for Living* (1933 on Broadway, 1939 in London). His 1934 *Point Valaine* (which did not appear on the British stage until 1947) provided another exception, experimenting with combining romantic storylines and violent, sexualised characterisation. New York audiences, who witnessed the first productions of *Point Valaine* in 1935, seemed perplexed by this departure from Coward's usual mix of playful frivolity and satirical merriment; *The Times'* New York correspondent expressed bewilderment that Coward should embark 'on the most turbulent of melodramatic seas, picturing ugly lust and violence [...] it is certainly not pretty and certainly from Mr. Coward it comes as something of a shock'.[54] Terence Rattigan also began his writing career in the 1930s with a witty comedy about language learning, *French Without Tears* (1936). However, then came *After the Dance* (1939), a more serious play about suicide and loss of youth. Again, as with Coward, Rattigan's 1930s work challenges preconceptions of him as an escapist, establishment figure, and demands a more nuanced reading of his oeuvre.

Against the foreboding 1930s backdrop, the theatre could also, however, provide reassuring light entertainment. Dodie Smith's *Dear Octopus* (1938), for instance, while acknowledging the changing nature of British family life, celebrated the enduring comfort of the 'dear octopus from whose tentacles we never quite escape, nor, in our inmost hearts, ever quite wish to'.[55] Smith represents a group of women playwrights in the 1930s, which included Gertrude Jennings (*Family Affairs*, 1934, and *Our Own Lives*, 1935), who are often overlooked by theatre history despite their interesting work. While subsequently ignored for writing '"realism" or "domestic comedy"' (as Maggie Gale puts it), actually, these women significantly broke into the 'male-dominated market'.[56] This was equally true for the art of acting, through the work of figures such as Edith Evans, Peggy Ashcroft, and Thorndike, as well as the managerial work of Lilian Baylis at the Old Vic. In fact, Baylis nurtured the talents of many actors who significantly advanced their careers in the 1930s: Laurence Olivier, Alec Guinness, John Gielgud, and Ralph Richardson, amongst others.[57]

Arguably the most significant event for British theatre in the 1930s, however, occurred well beyond the stage in the terrifyingly real theatres of war. In Spring 1939, on the cusp of a new international conflict, Coward wrote two new comedies: *Present Laughter* and *This Happy Breed*. Preparation for performance commenced, and the dress rehearsals took place on 30 and 31 August. On 3 September, Britain declared war and the plays did not actually appear on stage until 1942. This pattern was repeated across the British theatre world. Unity dropped its plans for a repertory theatre, theatres closed as blackouts were declared (though the Windmill and Unity reopened quickly), and Group faded away.[58] It appeared that war might irreparably destroy the British theatre scene. However, in reality, the Second World War transformed British theatre with the establishment of the Council for the Encouragement of Music and the Arts (CEMA) in 1940 (the forerunner of the Arts Council), the proliferation of touring companies that challenged the dominance of London, and the success of the Entertainments National Service Association (ENSA), which provided theatrical diversion for the troops and eventually paved the way for a National Theatre. Without over-stating the point, by the end of the war, Britain had a more egalitarian, democratic, geographically open theatre scene that acted as a stimulus for new generations of theatre-makers. The transformation of British theatre in the 1930s (with all its flaws, failures, and tensions) pre-empted the angry young men, radical agitational collectives, makers intent on break-ing down racial and/or gendered boundaries, in-yer-face experimental-ism, and cross-disciplinary innovations of the late twentieth and twenty-first centuries.

Notes

1. Stephen Spender, 'The Poetic Dramas of W.H. Auden and Christopher Isherwood', in *The Thirties and After: Poetry, Politics, People (1933–75)* (Basingstoke: Palgrave Macmillan, 1978), p. 61.

2. Maggie Gale, 'Theatre and Drama Between the Wars', in *The Cambridge History of Twentieth-Century English Literature*, ed. by Laura Marcus and Peter Nicholls (Cambridge: Cambridge University Press, 2004), pp. 318–34 (p. 332).

3. David Kuhns, *German Expressionist Theatre: The Actor and the Stage* (Cambridge: Cambridge University Press, 1997), p. 3.

4. Tyrone Guthrie, *A Life in Theatre* (London: Hamish Hamilton, 1961), p. 55.

5. Rebecca D'Monté, *British Theatre and Performance: 1900–1950* (London: Bloomsbury, 2015), p. 123; J. S., 'A New London Playhouse: Play and a Variety', *The Manchester Guardian*, 30 May 1930, p. 17.

6. Quoted in Maggie Gale, *J. B. Priestley* (London: Routledge, 2008), p. 174.

7. 'New Theatre', *The Times*, 23 February 1939, p. 12.

8. Christopher Innes, *Modern British Drama: The Twentieth Century* (Cambridge: Cambridge University Press, 2002), p. 4. See Claire Warden, *British Avant-Garde Theatre* (Basingstoke: Palgrave Macmillan, 2012), for more information about experimental performance in the pre-1945 period in Britain. In this book, I endeavor to illustrate that British theatre had decidedly more in common with avant-garde experiments on the Continent than conventional theatre historiographies have often imagined.

9. Olga Taxidou, *Modernism and Performance: From Jarry to Brecht* (Basingstoke: Palgrave Macmillan, 2007), p. 101.

10. W. H. Auden, 'The Future of English Poetic Drama', in W. H. Auden and Christopher Isherwood, *Plays and Other Dramatic Writings, 1928–1938*, ed. by Edward Mendelson (Princeton: Princeton University Press, 1988), p. 521.

11. T. S. Eliot, 'Murder in the Cathedral', in *The Complete Plays of T.S. Eliot* (New York: Harcourt, 1967), p. 50.

12. Ashley Dukes, *The Scene is Changed* (London: Macmillan, 1942). www .gutenberg.ca/ebooks/dukesa-sceneischanged/dukesa-sceneischanged-00-h-d ir/dukesa-sceneischanged-00-h.html [accessed 1 April 2016].

13. Sarah Bay-Cheng and Barbara Cole, *Poets at Play: An Anthology of Modernist Drama* (Selinsgrove: Susquehanna University Press, 2010), p. 14.

14. W. H. Auden and Christopher Isherwood, 'The Dog Beneath the Skin', in *Plays and Other Dramatic Writings*, p. 254.

15. Franklin J. Hildy, 'Playing Places for Shakespeare: The Maddermarket Theatre, Norwich', *Shakespeare Survey*, 47 (1994), 81–90 (p. 81).

16. Ralph Berry, 'Komisarjevsky at Stratford-Upon-Avon', *Shakespeare Survey*, 36 (1983), 73–84 (p. 73).

17. Michael Sidnell, *Dances of Death: The Group Theatre of London in the Thirties* (London: Faber and Faber, 1984), p. 258.

18. Ibid., p. 70.

19. Cited in ibid., p. 72.

20. Martin Puchner, *Stage-Fright: Modernism, Anti-Theatricality and Drama* (Baltimore: Johns Hopkins University Press, 2002).

21. Quoted in Sidnell, *Dances of Death*, p. 66.

22. I. Brown, 'Dance of Death: Group Theatre Season at the Westminster', *The Manchester Guardian*, 2 October 1935, p. 12.

23. The quotation from the subtitle is from W. H. Auden and Christopher Isherwood, 'The Ascent of F6', in *Plays and Other Dramatic Writings*, p. 298. Joe Kelleher, *Theatre & Politics* (Basingstoke: Palgrave Macmillan, 2009), p. 10.

24. Steve Nicholson. '"Irritating Tricks": Aesthetic Experimentation and Political Theatre', in *Rewriting the Thirties: Modernism and After*, ed. by Keith Williams and Steven Matthews (London: Longman, 1997), pp. 147–62 (p. 151).

25. Steve Nicholson, *The Censorship of British Drama 1900–1968: Volume One 1900–1932* (Exeter: University of Exeter Press, 2003), p. 174.

26. Dominic Shellard and Steve Nicholson with Miriam Handley, *The Lord Chamberlain Regrets: A History of British Theatre Censorship* (London: The British Library, 2004), p. 123.

27. Ibid.

28. Maggie Gale, 'The London Stage, 1918-1945', in *The Cambridge History of British Theatre*, vol 3, ed. by Baz Kershaw (Cambridge: Cambridge University Press, 2004), pp. 143–66 (p. 151).

29. Andrew Davies, *Other Theatres: The Development of Alternative and Experimental Theatre in Britain* (Totowa, NJ: Barnes and Noble, 1987), p. 94.

30. John Drakakis, *British Radio Drama* (Cambridge: Cambridge University Press, 1981), p. 7.

31. Davies, *Other Theatres*, p. 94.

32. Miles Malleson, *Six Men of Dorset* (London: Victor Gollancz, 1952), p. 110.

33. Robert Maclellan, *Toom Byres* (Glasgow: William Maclellan), p. 5.

34. See Warden, *British Avant-Garde Theatre*, p. 107.

35. 'The basis and development of the WTM (1932)' in *Theatres of the Left 1880–1935: Workers' Theatre Movements in Britain and America*, ed. by Raphael Samuel, Ewan MacColl, and Stuart Cosgrove (London: Routledge and Kegan Paul, 1985), p. 100.

36. Ness Edwards, 'The Workers' Theatre', in *Theatres of the Left*, ed. by Samuel et. al., p. 195.

37. G. B. Shaw, *Geneva* (1938). http://gutenberg.net.au/ebooks03/0300551h.htm l#e05

38. Nicholson, 'Irritating Tricks', p. 152.

39. See M. Wallis, 'Pageantry and the Popular Front: Ideological Production in the 'Thirties', *New Theatre Quarterly*, 10.38 (1994), 132–56.

40. Stephen Spender, *Trial of a Judge* (London: Faber and Faber, 1938), p. 108.

41. Colin Chambers, *The Story of Unity Theatre* (London: Lawrence and Wishart, 1989), p. 147.

42. This production caused significant ruptures in the landscape of political theatre in Britain and ushered in a new era which moved away from agitprop. See Chambers, *The Story of Unity Theatre*, pp. 43–5 for more details about this transition.

43. For more on the FTP, see Library of Congress online collection of historical documents and scripts: https://memory.loc.gov/ammem/fedtp/fthome.html

44. Colin Chambers, 'History in the Driving Seat: Unity Theatre and the Embrace of the "Real"', in *Get Real: Documentary Theatre Past and Present*, ed. by Alison Forsyth and Chris Megson (Basingstoke: Palgrave Macmillan, 2011), pp. 38–54 (pp. 43–5).
45. For further information about this play, see Warden, *British Avant-Garde Theatre*, pp. 27–9. The extant script is published in *Agit-prop to Theatre Workshop: Political Playscripts 1930–50*, ed. by Howard Goorney and Ewan MacColl (Manchester: Manchester University Press, 1986).
46. Chambers, *The Story of Unity Theatre*, pp. 151–7.
47. J. H. M. 'A Workers Theatre: Two American Plays', *The Manchester Guardian*, 16 June 1938, p. 14.
48. Walter Greenwood, 'Love on the Dole', in *Plays of the Thirties: Volume 1*, ed. by James Charlton (London: Pan, 1966), p. 192.
49. W. H. Auden, 'Manifesto on the Theatre', in *The English Auden: Poems, Essays and Dramatic Writings, 1927–1939*, ed. by Edward Mendelson (London: Faber and Faber, 1986), p. 273.
50. Janelle Reinelt, *After Brecht: British Epic Theater* (Ann Arbor: University of Michigan Press, 1996).
51. Peter Noble, *Ivor Novello* (London: White Lion, 1975), pp. 197–210.
52. James Ross Moore, 'Girl Crazy: Musicals and Revue Between the Wars', in *British Theatre Between the Wars: 1918–1939*, ed. by Clive Barker and Maggie Gale, pp. 88–112 (pp. 105–9).
53. Frances Gray, *Noel Coward* (London: MacMillan, 1987), p. 51.
54. 'Point Valaine', *The Times*, 29 January 1935, p. 10.
55. Dodie Smith, 'Dear Octopus', in *Plays of the Thirties*, p. 379.
56. Maggie Gale, 'Women Playwrights of the 1920s and 1930s', in *The Cambridge Companion to Modern British Women Playwrights*, ed. by Elaine Aston and Janelle Reinelt (Cambridge: Cambridge University Press, 2000), pp. 23–37 (p. 23).
57. Elizabeth Schafer, *Lilian Baylis: A Biography* (Hatfield: Hertfordshire University Press and Society for Theatre Research, 2006), p. 6.
58. Davies, *Other Theatres*, p. 123; Andrew Davies, 'The War Years', in *Theatre and War 1933–1945: Performance in Extremis*, ed. by M. Balfour (New York: Berghahn, 2001), pp. 54–64 (p. 55). There was an attempt to resurrect Group after the War but this was a largely fruitless enterprise. See Appendix E in Sidnell, *Dances of Death*, pp. 299–302.

CHAPTER 4

Publishing and Periodicals

Peter Marks

The 1930s was a decade energised by crisis and hope. It ended badly on many fronts, including (seemingly) that of literature. Robert Hewison labels the years 1939 and 1940 the 'grand slaughter of magazines', noting that *The Cornhill Magazine, Criterion, New Verse, Welsh Review, Voice of Scotland*, and a range of other journals 'all fell silent'.[1] John Lehmann, a leading young periodical editor, recalled how 'In the Christmas [1939] Number I announced the death of *New Writing*',[2] an innovative journal he had launched in 1936. Yet Hewison's depressing list incorporates periodicals begun in the previous decade, such as Eliot's *Criterion* (1922–39), and in the previous century – *The Cornhill* was first published in 1860. The 'deaths' of *Criterion* and *The Cornhill* are less surprising than that they survived as long as they did. Lehmann himself later admitted that he exaggerated the death of *New Writing*: 'In the early days of the war, it seemed to me that *New Writing* could scarcely hope to survive.'[3] Survive it did, until the autumn of 1941, as *Folios of New Writing*, demonstrating commendable (but not unique) endurance. The small, independent publisher The Bodley Head had published *New Writing*'s first 1936 number, before Lehmann moved the journal to the communist publishing firm Lawrence and Wishart, hoping to start a 'New Writing Library' there. That venture failed, so Lehmann moved *New Writing* to Leonard and Virginia Woolf's Hogarth Press, where he had worked in 1931 and 1932. Once the war began, Lehmann published a selection of *New Writing*'s pre-war output as *Penguin New Writing*, formalising an association with Penguin Books that continued until 1950. *New Writing* shows the complicated interplay between publishing and periodicals through a decade rich with possibility. Recent scholarship on 1930s literature, including work in this *Companion*, argues against the facile dismissal of the decade's writers for naively misunderstanding events. The decade's periodical and publishing activity demonstrates something more nuanced and enlightening: that writers and publishers were forward-looking and innovative, recognising a range of dangers while actively working to construct a better future.

Despite the overlap between periodicals and book publishing, economies of scale should be kept in mind. Journals tended to have small sales, so that, in the case of Ford Madox Ford's *The English Review* (1908–37), 'circulation never rose above about 1,000 copies a month',[4] while *The Criterion* had only 200 subscribers when Eliot brought it to a close in 1939.[5] Even the *Times Literary Supplement*, financially backed by Lord Northcliffe, 'very nearly died' in 1922 after its circulation 'almost halved' from a 1914 high of 44,000, according to a later editor, Jeremy Treglown. Indeed Treglown suggests that only Northcliffe's own death later that year saved the *Supplement*.[6] The *Left Review* sold 5,000 copies,[7] an impressive amount for a literary periodical in the 1930s. But, in that same year, Victor Gollancz's Left Book Club had 57,000 members, each committed to buying a book a month. Penguin Specials, first produced in 1937, might sell 250,000 copies. The latter was a publishing phenomenon but not unique, for, while the publishing market sat on notoriously unsteady ground, a successful commercial publisher such as Everyman's Library might have a print run of 10,000 copies and print multiple runs over time (as with the thirty-one printings of *David Copperfield*).[8] Book publishers and periodicals were in part speaking to different types of audiences or audiences with different interests. Periodicals were focused entities, with specific concerns and perspectives honed by editors and contributors. Their relatively brief shelf lives were invigorated by passion and controversy that contributed valuably to the aesthetic and political discourse in a traumatic decade. Although publishing was always a precarious affair, publishers aimed to entertain and inform larger audiences. Even relatively small entities such as Gollancz and the Hogarth Press fostered broad public debate, while the remarkable success of Penguin Books, established in 1935, had significant cultural effects for decades. This chapter assesses some of these contributions, incorporating lesser-known publications and adventuring beyond the usual London–Oxford–Cambridge triangle dominated by middle-class men; the decade was far more culturally complex than that.

Periodicals in Scotland and Wales

One small example of that far-flung richness was one of Hewison's 'casualties': *The Voice of Scotland* (1938–9). Its key figure, C. M. Grieve (better known under the pseudonym Hugh MacDiarmid), had proposed in an earlier periodical, *The Scottish Chapbook* (1922–3), to 'bring Scottish

Literature into closer touch with current European tendencies in technique and ideation'. Rejecting English cultural dominance, Grieve insisted 'upon truer evaluations of the work of Scottish writers than are usually given in the present over-Anglicised condition of British literary journalism'.[9] The Scottish Renaissance of the 1920s had rekindled interest in Scottish language and national identity. This dynamic continued in the 1930s, most substantially with *The Modern Scot* (1930–6), owned and edited by James Whyte. Margery McCulloch explains that Whyte's 'comfortable financial background' allowed him to 'conduct his magazine independently' and to pursue a commitment to that 1930s leitmotif, the 'interaction of the political and aesthetic'.[10] The early Spring 1932 number provides an instructive sample, including William Soutar's 350-line poem 'The Auld Tree' (complete with a glossary of Scots phrases such as 'Yirdlin' and 'Thowless') and Naomi Mitchison's 'A Socialist Plan for Scotland'. She rejects the large urbanised Socialism exemplified in the Soviet Union for smaller cooperatives with links to rural communities. Grant Duff addresses European perspectives characteristic of the Scottish Renaissance, writing about Benedetto Croce's place in post-war Italian philosophy. The initial 'Editorial Notes' discuss 'The Background of Present-Day Nationalism', declaring how 'few Nationalists could be found today to applaud, for example, [Heinrich von] Treitschke's and [Johann Gottlieb] Fichte's impassioned invocations of the racial superiority and achievements of the German people'. The article's 'today' is April 1932, before Hitler was appointed German Chancellor. The international situation changed rapidly, and periodicals adjusted accordingly.

McCulloch judges that '*The Modern Scot* was a splendidly interactive and cosmopolitan modern journal', more obviously fulfilling Grieve's 'early vision of an inspirational aesthetic and political Scottish periodical than did his own hand-to-mouth little magazines'.[11] The final phrase is informative, for all periodicals are vulnerable creatures. McCulloch suggests one local reason: 'the absence in Scotland of a sufficiently large and adventurous audience interested in the promotion of new ideas, both Scottish and emanating from beyond Scotland.'[12] *The Modern Scot* survived from 1930–6, then briefly merged with another literary periodical to form *Outlook* (1936–7). Grieve/MacDiarmid returned in 1938 with *The Voice of Scotland*, which Cairns Craig observes promoted MacDiarmid's take on Scottish culture. For Craig, even though MacDiarmid was positive about young Celtic writers and the significance of contemporary poetry in Scots, 'actually existing Scotland' remained 'the mere corpse of a cultured nation'.[13] McCulloch, however, emphasises how journals expanded the 'potentially inward-looking idea of an interwar "Scottish Renaissance" movement to include its international significance as a Scottish manifestation of modernism'.[14] Often short-lived, these journals collectively voiced an ever-evolving sensibility.

Chris Hopkins charts something similar in Wales. Two late 1930s journals, *Wales* (1937–9) and *Welsh Review* (1939–40), both 'generally socially minded and progressive', 'reflected concerns with the consequences, especially for Wales, of current crises in economics and politics and the probability of another war'.[15] Hopkins reckons that they 'had an enormous impact on the development of Welsh writing in English'.[16] In his first editorial in *Wales*, Keidrych Rhys declares that 'We are not a literary clique; once more we stress we are with the People',[17] and that *Wales* aims to give young writers 'an opportunity denied them in the English Literary Map'.[18] It published young artists including Dylan Thomas, Glyn Jones, and Idris Davies in its first series, which wound up on the eve of the Second World War. *Welsh Review* first appeared in January 1939, primarily published in English. While Hopkins notes that 'translations of works in Welsh were particularly sought',[19] Malcolm Ballin addresses the brute reality that 'a bilingual model would fail financially'.[20] Its August 1939 number illustrated the array of new creative and critical talent available, with stories by Walter Dowding and Gwyn Jones and poetry by Ursula Lavery. These precede James Guthrie's extended personal reminiscence of Edward Thomas.[21] J. Ellis Williams writes tartly about 'Welsh Drama To-Day', commenting that in 1930 'every Welshman who could afford a penny for a pencil was then busy writing a play', while in 1939 'companies all over Wales looking for new plays are to-day turning every stone to find one'.[22] *The Welsh Review* lasted only until November 1939, though, like *Wales*, it would have an afterlife in the 1940s. Such Scottish and Welsh examples advertise the vigour of independent critical and creative thought beyond London, Oxford, and Cambridge.

Journals from the Metropole

That said, many of the most influential journals did emanate from those three undeniably powerful cultural centres, providing spaces for new, often highly politicised writing. Cambridge, for example, harboured the fleeting and politically radical *Cambridge Left* (1933–4), but also *Scrutiny* (1932–1953), which achieved its great effect beyond the 1930s, becoming, under the proselytising eye of F. R. Leavis, one of the most influential journals of literary criticism of the twentieth century.[23] *Cambridge Left* offered a platform for rising literary figures such as John Cornford (later killed in the Spanish Civil War) to test out fusions of radical politics and poetics. The relatively circumscribed world of Oxbridge and London maintained a critical mass of writers and publishers that was impressive and generative, though sometimes metaphorically inbred. Undoubtedly, the literary component was male-dominated. Virginia Woolf's *A Room of One's Own* (1929) opens with the narrator chased off Oxbridge turf for being a woman, a powerful indictment of the high historical barriers women faced when men largely controlled literary production (as publishers or editors), literary reception (as reviewers), and the literary networks so vital to budding talent.

One notable exception was the London-based weekly *Time and Tide*, established in 1920 by wealthy activist Viscountess Margaret Rhondda. Jane Dowson explains that, from the outset, Rhondda 'championed free-thinking dialogue and the role of intellectual women as board members, journalists, writers, and influential figures in all areas of public life'.[24] The magazine quickly established itself in the 1920s as a champion of feminist thought, promoting 'the social equality of women and the working class'.[25] These concerns continued into the volatile 1930s, when *Time and Tide* expanded in size, focus, and circulation. The magazine's feminist slant, instanced in extracts from '*A Room of One's Own*, the serialisation of E. M. Delafield's *Diary of a Provincial Lady* [...] and the many essays by Winifred Holtby',[26] was never its sole reason for being. Muriel Mellown notes: 'As events in Europe took on an ever more ominous tone, the emphasis inevitably shifted to the pressing political issues – disarmament, isolationism, pacifism, the rise of the Nazi Party, the war in Spain.'[27] *Time and Tide*, which in the 1920s published the work of writers of the calibre of Katherine Mansfield, Sylvia Townsend Warner, and Aldous Huxley, maintained a high literary component, publishing the likes of Rebecca West, Storm Jameson, Holtby, and Mitchison in the 1930s. This latter group exemplifies how London literary networking might work in favour of women, with Janet Montefiore explaining that 'the closeness between these writers is cultural and political as much as personal'. They all lived in London, knowing 'each other as members of pacifist and/or anti-Fascist causes, as well as meeting on the pages of [...] *Time and Tide*, to which they all contributed'.[28] The magazine functioned as a capacious interactive space for progressive attitudes, with women prominent in its production and output.

Poetry and the People (1938–40) perhaps was the decade's most successful attempt to give working-class writers their own literary platform. Or, rather, working-class men, for, if middle-class women struggled to get published in the 1930s, working-class women faced far greater impediments. As Christopher Hilliard records with evident disappointment in his authoritative study of the period, 'efforts to uncover working-class women writers in the first half of the twentieth century have turned up very few'.[29] Working-class writers had few of the affiliations through education and social interaction that middle-class writers tended to enjoy and that enabled easier access to publishers or periodicals. Indeed, *Poetry and the People* itself required middle-class help, arising out of the Left Book Club, which activated discussion groups throughout Britain on fiction, theatre, and poetry. One product of this effort, the *Left Poets' News Sheet*, was reborn as *Poetry and the People* in July 1938. The journal aimed to publish poetry by workers, along with articles focussed on their lives. The materiality of the journal underscored its precarious existence; the 'first fourteen issues were typed and duplicated rather than printed, and ran to twenty pages'.[30] Still, Andy Croft calculates that, after a year, *Poetry and the People* 'was selling a thousand copies a month',[31] and it set up discussion groups along Left Book Club lines. The standard of poetry itself was variable, an editor noting that, while submission numbers were high, 'the general level of achievement is low. Most of the great volume of poetry we receive, frankly, is worthless as poetry.'[32] The journal drew well-established writers such as Cecil Day-Lewis, Charles Madge, and Louis MacNeice, all contributing articles and in some cases talks to the journal's writers. Ultimately, the idealism motivating *Poetry and the People* was undermined by larger social and political circumstances and by the pragmatics of production that threaten all periodicals. Revamped in 1939, it appeared only sporadically in 1940, its paper ration taken over by the left-wing middle-class writers behind a new venture, *Our Time* (1941–9). But *Poetry and the People* was less important for what it produced than what it stood for: the desire for workers to find an outlet for previously suppressed or undervalued creativity.

Working-class writers were also promoted in *Left Review*. Many of its guiding spirits were members of the Communist Party of Great Britain or fellow travellers, and initially it was the literary organ of the British Section of the International Union of Revolutionary Writers. First published in October 1934, *Left Review* created, in David Trotter's term, 'the main forum for Popular Front literary activity',[33] after the Communist Party switched from a belligerent attitude towards other left-wing parties to a broader-based anti-fascist struggle. *Left Review*'s first number carried a Writer's International declaration proclaiming the collapse of capitalist culture and the need for 'revolutionary writers' to oppose fascism and support the Soviet Union. While most of its contributors were politically engaged middle class, it did promote competitions to encourage working-class writers, asking them in December 1934 to describe 'an hour or a shift at work', or a strike (October 1935). One of the journal's initial editorial collective, Amabel Williams-Ellis, was the motive force behind these competitions, although another editor, Alick West, 'publicly deplored the literary advice she gave out and objected to the competitions as a sort of "patronage"'.[34] Hilliard makes the plausible criticism that the first group of editors might not have been 'particularly competent or diligent at building up a cadre of working-class writers',[35] a charge he qualifies in relation to *Left Review*'s later editors, Edgell Rickword and Randall Swingler. Whatever the case, Rickword cut back on such competitions and Swingler abandoned them.

Left Review was a regular booster for the Soviet Union and what many contributors considered the greater cultural freedom emanating from (putatively) the only extant socialist nation. While regularly taking aim at the 'decadence' of much contemporary British literature, the alternative approach of socialist realism, which had emerged from the 1934 All Union Congress of Soviet Writers in Moscow, failed to find sufficient *Left Review* adherents to generate a creative critical mass. The vital conflict during its time was the Spanish Civil War and, in 1937, the journal published a survey of writer commitment, *Authors Take Sides on the Spanish War*. The vast majority of respondents favoured the left-wing Republican government, although Laura Riding, Evelyn Waugh, and others pointedly supported the Franco-led rebellion. Whether the journal presented a unified political voice is debatable, the assortment of writers published arguing against it as being merely a Communist Party organ – and indeed Benjamin Kohlmann's chapter in this *Companion* finds in it evidence of the post-war New Left. The July 1936 number, for example, contains work by Rebecca West, H. G. Wells, Gerald Heard, André Malraux, Julian Benda, and Ernst Toller. Admittedly, this issue celebrated a recent International Writers convention, which might be seen as a Communist Party propaganda vehicle, but in general *Left Review* was internationalist in perspective rather than a party-political loudspeaker. For all its energy and cultural engagement, though, Swingler wound up *Left Review* in 1938. The precise reasons for its demise are unclear. While it shared an address with Lawrence and Wishart, it might be that a proposed deal with the more commercial publisher Penguin Books fell through.[36]

Hogarth Press and the Left Book Club

Penguin Books itself was one of the significant publishing successes of the decade (and will be dealt with later in this chapter), but smaller presses also contributed tellingly. Hogarth Press exemplifies how publishers responded, and contributed, to the tenor of the times. Established in 1917 by Leonard and Virginia Woolf in their London home, the press published work the Woolfs thought worthy but likely to find only a small audience. Virginia Woolf already had published *The Voyage Out* (1915), but Hogarth became the vehicle for subsequent novels and non-fiction, helping to employ her troubled brilliance. Leonard ran the business. Begun with the Woolfs hand printing volumes at home (before becoming a more commercial affair), Hogarth was no mere vanity press. The couple's solicitous oversight published creative work by Woolf, Katherine Mansfield, T. S. Eliot, E. M. Forster, and Vita Sackville-West, alongside Leonard Woolf's socially engaged writing, translations of Rilke, Freud's *The Ego and the Id*, and new analyses by Maynard Keynes. The 1930s stamped its mark on the press, for, alongside Virginia Woolf's challenging creative work, such as *The Waves* (1931), which sold 10,000 copies in six months, J. H. Willis comments that the decade 'was the period when Leonard Woolf's political interest provided almost a new identity for Hogarth. The press soon averaged eight titles a year on a variety of political and social subjects.'[37] One of the most noteworthy was Virginia Woolf's 1938 searing anti-war critique, *Three Guineas* (considered in later chapters of this *Companion*).

A revealing aspect of Hogarth's 1930s was its publication of politically aligned young writers. A key figure promoting these new voices was one of its members, John Lehmann. Lehmann was in his early twenties when he joined the press in 1931, and, although he left acrimoniously after eighteen months, he returned in 1938. Lehmann enlisted a fellow Oxbridge graduate, Michael Roberts, who chose nine young poets, many on their way to being internationally recognised and most from Oxford or Cambridge: W. H. Auden, Cecil Day-Lewis, William Empson, Stephen Spender, Lehmann, and others. The result, *New Signatures: Poems by Several Hands* (1932), part of the Hogarth Living Poets series, announced authors united not by political orthodoxy but by increased social awareness. John Fuller comments that some of Auden's contributions 'represented a conscious flirtation with Communism',[38] which might be true generally for the volume. Roberts followed this with *New Country: Prose and Poetry by the Authors of New Signatures* (1933).

The prose section especially allowed for more overtly political material, including Spender's essay 'Poetry and Revolution' and Day-Lewis's 'Letter to a Young Revolutionary', which begins portentously: 'Dear Jonathan. So you are thinking of joining the Communist Party.'[39] In the long term, most contributors moved away from the overtly leftist attitude struck in this volume, but *New Country* and *New Signatures* mark significant moments in the expression of political intent by young writers under the Hogarth banner.

Those writers were all men. Not surprisingly, and even given Virginia Woolf's agonistic relationship with feminism, the Hogarth Press gave space to feminist-oriented works. Examples from the 1920s include Willa Muir's *Women: An Enquiry* (1925), the pamphlet *Leisured Women* (1928) by *Time and Tide's* Viscountess Rhondda, and Woolf's inventive polemic *A Room of One's Own*. The press published *Life as We Have Known It* in 1931, a remarkable first-hand account of the struggle of working-class women in the early twentieth century who had found common cause through association with the Women's Co-operative Guild. Hogarth also released *Our Freedom and Its Results* (1936), edited by the feminist Ray Strachey, a collection of five middle-class women supplying assessments of women's history, their contemporary situation, and what the future might hold. Willis notes that Virginia Woolf 'did not involve herself in the project', adding 'it is unclear' whether she ever read the completed book. She did, however, make her own powerful, idiosyncratic contribution to feminist writing with *Three Guineas*, a work that remains a tribute to the sort of independent thinking a small, independent press can introduce into public discourse. As with *A Room of One's Own*, its influence far outlasted the decade.

Where the Hogarth Press both began before and continued briefly after the 1930s, the rise of the Left Book Club seems particularly reflective of the decade. Victor Gollancz, an independent publisher since 1927, initiated it in 1936. Gollancz had moved leftward politically, his socialist allegiances manifest in works published in the early 1930s such as G. D. H. Cole's 1934 study *What Marx Really Meant* (which Gollancz commissioned) and John Strachey's *The Coming Struggle for Power* (1932), which ends stirringly with the vision of British workers potentially 'taking a decisive role in the establishment of world communism'.[40] In the increasingly troubled world of international politics, and in response to the National Government's election victory in 1935, Gollancz proposed a strategic approach to disseminating left-wing thought: a book club requiring members to purchase a Selection of the Month for at least six months, at the reduced price of two shillings and sixpence. Non-members could purchase these books at a higher price. Books would be chosen by the Left Book Club's selectors: Gollancz, Strachey, and Harold Laski (a Labour Party radical and politics professor). Both Strachey and Laski had communist sympathies, while Gollancz, though less in thrall, was also supportive of the Party. But the LBC, as it quickly became known, was no clumsy propaganda unit. Its members were voluntary, the initial 9,000 who signed up by May 1936 far outstripping Gollancz's hope of 2,500 subscribers. Membership would reach 57,000 by April 1939, revealing a progressive audience hungry for left-wing analyses and proposals.

Many of the initial 1936 selections, in distinctive orange covers, spoke to compelling international concerns from an overseas perspective: the exiled German Rudolf Olden's *Hitler the Pawn* (June), Frenchman André Malraux's *Days of Contempt* (August), the Italian Gaetano Salvemini's *Under the Axe of Fascism* (October), and *Spain in Revolt* (December) by the Americans Harry Gannes and Theodore Repard. Club members also received a monthly newsletter, *Left Book News*. It initially had a regular column, 'The USSR Month by Month', by the communist and noted film critic Ivor Montagu, applauding Soviet life and institutions, including the Moscow Show Trials. By February 1937, the LBC could hire out the Albert Hall for a mass rally, Ruth Dudley Edwards noting that by then:

> The *Left Book News* (now the *Left News*) was over thirty pages long. 'Additional', 'Supplementary', and 'Topical' books were available as extras and the 'Educational' category was at the planning stage. Weekend schools had begun, provincial rallies were being arranged, and most significant of all, there were already between three and four hundred discussion groups nationwide.[41]

The LBC quickly approximated a political movement. This very success generated tensions, Gollancz's own wish to nurture a Popular Front inclusiveness as the necessary defence against fascism at odds with more radical elements, including Strachey and Laski, who wanted the Club to support the Communist Party. Party members infiltrated discussion groups around the country that met regularly to consider the Monthly Selections, and that created offshoots such as *Poetry and the People* and the LBC Theatre Guild. At the height of its popularity, the LBC boasted 1,200 discussion groups nationwide, as well as international branches as far afield as Australia, which had 4,500 members.[42]

One criticism was that the Club spoke less to the working class it ostensibly championed than to middle-class intellectuals. True, it did publish *The Problem of the Distressed Areas* (November 1937) by National Unemployed Workers' Movement leader Wal Hannington, and B. L. Coombes' *These Poor Hands: The Autobiography of a Miner in South Wales* (June 1939), as well as Labour MP 'Red Ellen' Wilkinson's *The Town That Was Murdered: The Life-Story of Jarrow* (September 1939). Like the work of Hannington and Coombs, Wilkinson's book, a polemical history of the Tyneside town famed as the starting point for the 1936 march of unemployed men to Parliament, presented a world to readers who had little experience of the conditions described. A more representative, if more controversial, study was George Orwell's *The Road to Wigan Pier* (March 1937), which gave an expressly middle-class account of working conditions in the north of England soldered roughly on to Orwell's autobiographical and consciously provocative take on socialism. The LBC version of this book came with a preface by Gollancz explicitly challenging, if not bluntly dismissing, the polemical sections of the book, while accepting its documentary-like first half as a vivid and compelling portrait of working-class conditions. Gollancz refused to publish Orwell's next book, *Homage to Catalonia* (1938), assuming correctly that it would prosecute an unorthodox case on the Spanish Civil War. Fredric Warburg, sometimes attacked as a 'Trotskyist' publisher, published it instead. The Spanish Civil War would prompt some of the LBC's best work, including Frank Jellinek's *The Civil War in Spain* (June 1938) and Arthur Koestler's *Spanish Testament* (December 1937), which Koestler backed up with a speaking tour. 'State of the nation' studies such as G. D. H. and M. I. Cole's *The Condition of Britain* (April 1937) were published alongside positive reviews of the Soviet Union, most notably, in October 1937, a reprint of Sidney and Beatrice Webb's 1935 *Soviet Communism: A New Civilisation*, revealingly with the original question mark in the title taken out. Works of political theory such as the Emile Burns–edited *A Handbook of Marxism* (July 1937) and anti-war arguments, exemplified by Eleanor Rathbone's *War Can Be Averted* (January 1938), register the LBC as a significant contributor to political discussion.

The Club was not without its deficiencies and critics. Although husband and wife teams such as the Coles and the Webbs were published, Rathbone's book was unusual, for, along with Wilkinson's *The Town That Was Murdered* and Hilary Newitt's *Women Must Choose* (June 1937), it was among the few sole-authored by women. Newitt presented a comparative account of women's positions under different European political systems, while Georgi Serebrennikov's *The Position of Women in the USSR* (January 1937) was another rarity in dealing specifically with women. This absence of a strong feminist voice was not raised in *Left News*, perhaps because these concerns were submerged beneath national and international politics, but likely because, for all its progressive energy, the LBC was still essentially dominated by men, and less concerned with the feminist issues that activated a journal such as *Time and Tide*. The Club also had political critics on the political left, Dudley Edwards noting that in 1937 the *New Statesman and Nation* indicted 'a membership composed of "intellectual sheep" led by "dictator Gollancz"'.[43] She suggests that for the Labour Party leadership the Club 'was at best an irritant, and at worst a serious threat'.[44] As a form of counter-measure, Clement Attlee's *The Labour Party in Perspective* (August 1937) attempted to connect to LBC members by explaining Labour's practical approach to socialism via a non-revolutionary road. Orwell also was critical, mocking a club meeting in *Coming Up For Air* (1939), where his narrator George Bowling judges that 'Invariably half the people come away without a notion of what it's all about'.[45] To his credit, Gollancz published the novel.

Through the late 1930s, while the Club's membership and influence grew, Gollancz's concerns grew about its direction. He slowly took against the Soviet Union and the motives of the Communist Party within Britain and beyond. The worrying prospect of European war was a staple of LBC choices, heightening the sense of threat and possibility. These factors simultaneously buttressed the argument for the Club's existence and accentuated the need for independent thinking if war was to be avoided. In a November 1938 editorial 'Thoughts After Munich', Gollancz admits that, while the LBC 'set out as an educational body', he had allowed himself 'to become too much of a propagandist and too little of an educator'. He adds that 'only by the clash of ideas does a mind truly become free', and that the Club had concentrated 'on two or three points of view'.[46] In early 1939, he began to break alliances with the Communist Party, the Nazi–Soviet Pact later that year sealing the division. While the Party in the early part of the war argued the case for a People's Movement against war, Gollancz proselytised in favour of the war effort, later editing and contributing to *The Betrayal of the Left: An Examination and Refutation of Communist Policy*, published as an 'Additional' Book in February 1941. While it was still productive and progressive, LBC's influence and energy declined through the enervating and disruptive war years, never realising Gollancz's hope that it could become a major political force. In the second half of the 1930s, though, the Club galvanised a serious-minded section of the people to engage with political issues from a leftist perspective. A *Left News* article in April 1939 noted that, as a result of the thirty-five Monthly

Selections published to that point '1,566,700 copies of democratic, anti-fascist, anti-war or pro-socialist books have been put into circulation [. . .]. Under conditions existing before the Left Book Club was formed, the majority of such books would never have seen the light of day.'[47] Gollancz wound up the LBC in 1948, but it had contributed dynamically to 1930s public debate.

Penguin Books

Another publishing venture inaugurated in the 1930s would be far more enduring: Penguin Books. As with the LBC, an energising individual established the firm in 1935, in this case Allen Lane. Lane had established himself as a dynamic force while at The Bodley Head, but his new venture tapped a market created by an increasing, better-educated readership, and the economic viability of the cheap, well-made paperback. Penguin was a bold venture in the mid-1930s, given that book production was pressured from other sources. Publishers competed with radio, film, and newspapers for audiences in what David Trotter has labelled the First Media Age. To that end, Lane strove to present Penguin as a distinctive brand, its books instantly recognisable by their banded covers that promoted a 'modern' feel and identified them as fiction (orange bands), biography (dark blue), or mystery and crime (green). Their small size made them a convenient product, able to be carried in a jacket pocket or handbag. They were extraordinary value for money at just sixpence, when the average new piece of hardback fiction cost seven shillings and sixpence (or fifteen times as much) and even cheap editions of books cost three shillings and sixpence. The low price was economically risky, and Penguin initially was understood by mainstream publishers as a threat to profits traditionally underpinned by sales of far more expensive hardback editions, followed by their own cheaper editions. Penguin challenged the business model for publishing; its success proving transformative across the industry. In the process it brought an illuminating array of high-quality fiction, thoughtful non-fiction, literary and cultural classics, and more to a reading public it did much to foster and educate. It says something for Lane's chutzpah that Penguin No. 1 might not seem an obvious choice: André Maurois's *Ariel*, a biography of Shelley. But Lane's old firm, The Bodley Head, had published the hardback edition, and Lane understood its worth. Penguin No. 2 had more obvious popular appeal: Ernest Hemingway's 1929 classic, *A Farewell to Arms*. These two, along with Agatha Christie's *The Mysterious Affair at Styles* and seven other works, were published simultaneously on

30 July 1935, a momentous day in the publishing history of the century, let alone of the decade.

Penguin published more than 200 titles in its main series during the late 1930s, and, while many of those authors and texts are forgotten, the impact of the price and format was immense. Penguin almost immediately succeeded in economic and cultural terms. Lane, though, harboured plans to introduce high-quality non-fiction and social analysis, embodied in two new series launched in 1937: Pelican Books and Penguin Specials. Pelicans were reprints of thought-provoking texts intended for intellectually adventurous readers. The first nine, published on 21 May 1937, included George Bernard Shaw's two-volume *The Intelligent Woman's Guide to Socialism, Capitalism, Sovietism and Fascism*, G. D. H. Cole's *Practical Economics*, Olaf Stapledon's speculative 'future history' *Last and First Men*, and Julian Huxley's *Essays in Popular Science*, quickly followed in October by Leonard Woolf's *After the Deluge: A Study of Communal Psychology* and Roger Fry's *Vision and Design*. The following year would see the Pelican editions of Freud's *Psychopathology of Everyday Life* and *Totem and Taboo*, Virginia Woolf's *The Common Reader*, and Beatrice Webb's two-volume autobiography *My Apprenticeship*, among many others. Sixty Pelicans were published between 1937 and the end of the decade, on subjects scientific, literary, aesthetic, archaeological, political, and sociological. The final three numbers of the 1930s underline the expansive scope of the series: Holbrook Jackson's *The Eighteen Nineties* (a review of arts and ideas in that decade), astronomer Sir James Jeans's *The Stars in Their Courses*, and Margery Rice's *Working Class Wives: Their Health and Conditions*. Where Penguins brought quality fiction to a large audience, Pelicans seeded high-quality thinking among the serious readers; all for sixpence.

Penguin Specials, first published in November 1937, had a more contemporary purpose, designed to inform readers on the political state that was deteriorating alarmingly. They addressed concerns canvassed by the LBC, but with less overtly ideological intent. Jeremy Lewis judges that the Penguin Specials were 'shorter and more accessible than the LBC choices, and whereas Gollancz's books were sold in large numbers to the converted, Lane's reached a far wider and less ideologically committed market'.[48] Where LBC books might sell more than 50,000, itself a considerable number, Penguin Specials might 'sell a quarter of a million copies or more'.[49] Because of the inherent peril of the international situation, speed of production was vital, books sometimes appearing a week after the typescript was delivered. The early list signals strong international concerns, *Germany Puts Back the Clock*, *Mussolini's Roman*

Empire, the Duchess of Atholl's *Searchlight on Spain*, and a translation of the French historian Geneviève Tabouis's *Blackmail or War* being the first four Specials issued. Tabouis would later flee France in advance of the German occupation. But the Specials allowed contrary views, including C. E. M. Joad's pro-pacifist *Why War?* (March 1939), the cover of which carried Joad's argument that war is not inevitable. The Marquis of Londonderry's *Ourselves and Germany* (December 1938) was more provocative still, its cover declaring: 'Should Britain Regard Germany As Her Potential Enemy, or Seek Her Friendship? Lord Londonderry Thinks That We Should Adopt a Policy of Friendship With Hitler and A Better Understanding of Germany's Aims.' Events would invalidate Londonderry's argument. Yet Penguin's willingness to publish such a view late in 1938 indicates Lane's desire for active discourse initiated through inexpensive, quality editions by contemporary thinkers. And, while as early as 7 November 1939 Harold Nicolson could explain the present, in a Penguin Special, *Why Britain Is At War*, the series also looked to the future, most significantly in H. G. Wells's *The Rights of Man, or What Are We Fighting For?* (March 1940). There, Wells sets out arguments that fed into the United Nation's Declaration of Human Rights in 1948.

Penguin's importance to political and cultural thinking and discussion in the late 1930s was substantial. As early as autumn 1938, Lane could boast that 'he had sold over 17 million books in the previous three years, was shifting six tons of books a day, and never printed fewer than 50,000 copies of any new title'.[50] Penguin's range was astonishing, including the quirky series King Penguins, first published in November 1939, after the war began but before the decade ended. The series indicates the decade's complexities, the first two numbers being one-shilling hardback editions: *British Birds on Lake, River and Stream*, and *A Book of Roses*, both with sixteen colour plates. It is possible to see these and subsequent King Penguins as indulgences, the result of the company's massive success in only five years. Or they could be understood, along with Penguin's other publications and the publishers and periodicals explored in this chapter (only a tiny sampling of the whole), as indicative of a diverse, engaged, and energetic cultural environment. That environment was drastically modified by the onset of war, naturally enough, Hewison's slaughter of the periodicals a clear manifestation of the new climate. As Adam Piette explains, 'The Ministry of Supply cut [paper] quotas to publishers down a third by 1943, their Paper Control stipulating page limits, words per page, and minimizing unnecessary design. Literary periodicals suffered badly under the new regime.'[51] By comparison, the 1930s proved a boom time for periodicals, their editors and

staff, contributors, and readers. The variety of individual and group positions and responses called forth by that complicated, ambiguous, and
endlessly morphing decade required and produced something far more
than W. H. Auden's persistent epitaph for the 1930s in 'September 1, 1939'
as a 'low dishonest decade'. He would later reject the poem, arguing that its
'rhetoric is too high flown'.[52] It might be equally valid to see the poem as
simplistically dismissive, disparaging the efforts, idealism, and diversity of
people who, even when wrong, faced the future, part of a variegated reality
that exposes the so-called Red Decade as monochromatic myth.

Notes

1. Robert Hewison, *Under Siege: Literary Life in Britain 1939–1945* (Oxford:
   Oxford University Press, 1988, rev. ed.), p. 12.
2. John Lehmann, *Folios of New Writing* 1 (1940), p. 5.
3. Ibid.
4. Cliff Wulfman, 'Ford Madox Ford and *The English Review* (1908–37)', in *The
   Oxford Critical and Cultural History of Modernist Magazines, Volume 1: Britain
   and Ireland 1880–1955*, ed. by Peter Brooker and Andrew Thacker (Oxford:
   Oxford University Press, 2009), pp. 226–39 (p. 235).
5. Peter Ackroyd, *T. S. Eliot* (London: Penguin, 1993), p. 248.
6. Jeremy Treglown, 'Literary History and the "Lit. Supp."', *The Yearbook of English
   Studies*, 16, Literary Periodicals Special Number (1986), 132–49 (pp. 134–5).
7. Andy Croft, *Red Letter Days: British Fiction and the 1930s* (London: Lawrence
   and Wishart, 1990), p. 50.
8. Terry I. Seymour, 'Great Books by the Millions: J.M. Dent's Everyman's
   Library', in *The Culture of the Publisher's Series, Volume 2: Nationalisms and
   the National Canon*, ed. by John Spiers (Basingstoke: Palgrave Macmillan,
   2011), pp. 166–72 (p. 167).
9. C. M. Grieve, 'Editorial', *The Scottish Chapbook, A Monthly Magazine of
   Scottish Arts and Letters*, 1.3 (1922), p. iii.
10. Margery Palmer McCulloch, *Scottish Modernism and Its Contexts 1989–1939:
    Literature, National Identity and Cultural Exchange* (Edinburgh: Edinburgh
    University Press, 2009), p. 22.
11. Ibid., p. 23.
12. Ibid., pp. 23–4.
13. Cairns Craig, 'Modernism and National Identity in Scottish Magazines', in
    The Oxford Critical and Cultural History of Modernist Magazines, Volume 1,
    ed. by Brooker and Thacker, pp. 759–784 (pp. 781–2).
14. McCulloch, p. 1.
15. Chris Hopkins, '*Wales* (1937–9), *The Welsh Review* (1939–40)', in *The Oxford
    Critical and Cultural History of Modernist Magazines, Volume 1*, ed. by Brooker
    and Thacker, pp. 714–34 (p. 732).

16. Ibid., p. 733.

17. Keidrych Rhys, *Wales*, August 1937, p. 36.

18. Rhys, *Wales*, p. 37.

19. Hopkins, '*Wales*', in *The Oxford Critical and Cultural History of Modernist Magazines*, ed. by Brooker and Thacker, p. 730.

20. Malcolm Ballin, *Welsh Periodicals in English: 1882–2012* (Cardiff: University of Wales Press, 2013), p. 86.

21. James Guthrie, 'Edward Thomas', *The Welsh Review*, 2.1 (August 1939), pp. 23–30. See www.modernistmagazines.com/index.php (accessed June 14, 2016).

22. J. Ellis Williams, 'Welsh Drama To-Day', *The Welsh Review*, 2.1 (August 1939), pp. 32–6 (p. 32). See www.modernistmagazines.com/index .php (accessed 14 June 2016).

23. Christopher Hilliard, *English as a Vocation: The Scrutiny Movement* (Oxford: Oxford University Press, 2012), p. 16.

24. Jane Dowson, 'Interventions in the Public Sphere', in *The Oxford Critical and Cultural History of Modernist Magazines, Volume 1*, ed. by Brooker and Thacker, pp. 530–551 (p. 530).

25. Ibid., p. 531.

26. Muriel J. Mellown, 'Time and Tide', in *British Literary Magazines: The Modern Age, 1914–1984*, ed. by Alvin Sullivan (New York, Greenwood Press, 1986), pp. 441–52 (p. 446).

27. Ibid.

28. Janet Montefiore, *Men and Women Writers of the 1930s: The Dangerous Flood of History* (London: Routledge, 1996), p. 164.

29. Christopher Hilliard, *To Exercise Our Talents: The Democratization of Writing in Britain* (Cambridge, MA: Harvard University Press, 2006), p. 100.

30. Peter Marks, 'Art and Politics in the 1930s', in *The Oxford Critical and Cultural History of Modernist Magazines, Volume 1*, ed. by Brooker and Thacker, pp. 623–46 (p. 642).

31. Andy Croft, *Comrade Heart: A Life of Randall Swingler* (Manchester: Manchester University Press, 2003), p. 79.

32. Walter Ford, 'Poetry and Who Cares Anyway', *Poetry and the People*, 8 February 1939, p. 14.

33. David Trotter, *Literature in the First Media Age: Britain Between the Wars* (Cambridge, MA: Harvard University Press, 2013), p. 197.

34. Christopher Hilliard, 'Producers By Hand and By Brain: Working-Class Writers and Left-Wing Publishers in 1930s Britain', *The Journal of Modern History*, 78.1 (2006), 37–64 (p. 44).

35. Ibid.

36. Ibid., 42.

37. J. H. Willis, Jr., *Leonard and Virginia Woolf As Publishers: The Hogarth Press, 1917–41* (Charlottesville: University of Virginia Press, 1992), p. 259.

38. John Fuller, *A Reader's Guide to W. H. Auden* (London: Thames and Hudson, 1970), p. 49.

39. C. Day-Lewis, 'Letter to a Young Revolutionary', in *New Country: Prose and Poetry by the Authors of New Signatures*, ed. by Michael Roberts (London: Hogarth Press, 1933), p. 25.
40. John Strachey, *The Coming Struggle for Power* (London: Victor Gollancz, 1934), p. 296.
41. Ruth Dudley Edwards, *Victor Gollancz: A Biography* (London: Victor Gollancz, 1987), p. 238.
42. John Arnold, 'The Left Book Club in Australia: Achieving Reform and Change Through Reading and its Attempted Suppression', *Journal of Australian Studies*, 25.69 (2001), 103–12.
43. Dudley Edwards, *Gollancz*, p. 262.
44. Ibid., p. 264.
45. George Orwell, *Coming Up For Air*, in *The Complete Works of George Orwell, Volume 7*, ed. by Peter Davison (London: Secker and Warburg, 1997), p. 154.
46. Victor Gollancz, 'Editorial: Thoughts After Munich', *The Left News*, 31 (November 1938), p. 1035.
47. *The Left News*, 30 (April 1939), p. 1218.
48. Jeremy Lewis, *Penguin Special: The Life and Times of Allen Lane* (London; Penguin Books, 2006), p. 134.
49. Ibid., p. 135.
50. Ibid., p. 145.
51. Adam Piette, 'War Poetry in Britain', in *The Cambridge Companion to Literature of World War II*, ed. by Marina MacKay (Cambridge: Cambridge University Press, 2009), pp. 13–25 (p. 13).
52. See www.youtube.com/watch?v=co84ZNeMzKE (5:28. Accessed September 1, 2016).

CHAPTER 5

The Middlebrow and Popular

Isobel Maddison

To be classified as 'popular' or 'middlebrow' is to be damned with imprecise and, often, faint praise. This is particularly true in the 1930s when questions of literary 'taste' and 'value' increasingly shifted the parameters of critical reception in Britain by drawing distinctions between the popular and highbrow while airing the notion of the 'middlebrow' as a third classification. These categorisations accelerated debates about the rise in commercial writing in the period while lamenting the wider effects of mass culture on society. Fundamentally, this discussion became a struggle over ideas of cultural and intellectual authority that broadly coincided with a proliferation of novels written predominantly for a wide readership, particularly of middle-class women, under the classification 'middlebrow', as Nicola Humble's groundbreaking study *The Feminine Middlebrow Novel, 1920s–1950s* establishes.[1] Books such as Daphne du Maurier's *Rebecca* (1938), Jan Struther's *Mrs Miniver* (1939), the novels of Rosamond Lehmann, and the works of Elizabeth von Arnim and Elizabeth Taylor have all been considered in the light of this classification which, by 2007, Hammill considers 'a productive, affirmative standpoint for writers who were not wholly aligned with either high modernism or popular culture'.[2] The writing of Somerset Maugham could also be considered 'middlebrow', while J. B. Priestley actively engaged with the increasingly brow-bound debate that characterised the 1930s by introducing the notion of the 'Broadbrow', having turned his back on academia to write for literary magazines such as *The London Mercury* and the *Saturday Review*, before becoming the lead reviewer of the influential *London Evening Standard*.[3] To date, much of the scholarship about the 'Battle of the Brows' has centred on writing specifically aimed at women, but the debates are widening. It is in this spirit, and in the context of the 1930s, that this chapter explores these debates and also considers the 'Golden Age' of detective fiction associated with, amongst others, Agatha Christie, Margery Allingham, and Dorothy L. Sayers (the 'Queens of Crime'),[4] and the

81

development of espionage fiction, particularly that of Eric Ambler who published several highly influential novels in this decade.

Battle of the Brows

It is fair to say that, though the rise in commercial fiction in the 1930s was accompanied by anxieties about cultural authority, drawing clear distinctions between the terms through which this debate progressed is no easy task for the responsible critic. Popular writing has been variously defined as 'lowbrow', 'the literature of escape',[5] and, in respect of crime fiction, the literature of 'sensation' and 'pulp fiction',[6] a mode of writing that grew out of pamphlets, broadside ballads, gallows confessions, and publications based on *The Newgate Calendar* from 1773 onwards.[7] Much later, Clive Bloom's definition of the difference between popular and literary fiction draws the following distinctions: 'Art fiction highlights its style, and delights in it and makes of style a fetish. Popular fiction neutralises style [...] and delights in making language invisible in order to tell a tale.'[8] This is a nod towards the idea that in popular fiction language is employed as an uncomplicated method of transferring stable meanings that reflect a fundamental truth outside their operation, rather than (as Marjorie Nicolson would have it in 1929) the result of a disinterested activity of privileging the 'formless' excesses of 'subjectivity' which have become associated with high modernism.[9] Whatever view we take towards the definition of 'the popular', it is usually regarded as an 'expression of mass, industrial and consumer society',[10] associated with a condition of reading that has been, to quote Bloom, '*proletarianised*', that is, associated with reading patterns assumed to be those of the lower classes though, of course, it is always difficult to ascertain who actually reads what in private or, more pointedly, which books some will admit to reading.[11] It is nevertheless the case that popular fiction has come to be regarded as a lesser subsection of 'proper' literature.

The 'middlebrow' is also a notoriously unstable classification and this is especially true in the interwar period when critics and commentators increasingly imposed a hierarchy of cultural values along a continuum of taste.[12] The first recorded use of the term 'middlebrow', to date, appeared in a copy of the Irish *Freeman's Journal* on 3 May 1924, and recent scholarship, most notably that edited by Erica Brown and Mary Grover in *Middlebrow Literary Cultures* (2012), has developed the debate by tracing the changing definitions of the term 'middlebrow' and the implications for those artists classified as such during the period 1920–1960.[13] More recently, Kate Macdonald has rightly pointed out that the so-called middlebrow was not a coherent movement and this has sometimes been problematic for those studying the subject. The 'Middlebrow never had its own manifesto',[14] she argues, unlike, for example, the Imagists or Futurists.[15] Rather, the middlebrow emerged as 'a miasmic force'[16] that existed primarily through market economics, the apotheosis of vilification of the middlebrow arriving in the early 1930s.[17] This is clear, as Macdonald suggests, in a defence of middlebrow values that appeared in the weekly paper *London Opinion* on 16 August 1930:

> In the matter of public exhibition the 'high' and the 'low' have had it all their own way. The one has slung its arrows, the other its bricks across this fair, smiling country of the 'in-betweens', and the in-betweens have looked up, wondered what all the fuss was about, and gone on with their job.
>
> Frankly, we like this middlebrow country; it comprises the majority of decent men and women, and seems to us to stand for balance, sanity, substance, humour [. . .].
>
> It lacks the precious posturing of the one extreme, the crude sensationalism of the other [. . .]. It [. . .] bridges all classes and ages and most activities.
>
> It is probably six people out of every ten one passes [. . .] and so it has, in the end, the casting vote. It counts.[18]

This defence is firmly rooted in the perceptions and sensible tastes of the majority: how can the views of so many fuss-free authors and sane 'balanced' readers be so wrong? But this is precisely the point on which the debate in the 1930s turns, and where cultural anxiety sometimes tips over into intellectual snobbery. For instance, Virginia Woolf's well-known essay 'Middlebrow' (written as an unsent letter in 1932, published ten years later) bristles with the rhetoric of class analysis circulating in the 1930s.[19] In a particularly memorable putdown, she defines middlebrow culture as a 'mixture of geniality and sentiment stuck together with a sticky slime of calves-foot jelly' and associates the middlebrow with an imprecise middling condition 'betwixt and between' the high and the low, defining the middlebrow only by negation and so creating a lacuna in which possible definitions are left to oscillate.[20] It is also worth pointing out that Woolf was responding to a clash on the BBC radio in 1932 between J. B. Priestley and Harold Nicolson whose series of talks were aired under the general title 'To an Unnamed Listener'. Priestley began the exchange with a talk, 'To a High-Brow', and Nicolson responded the following week with 'To a Low-Brow', a situation Virginia Woolf rightly described as 'a Battle of the Brows' that was literally troubling the 'evening air'.[21]

Such exchanges exemplify the apparently semi-organised efforts of some writers and critics in the 1930s who set out to embarrass the consumers of commercial fiction. At the same time, there were those who sought to educate the growing reading public out of so-called lowbrow reading towards an appreciation of high art. This is the decade in which Virginia Woolf asked 'How Should one Read a Book?' (1932), before explaining one could train one's taste away from 'rubbish-reading',[22] and the period when Arnold Bennett's 1909 *Literary Taste and How to Form it* was reissued (in 1938), with additional lists by Frank Swinnerton.[23] The year 1932 is, of course, the same year that Q. D. Leavis published *Fiction and the Reading Public* where she lambasted the middlebrow for 'touching grossly on fine issues' before ultimately defining the middlebrow as 'the *faux-bon*'.[24]

Material Culture

The conditions under which literary texts were produced in the 1930s augmented ideas of hierarchy and separation rather than of declassification and connection. The proliferation of national newspapers, for instance, became an inescapable force in British culture and this played its part in the construction of ideas about both popular and middlebrow culture. As Adrian Bingham argues, 'the newspaper became a key motif of fiction and art; a prime symbol of the emerging urban mass culture; and one of the most acute guides to the stratification of British society'.[25] Moreover, in 1933, Patrick Balfour, 'a high-profile society columnist', noted 'the "immense" development and expansion of the modern newspaper' which was '"a mixed bag of tricks, providing sufficient material to occupy the whole of the average man's leisure time"'.[26] Crucially the newspapers fashioned, as well as reflected, taste by informing readers of contemporary culture, books, films, and plays while, Bingham argues, papers like *The Mail*, *The Express*, and *The Weekly Dispatch* provided 'powerful cultural and commercial support for the middlebrow section of the market'.[27]

As these markets grew, there were those who aimed to maximise the financial benefits. As McAleer has noted, in 1930 *The Publishers' Circular* described books as one of 'the "indispensable necessities of life", and condemned the "intellectual snobbery" of booksellers and publishers who still regarded the trade as a sacred luxury', rather than '"the business of selling"' for '"a reasonable profit"'.[28] There is no emphasis here on establishing or maintaining literary hierarchies. Instead, the reader is primarily a consumer, and at a time when publishers were trying to cope with the burgeoning demand for reading material. Certainly, as McAleer argues, the reading boom that began in Britain in 1870 was hardly diminished in the early decades of the twentieth century. In both the First and Second World Wars restrictions on leisure activities and expenditure, plus paper rationing, only intensified the demand for reading, and this was sustained in peacetime. These reading habits were fostered in the 1920s and 1930s by the Depression, the growth in cheap facilities for borrowing books, Penguin's founding of its mass-market paperback in 1935 (as addressed in Peter Marks's chapter), and by the cinema.[29] It is interesting to observe, for example, that John Buchan's novel *The Thirty Nine Steps* (serialised in 1915) had its first airing as a film in 1935, tapping into the growing interest in spy narratives that arose at a time when readers and viewers increasingly feared for the future in the light of German rearmament. Indeed, by the 1930s, the fashionable black-and-white 'talkies' had become a 'mass medium',[30] with popular taste dictating the subject matter of many films which attracted approximately 963 million cinema admissions annually in Britain at no more than a shilling a seat.[31] Consequently, the cinema was an affordable and pleasurable form of mass entertainment which became increasingly upwardly mobile in the 1930s and 1940s, its ever more middle- and upper-class audience simultaneously widening its social and political interests in the era of Mass Observation.[32] Even so, in 1932, Q. D. Leavis argued that 'the cinema, rather like listening to the gramophone or wireless', was fundamentally a 'passive' amusement as well as, regrettably, a 'standardising' force that (like large-circulation newspapers and magazines) had destroyed 'traditional' culture.[33]

While the cinema attracted audiences novelists could only dream of, there was a similar exponential rise in cheap and accessible reading material. This was an era when men and women regarded books as one of the most satisfying and inexpensive forms of amusement,[34] so much so that by 1939 *The Publishers' Circular* concluded that '"the great British book-buying public are [...] choosing [...] lighter books these dark days, and leaving the heavier ones for future happier times and occasions"'.[35] Access to this 'lighter' reading material was aided by the establishment of the 'Pay-as-You-Read', 'No Deposit', or 'tuppenny' libraries. These offered a wider selection of fiction than the public libraries. Mostly attached to news agencies, department stores, and tobacconists, these commercial lending libraries catered to the requirements of a new reading public who had seen their wages rise by one-third between 1913 and 1938, allowing for increased consumer expenditure.[36] As McAleer suggests, the growth of commercial libraries during the 1930s is one indication that the lower-middle and working classes now had sufficient disposable income to spend on reading,[37] even if, again, Q. D. Leavis appears to be unimpressed with the choice of subject matter.

Evidently, the rise of critical discourse amongst the intelligentsia, and taste-makers in the 1930s more generally, helped create a particular atmosphere in which accessible writing considered entertaining and pleasurable became increasingly associated with degraded literary production and the betrayal of artistic integrity. Nevertheless, the debate did not provide a clear definition of either 'the popular' or 'the middlebrow', and it remains the case that these terms are entangled: both are still largely understood only in opposition to 'highbrow' writing, or in contrast to the work of the avant-garde or as simply 'not modern'. It is for this reason that an exclusive separation between works of literature designated as 'serious' or 'proper' and those classified as either 'middlebrow' or 'popular' is now regarded as unhelpful for understanding this kind of literary production. As Bourdieu argues (more than fifty years after Virginia Woolf wrote 'Middlebrow'), 'the same object which is today typically middlebrow [...] may yesterday have figured in the most "refined" constellation of tastes and may be put back there at any moment by one of those taste-maker's coups which are capable of rehabilitating the most discredited object'.[38] Humble may have glossed some of the ideas associated with the middlebrow and argued that novels classified as such tend to include an intense interest in domestic details, notions of correct taste including the literary, and a fascination with bohemianism accompanied by a 'faint suspicion of intellectuality',[39] but this is always underpinned by an awareness that the classification itself is inherently unstable. With this in mind, recent scholarship has increasingly focussed on canon-formation, the role of material culture in creating particular markets for readers, and the ways in which critical discourse defines the terms within which its own narrative operates. This approach provides a clearer understanding of the limits of critical discourse as it has emerged on this topic. As Humble argues, and as Bloom confirms in *Bestsellers*, the 'provisionality' of the term middlebrow (and implicitly of 'the popular') 'is precisely what draws' scholars to these areas of 'study'.[40] Nonetheless, we need to be mindful that using the terms 'popular' and 'middlebrow', which are themselves frequently inseparable, often unwittingly entrenches the assumptions these classifications appear to air and challenge, at least to those uninitiated in this particular branch of literary revision.

Women and the Middlebrow

The discussion about the critical neglect of so-called middlebrow authors writing specifically for women has been well-rehearsed. It is nevertheless useful to reiterate some of the common features thought to be shared by these texts, focussing on two less-obvious authors. As Humble argues, in the broadest sense, 'middlebrow' books often include 'the enjoyable feminine "trivia" of clothes, food, family, manners and romance', while communicating to a predominantly female readership an element of wry self-consciousness that draws attention to the superficiality of the topics discussed.[41] The expectation is that these books are greeted in a spirit of 'pure self-indulgence' by the reader, rather than drawing serious critical analysis, and this is significant in terms of classification.[42] Humble argues convincingly that one of the most important reasons for the lack of scholarship on 'the major part of the fiction published in Britain', especially in the universities between the 1920s and 1950s, is that it was primarily 'written and consumed by women'.[43] An overview of the critical vocabulary frequently used in the 1930s and beyond to discuss the novels of Elizabeth von Arnim and Rosamond Lehmann helps explain the previous dearth of 'serious' scholarship on these writers. For instance, as early as 1920 the *Daily Mail* is somewhat contradictory in its assessment of von Arnim's *In the Mountains* (1920). While the review stops short of categorising this book as 'middlebrow', the reviewer argues instead that, though the work is genuine 'literature', it is not 'Highbrow stuff', leaving the novel hovering tantalisingly betwixt and between classifications.[44] Moreover, the words 'delightful' and 'charming' appear often in reviews of von Arnim's work when, in fact, much of it could equally be considered biting satire. For example, the *Canadian Bookman* and the *New York Times* draw attention to von Arnim's charm and her 'delightful style',[45] before a later reviewer of the *New York Times* develops these assessments in 1931: '*Father* is not only an excellent romance [...] it is a charming, restrained and intelligent comedy' which is 'delightfully and rather sharply spiced with malice'.[46] H. G. Wells, who is thought to have been von Arnim's lover, highly praised her next novel, *The Jasmine Farm* (1934), although he also acknowledged that it might be dismissed by university-trained writers, presumably because it did not carry the fashionable markers of obvious seriousness and literary experimentation.[47] It is a relief, therefore, to find a suitably perplexed E. E. Mavrogordato reviewing *Father* in the *Times Literary Supplement* in November 1934 and conceding that 'no category [...] suggests itself as appropriate'.[48] In fact many struggled to find a suitable vocabulary to explore what is essentially stylish, satiric, and hybrid writing that moves deftly between outright social satire dense with intertexual allusion, the country house novel, the romance, and the gothic genre.

Similarly, Wendy Pollard explores the novels of Rosamond Lehmann amidst the increasingly hierarchical critical context in which her work appeared. To this end, Pollard points out that Lehmann's first novel, *Dusty Answer* (1927), achieved that rare combination of 'substantial critical respect and exceptional popular success', before she moves on to a discussion of the reception of Lehmann's work in the 1930s.[49] While in 1930 *A Note in Music* provoked comparisons with Jane Austen, Pollard explains that the adjectives 'charming' and 'delightful' appear in reviews of Lehmann's work repeatedly in, for instance, *The Daily Telegraph*, *Morning Post*, *The Times*, and *The Sunday Times*. Furthermore, 'other adjectives which constantly appear as an integral part of the praise' simultaneously undermine it, including the diminutives 'little, light and slight'.[50] It is fitting, therefore, that Pollard's book draws out the impact of critical discourse on the changing reception of Lehmann's work in a monograph that has as its subtitle 'The Vagaries of Literary Reception'. This seems especially apt given Bourdieu's belief in the changing status of various kinds of literature and the possible 'rehabilitation' of 'discredited' work. It is also entirely right that in this current volume MacKay includes Lehmann in her chapter on the 'Literary Novel' of the 1930s in a welcome departure from the drive towards the rigid literary hierarchies that overshadowed this decade. As MacKay suggests in her chapter for this book, the definition of 'literary' now 'routinely overlaps with a range of forms', a situation many critics in the 1930s struggled to acknowledge, overwhelmed as they were by the flourishing discourse of classification favoured by the makers of taste.

The Golden Age of Detective Fiction

It is with these ideas in mind that we briefly approach the 'Golden Age' of detective fiction, being careful not to fall into the trap of assigning critical labels while remaining mindful of the context within which these works were judged. As Dorothy L. Sayers argues of her best-known novel, 'I doubt very much whether, if *Gaudy Night* had been written in 1922 [rather than published in 1935], it would ever have seen the light. The detective story of that period enjoyed a pretty poor reputation, and was not expected to contain anything that could be mistaken for "serious" reading.'[51]

Whatever its reputation at the time, or its neglect in subsequent histories of the era, we can be sure of the popularity of detective fiction in the 1930s, and there are interesting contextual questions to consider that flow from this fact. These novels were read by the majority of people, 'either aggressively or shamefacedly by nearly everyone' argues Joseph Krutch retrospectively in 1944.[52] The genre even drew serious engagement from so-called highbrow modernists. W. H. Auden believed detective stories had 'a magical function' and considered them 'an addiction like tobacco or alcohol', though he also declared that those of the clue-puzzle variety, exemplified by writers such as Agatha Christie and considered the dominant form in the 1930s, had 'nothing to do with works of art'.[53] Rather, in his opinion, these books were escapist, in that the reader identifies with the investigator as an heroic figure as he or she apprehends the guilty party and so restores society to an innocent state: an appealing act of redemption at a time of escalating interwar ills. T. S. Eliot also joined the debate and set out, perhaps unsurprisingly, to devise rules for detective stories where, for example, 'disguises must only be occasional and incidental' and where the detective should be 'highly intelligent but not superhuman'.[54] Eliot was extremely keen on the idea of fair play: 'We should feel that we [the reader] have a sporting chance to solve the mystery ourselves.'[55] Indeed, this is a key element of the clue-puzzle genre in books such as Agatha Christie's *Murder at the Vicarage*, published in 1930, where Miss Marple first appeared. Here the reader is drawn into the artificiality of the detection game from the start: 'If this were only a book', one of the villagers states.[56] Later, the Vicar argues, 'you underestimate the detective instinct of village life [. . .]. There is no detective in England equal to a spinster lady of uncertain age with plenty of time on her hands'[57] – surely gesturing towards the leisured clue-busting and ideal reader of detective novels at a time when the lending libraries were the basic medium of dissemination of the clue-puzzle novels and 75 per cent of this readership was female.[58] Fair play also features in the amusing oath drawn up by members of The Detection Club. Established in 1930, the Club attracted the most distinguished names in British detective fiction and contributed to the idea of a 'Golden Age'. Dorothy L. Sayers, G. K. Chesterton, A. A. Milne, Hugh Walpole, and Agatha Christie were among the first twenty-eight members to be elected and all lauded fair play as a necessary element of their work.[59] All of which points to the necessity that the clue-puzzle invite the reader to participate in the seemingly democratic act of mutual detection. This is aided by the flat style of writing, the reader remaining undistracted by the frequently two-dimensional characterisation while negotiating the escalating clues and trying to avoid the deliberate red herrings. The author's implication is that the reader could be as intelligent, or even cleverer, than the fictional detective and, as the form became consolidated in practice, the enterprise of reading became more a game of logical deduction than of imaginative sympathy. As Dorothy L. Sayers argued, 'In its severest form, the mystery-story is a pure analytical exercise and, as such, may be a highly finished work of art, within its highly artificial limits', though it 'never' can, she added, 'attain the loftiest level of literary achievement' because 'it rarely touches the heights and depths of human passion'.[60]

What the clue-puzzle genre was able to do, however, was tap into the contextual interests and pastimes of the majority. The pages of magazines during the 1920s and 1930s swarmed with enigmas, acrostics, and cross-words as well as detective stories, Sayers believing these offered a 'sort of catharsis or purging of [...] fears' both personal and national – at one level another form of absorbed escapism in which anxieties are displaced by intellectual satisfaction.[61] There are nevertheless limits to the contextual resonances we can read into these books. For example, the social worlds presented in Agatha Christie are not those of the unemployed Jarrow Marchers of 1936. Instead, the settings tend towards the comfortable and conservative; events develop in secluded country houses or hotels in which a narrow range of people come together briefly, all of whom appear to be equipped with motives for murder as the plot drives towards its frequently theatrical denouement. Subsequent scholarship offers fresh perspectives on these texts,[62] but it is perhaps Marjorie Nicolson in 1929 who is best placed to capture the mood of the age from an academic's perspective in her essay 'The Professor and the Detective'. The detective story is, she argues, 'an escape' from the kind of 'literature' that presents 'long-drawn-out dissections of emotion' (for which we read modernism) in favour of an appeal to the 'intellect'. Reading detective fiction is a 'revolt against the "psychological novel"' especially by those who teach English in universities. Furthermore, it is a move 'from formlessness to form' and, crucially, a welcome 'return' to earlier kinds of fiction where 'it is still possible to tell a story'.[63] The clue-puzzle genre so popular in the 1930s may not tell us much about the very real anxieties experienced by many in the decade, but here, at least, Nicolson adds refreshing complication to our understanding of literary production and a little to its critical reception in the period.

The Spy Novel and Eric Ambler

Arguing retrospectively in 1983, Eric Ambler offers a now familiar assessment: 'When *Epitaph for a Spy* [1938] was written spy stories were generally considered a very low form of life indeed, and few self-respecting critics were prepared to notice them [. . .]. The spy novel had to become a social phenomenon before it could draw academic fire.'[64] Or, as David Trotter puts it in 2015, there is 'no margin seedier' than that 'traversed by the protagonists' of the spy novel, whether we choose to interpret this as risky exploration beyond established boundaries or as a further nod towards a sidelined and degraded form of literary production.[65]

Unlike the 'Golden Age' clue-puzzle novel, the work of Eric Ambler is keenly engaged with the difficult and changing pre-war context within which it was published. As Michael Denning argues, Ambler wished to align the thriller with 'contemporary reality', a claim that suggests a development away from the heightened rhetoric of polemical anti-invasion literature published in the first decade of the twentieth century such as that of William Le Queux.[66] Accordingly, Ambler's work is tied up with the anxiety-ridden 1930s and with ideas of European political duplicity communicated in a nuanced register beyond that of simple propaganda. His 1939 short story 'The Army of Shadows',[67] for example, sponsored in aid of the war effort, engages directly with the impending Second World War and draws a sharp and deliberate distinction between the good motives of the 'German people' and 'Nazi Tyranny'[68] at a time when Ambler believed he would be called up to fight in the army 'somewhere near the blunt end'.[69] As in Ambler's novels, in this story the 'truth' is constantly revealed as unstable and relative: almost simultaneously, claims about 'true' identity are doubted, the dominant narrative of Nazi propaganda is undermined by those constructing a welcome, alternative, and written perspective in a short story where, stylistically, the framing narrator admits that the story appears both unfinished and incoherent because he is actually communicating real events. The overarching question posed by the story becomes one of narrative veracity: what are we meant to believe if all narratives create provisional meanings and all are suspect in one way or another? Similarly, notions of compromised loyalties, betrayal, double-dealing, and the psychological complications of moral questions feature largely in Ambler's novels, while political situations beyond the text are recorded with an eye for historical detail. In *Coffin for Dimitrios* (1939),[70] for example, the Turkish-Greek war of 1922, and the occupation of Smyrna by the Turkish National Army on 9 September, appear in a detailed political and contextual narrative of the conflict. However, even as the context is carefully reconstructed, the artificiality of the writing process is foregrounded, and the first thirty pages of the novel are largely concerned with the interplay between murder 'in reality' and the fictional variety. We read, for instance, that murder is of course 'Incomplete. Inartistic': 'No detection, no suspects, no hidden motives', real murder is 'merely sordid' and just 'Another unfinished story'.[71] For the writer, however, 'Everything must be tidy, artistic, like a *roman policier*'[72] though, in an act of misdirection and as with several of Ambler's central protagonists, in *Coffin* we follow the progress of an anti-hero as he is plunged into a world he struggles to understand, especially because the line between reality and fiction is frequently and deliberately blurred. False clues are communicated through shifting viewpoints: spies are merged within the general population; the double agent tells two opposing tales, of course; while the intense self-reflexivity of the writing foregrounds the role of narrative as a shaping, if dubious, force through which the reader needs to chart a careful course. And, in part, it is this that separates Ambler's work from the aims of those writing the clue-puzzle novel in the 1930s. Where the work of Agatha Christie, for instance, relies on drawing the reader into a predominantly inward-looking genre where the detective and reader are engaged in the comforting enterprise of uncovering the truth of the criminal situation, the tendency of Ambler's work is to obfuscate the evidence, look outwards to the wider conflicted, and 'continental', context while destabilising the reader and resisting closure. The two genres may have been popular in the 1930s in the simplest sense because they are absorbing, escapist, and both pose an intellectual problem, but the difference in structure, style, and effect is marked and significant. As Synder argues, Ambler 'make[s] us question our grounds for trusting the sufficiency of ratiocinative deduction'.[73] Logic is not necessarily a direct route to uncomplicated 'truth'.

While spy fiction has become the subject of increasing academic interest, including recent attention to its development in the 1930s,[74] it remains the case that genre fiction, including that of Ambler, has not yet been fully 'rehabilitated'. It is therefore unsurprising to find that in 2011 Synder feels the need to attribute Ambler's low profile within the scholarly community to his 'categorization as a "spy novelist"'.[75] And, as if to underscore the point, Synder's 'Introduction' has the subtitle, 'Reconnoitering a Disreputable Genre'.[76] It may be the case that the 'reputation of espionage fiction has lagged far behind that of the detective story, even though they are closely related literary forms'.[77] But, rather like those writers classified as 'middlebrow', and to a lesser extent the 'Queens of Crime', these authors negotiated the critical climate of the 1930s by combining elements from different modes that complicate the apparent simplicity with which their work was received. It is true, however, that the 'Battle of the Brows' exerted pressure on the wider cultural context, degrading work that was commercial and entertaining. But, as Woolf argues in 1932 in a moment when perhaps the democratic impulse supersedes her engagement with this brow-bound discourse, 'behind the erratic gunfire of the press' there is 'another kind of criticism, the opinion of people reading for the love of reading, slowly and unprofessionally, and judging with great sympathy and great severity'.[78] In the case of the authors discussed here, they too thought it best to keep a wide and open eye on their discerning readership whatever the vagaries of literary fashion, just as it seems likely they chose to squint, even if ever so slightly, at the professional critics.

Notes

1. Nicola Humble, *The Feminine Middlebrow Novel, 1920s to 1950s: Class, Domesticity and Bohemianism* (Oxford: Oxford University Press, 2001).
2. Faye Hammill, *Women, Celebrity, and Literary Culture between the Wars* (Austin: University of Texas Press, 2007), p. 6. For discussions of von Arnim's writing from this perspective, see Erica Brown, *Comedy and the Feminine Middlebrow Novel: Elizabeth von Arnim and Elizabeth Taylor* (London: Pickering and Chatto, 2013), and Isobel Maddison, *Elizabeth von Arnim: Beyond the German Garden* (Farnham: Ashgate, 2013).
3. See J. B. Priestley, *Angel Pavement* (London: Heinemann, 1930), and 'High, Low, Broad', *Saturday Review*, Feb 1926; reprinted in *Open House: A Book of Essays* (London: Heinemann, 1929). Priestley argued that the Broadbrow's critical faculty achieved a balance between emotion and reason, permanence and change, producing works defined by an eclecticism in taste (p. 165).
4. Stephen Knight, 'The Golden Age', *in The Cambridge Companion to Crime Fiction*, ed. by Martin Priestman (Cambridge: Cambridge University Press, 2003), pp. 77–94. Knight argues that 'The Golden Age of crime fiction is usually taken as the period between the two world wars' (p. 77).
5. Marjorie Nicolson, 'The Professor and the Detective', in *The Art of the Mystery Story: A Collection of Critical Essays*, ed. by Howard Haycraft (New York: Simon and Schuster, 1946), pp. 110–27 (p. 112). This essay was first published in 1929.
6. Joel Black, 'Crime Fiction and the Literary Canon: Popular versus Literary Crime Fiction', in *A Companion to Crime Fiction*, ed. by Charles J. Rzepka and Lee Horsley (Oxford: Blackwell, 2010), pp. 76–89 (p. 78).
7. Martin Priestman, *Detective Fiction and Literature: The Figure on the Carpet* (London: MacMillan, 1990), p. 2.
8. Clive Bloom, *Bestsellers: Popular Fiction since 1900* (Basingstoke: Palgrave, 2002), p. 21.
9. Nicolson, 'The Professor and the Detective', p. 114.
10. Bloom, *Bestsellers*, p. 17.

11. Ibid., p. 28. Bloom argues that mass literature has nothing per se to do with working-class readers.

12. *Transitions in Middlebrow Writing, 1880–1930*, ed. by Kate Macdonald and Christoph Singer (London: Palgrave, 2015), p. 3.

13. The recorded use is: 'Ireland's musical identity, in spite of what highbrows and middlebrows say, is ultimately bound up with festivals'. Quoted from *Middlebrow Literary Cultures: The Battle of the Brows, 1920–1960*, ed. by Erica Brown and Mary Grover (Basingstoke: Palgrave, 2012), p. 19.

14. *Transitions in Middlebrow Writing*, ed. by Macdonald and Singer, p. 5.

15. See *Manifesto: A Century of Isms*, ed. by Mary Ann Caws (Lincoln: University of Nebraska Press, 2000).

16. *Transitions in Middlebrow Writing*, ed. by Macdonald and Singer, p. 5.

17. *The Times*, 6 January 1922, p. 5.

18. Anon, 'Come in! And let's talk about . . . Middlebrows', *London Opinion*, 16 August 1930, pp. 136–7.

19. Virginia Woolf, 'Middlebrow', in *Collected Essays, Volume 2* (London: Hogarth, 1966), pp. 196–203.

20. Ibid., pp. 200, 198.

21. Ibid., p. 196.

22. Virginia Woolf, 'How Should One Read a Book?', in *Collected Essays, Volume 2*, pp. 1–11 (p. 5).

23. Arnold Bennett, *Literary Taste and How to Form It* (Harmondsworth: Penguin, 1938).

24. Q. D. Leavis, *Fiction and the Reading Public* (London: Chatto and Windus, 1965), pp. 65, 39.

25. Adrian Bingham, 'Cultural Hierarchies and the Interwar British Press', in *Middlebrow Literary Cultures*, ed. by Brown and Grover, pp. 55–68 (p. 55).

26. Ibid., p. 57.

27. Ibid., p. 56.

28. Joseph McAleer, *Popular Reading and Publishing in Britain 1914–1950* (Oxford: Clarendon, 1992), p. 42.

29. Ibid., p. 43.

30. Lara Feigel, *Literature, Cinema and Politics 1930–1945* (Edinburgh: Edinburgh University Press, 2010), p. 3.

31. Ibid.

32. The Mass Observation movement was founded in 1937 as a social research organisation, recording life in Britain through volunteer observers.

33. Q. D. Leavis, *Fiction*, pp. 55, 193.

34. This was reported in *The Publishers' Circular* in 1931. Paraphrased from McAleer, *Popular Reading*, p. 73.

35. Ibid.

36. Ibid., p. 49.

37. Ibid., p. 51.

38. Pierre Bourdieu, *Distinction: A Social Critique of the Judgement of Taste* (Cambridge, MA: Harvard University Press, 1984), p. 327.

39. Humble, *Feminine*, p. 8.
40. Nicola Humble, 'Sitting Forward or Sitting Back: Highbrow v Middlebrow Reading', *Modernist Cultures*, 6.1 (2011), 41–59 (p. 42).
41. Humble, *Feminine*, p. 5.
42. Ibid., p. 6.
43. Ibid., p. 2.
44. Hamilton Fyfe, 'Books and their Writers: A Dean in Love', *Daily Mail*, 20 August 1920, p. 7.
45. Anon, 'Elizabeth again: "The Enchanted April"', *Canadian Bookman*, March 1923, p. 72; Anon, 'Delicate Irony' (review of *Expiation*), *New York Times Book Review*, 3 February 1929, p. 8.
46. Anon, 'Father and some other Recent Works of Fiction', *New York Times Book Review*, 31 May 1931, pp. 6–7 (p. 6).
47. See Isobel Maddison, *Elizabeth von Arnim: Beyond the German Garden* (Farnham: Ashgate, 2013), p. 42.
48. E. E. Movragordato, 'New Novels' (review of *The Jasmine Farm*), *Times Literary Supplement*, 29 November 1934, p. 854.
49. Wendy Pollard, *Rosamond Lehmann and Her Critics: The Vagaries of Literary Reception* (Aldershot: Ashgate, 2004), p. 1.
50. Ibid, p. 78.
51. Dorothy L. Sayers, 'Gaudy Night', in *The Art of the Mystery Story*, ed. by Haycraft, pp. 208–21 (p. 208).
52. Joseph Wood Krutch, 'Only a Detective Story', in *The Art of the Mystery Story*, ed. by Haycraft, pp. 178–85 (p. 179).
53. W. H. Auden, 'The Guilty Vicarage', in *Detective Fiction: A Collection of Critical Essays*, ed. by Robin W. Winks (Englewood Cliffs, NJ: Prentice Hall, 1980), pp. 15–24 (p. 15).
54. Quoted in Martin Edwards, *The Golden Age of Murder: The Mystery of the Writers Who Invented the Modern Detective Story* (London: HarperCollins, 2015), p. 113.
55. Ibid.
56. Agatha Christie, *The Murder at the Vicarage* (London: HarperCollins, 1930), p. 16.
57. Ibid., p. 33.
58. Knight, p. 81.
59. 'The Detective Club Oath', in *The Art of the Mystery Story*, ed. by Haycraft, pp. 197–99.
60. Dorothy L. Sayers, 'The Omnibus of Crime', in *The Art of the Mystery Story*, ed. by Haycraft, pp. 71–109 (p. 101).
61. Sayers, p. 72.
62. See *Murdering Miss Marple: Essays on Gender and Sexuality in the New Golden Age of Women's Crime Fiction*, ed. by Julie H. Kim (London: McFarlane, 2012); Jessica Mann, *Deadlier than the Male: An Investigation into Feminine Crime Writing* (Newton Abbott: David Charles, 1981); Melissa Schaub, *Middlebrow Feminism in Classic British Detective Fiction: The Female*

Gentleman (Basingstoke: Palgrave, 2013); and J. C. Bernthal, *Queering Agatha Christie: Revisiting the Golden Age of Detective Fiction* (London: Palgrave Macmillan, 2016).

63. Nicolson, 'The Professor and the Detective', pp. 114, 116.
64. Eric Ambler, preface to *Epitaph for a Spy* (Bath: Chivers, 1983), p. 6.
65. David Trotter, 'Mobility, Network, Message: Spy Fiction and Film in the Long 1930s', *Critical Quarterly*, 57.3 (2015), 10–21 (p. 10). See also Phyllis Lassner, *Espionage and Exile: Fascism and Anti-Fascism in British Spy Fiction and Film* (Edinburgh: Edinburgh University Press, 2016), which gives important attention to the political context of 1930s spy novels.
66. Michael Denning, quoted in Robert Snyder, *The Art of Indirection in British Espionage Fiction: A Critical Study of Six Novelists* (London: McFarland, 2011), p. 25. Le Queux published 'The Invasion of 1910' in the *Daily Mail*, March 1906. For a fuller discussion of anti-invasion literature, see Isobel Maddison, 'The Curious Case of Christine', *First World War Studies*, 3.2 (2012), 183–200.
67. Eric Ambler, 'The Army of Shadows', in *Waiting for Orders: The Complete Short Stories of Eric Ambler* (New York: Mysterious Press, 1991).
68. Ambler, 'Introduction', *Waiting for Orders*, p. 4.
69. Ibid., p. 3.
70. Ambler, *A Coffin for Dimitrios* (London: Vintage: 2001). This work was also published under the title *The Mask of Dimitrios*.
71. Ibid., p. 27.
72. Ibid., p. 23.
73. Synder, *The Art of Indirection*, p. 30.
74. See Trotter, 'Mobility, Network, Message'.
75. Synder, *The Art of Indirection*, p. 45.
76. Ibid., p. 3.
77. Ibid., 'Preface', p. 1.
78. Woolf, 'How Should One', p. 11.

CHAPTER 6

Modernism

Tyrus Miller

In a lecture delivered early in 1936 entitled 'Poetry and Film', W. H. Auden offered a Marxist-shaded characterisation of modernism within a brief, reductive account of the historical division of high and low art. The class divisions that grew out of the Industrial Revolution, Auden asserted, had also given rise to an intermediate social element, 'a class of people living apart from industry but supported by its profits – the rentier class'.[1] Modernism, Auden claims, can be understood as nothing other than 'rentier art', an artistic expression of the outlook of this dependent, impractical side-branch of the industrial ruling class: 'A distinct type of art arose [...] developing through Cezanne, Proust and Joyce.'[2] In what follows, Auden does not further linger over this dismissive account of three great innovators of modern art and literature, but hastens on to the real focus of his lecture, which is popular art and specifically the art of film. In his 'Letter to Lord Byron' (1936), he put this view more wittily, but no less dismissively, measuring the fluctuating aesthetic capital of the great modernists on a kind of snob's cultural bourse:

> Joyces are firm and there there's nothing new.
> Eliots have hardened just a point or two.
> Hopkins are brisk, thanks to some recent boosts.
> There's been some further weakening in Prousts.[3]

Yet, later in the poem, Auden (more self-aggrandisingly) interpolates himself and his poet-friends among the eminences of the modernist generation to compose a flock of 'several singing birds' who can still soar in writing today.[4] In a single seven-line verse, imploring his interlocutor to 'Cheer up!', Auden links Stephen Spender, Louis MacNeice, and implicitly himself to T. S. Eliot, who 'has really stretched his eagle's wing', alluding to the despairing 'agèd eagle' of the older poet's *Ash-Wednesday* (1930)

97

sequence; to W. B. Yeats, who has 'helped himself to Parnell's heart'; and to Wyndham Lewis, 'That lonely old volcano of the Right'.[5]

In 'Inside the Whale' (1940), a celebrated review of Henry Miller's novels of the 1930s and a broader retrospective stocktaking of the literary decade just past, George Orwell, too, could without hesitation write in his opening paragraph that several of the renowned writers who praised Miller's *Tropic of Cancer* when it appeared in 1935 – including T. S. Eliot, Herbert Read, Aldous Huxley, John Dos Passos, and Ezra Pound – were essentially obsolete. They were, 'on the whole, not the writers who are in fashion at this moment'.[6] Orwell's treatment of these writers, and others he discusses such as E. M. Forster, D. H. Lawrence, and James Joyce, is somewhat more appreciative than Auden's (despite Auden's own greater stylistic proximity to modernism in much of his poetry, experimental prose, and verse drama). Yet, on the whole, Orwell agrees with Auden's blithe characterisation of modernism as a privileged, detached, and unpractical 'rentier' art written by those who could afford to give vent, in high style and experimental form, to pessimistic laments about the human and superhuman condition. Orwell goes so far as to diagnose a causal nexus between the comfortable conditions taken for granted by the rentier class of the 1920s and the pessimistic, self-involved artistry of modernism:

> Was it not, after all, *because* these people were writing in an exceptionally comfortable epoch? It is just in such times that 'cosmic despair' can flourish. [. . .] As for the 'twenties, they were the golden age of the *rentier*-intellectual, a period of irresponsibility such as the world had never before seen.[7]

Though this description of modernism is certainly not free of moralism, Orwell's more telling point is that the social conditions that once supported modernist art and literature, along with the leisure-class intellectuals who produced and appreciated it, are now untenable in the new European horizon of economic depression, mass unemployment, spreading fascism, and rearmament for total war. Neither prosperity nor high-toned aesthetic detachment are, in Orwell's judgment, permitted by the objective historical situation of the moment. Thus, after only twenty years, high modernism already appeared to Orwell a distant fossil, an artistic anachronism without a future. Any future age of major literature and art, he concludes, cannot come to pass until 'the world has shaken itself into its new shape'.[8]

Orwell's diagnosis was not, it seems, simply idiosyncratic, or representative solely of the viewpoint of a younger, more left-leaning literary generation. At the conclusion of his critical survey of what he took to be the dregs of a failed modernist movement, Wyndham Lewis ended *Men Without Art* (1934) with an address to the reader, hoping that he had 'directed your attention to a question of great moment – namely, whether the society of the immediate future should be composed, for the first time in civilised history, of *Men without art*'.[9] Analogously, in his final essay for *The Criterion* in January 1939, T. S. Eliot sounded a valedictory note not just for the journal but for the sort of culture that he and its contributors had sought to represent:

> Only from about the year 1926 did the features of the post-war world begin clearly to emerge – and not only in the sphere of politics. From about that date one began slowly to realize that the intellectual and artistic output of the previous seven years had been rather the last efforts of an old world, than the first struggles of a new.[10]

'For this immediate future, perhaps for a long way ahead', Eliot concludes, 'the continuity of culture may have to be maintained by a very small number of people indeed – and these not necessarily the best equipped with worldly advantages.'[11]

High Modernism

What, however, of the modernist writers that Auden and Orwell (and even Lewis and Eliot themselves) cast as grand if already somewhat hollow statues of the previous decade, with a nearly defunct relation to the currents of the present day? As we well know, it was not as if, on the final day of 1929, the key representatives of high modernism had simply vaporised, ceasing ever again to write or opine about the state of literature and the world. Works by major modernists continued to appear, such as Eliot's verse drama *Murder in the Cathedral* (1935), Woolf's *The Waves* (1931) and *The Years* (1937), Wyndham Lewis's *The Apes of God* (1930) and *The Revenge for Love* (1937), Aldous Huxley's *Brave New World* (1932) and *Eyeless in Gaza* (1936), Djuna Barnes's *Nightwood* (1936), Rebecca West's *The Thinking Reed* (1936), Dorothy Richardson's four-volume *Pilgrimage* (1938), and James Joyce's *Finnegans Wake* (1939). The decade also saw the emergence of newer voices adapting modernist idioms to new contexts such as David Jones, Elizabeth Bowen, Jean Rhys, Christopher Isherwood, Rex Warner, Samuel Beckett, Lewis Grassic Gibbon, Flann O'Brien, Malcolm Lowry, and Lawrence Durrell.

It is true that some of the key works of the 1930s written by established modernist authors remained strongly rooted in the modes, concerns, or even material texts of prior decades. This is most striking in the case of James Joyce, who began what was to eventually become *Finnegans Wake* (1939) in the early 1920s, and published key parts of it under the working title *Work in Progress* beginning in 1924 in avant-garde little magazines such as *Transition, Transatlantic Review, This Quarter*, and *Two Worlds*. Already before the turn of the decade, a collection of critical essays, *Our Exagmination Round His Factification for Incamination of Work in Progress* (1929), had been dedicated to the work – implicitly canonising it within the framework of the Anglo-American high modernism for which Joyce's own work of the 1910s and 1920s was foundational. Wyndham Lewis's notorious criticisms of Joyce in *Time and Western Man* (1927) and his appropriation of Joyce's manuscript for parody in *The Childermass* (1928), which occasioned Joyce's hilarious ripostes in *Work in Progress/ Finnegans Wake*, had, likewise, largely run their polemical course by the time the 1930s rolled around. Though Joyce worked on his last book throughout the 1930s, his poor health, family worries, and increasing blindness hampered the completion and publication of the definitive *Finnegans Wake*. By the time of the book publication of *Finnegans Wake* in 1939, with the outbreak of the Second World War following shortly, its impact had already been significantly blunted by the unfavourable context for its reception. Its contemporary influence was confined largely to the small avant-garde Parisian clique around Joyce in the 1920s, with a few singular heirs like the young Samuel Beckett's aborted novel *Dream of Fair to Middling Women* (1932) and the remnants of it that went into *More Pricks Than Kicks* (1934), and Flann O'Brien's *At Swim Two Birds* (1939). Its real heyday of reception was among the various neo-avant-gardes of the 1960s (especially through experimental novelists ranging from Samuel Beckett and Christine Brooke-Rose to Philippe Sollers, Maurice Roche, and Arno Schmidt). One might then reasonably characterise *Finnegans Wake* as a major modernist work partially produced and eventually published *in* the 1930s, yet not, in the stronger literary historical sense of 'period' style and themes, fully *of* the 1930s.

Though not as marked as in the case of Joyce, T. S. Eliot, too, recapitulated and extended the concerns of his earlier modernist works in his first significant publication of the 1930s, the serial poem *Ash-Wednesday* (1930). Individual parts of it had already appeared separately in earlier publication; Eliot montaged them together with new segments in a sequence recognisably related to *Gerontion* (1920), *The Waste Land* (1922), and *The Hollow Men* (1925) in idiom and thematic concerns, despite *Ash-Wednesday*'s further heightening of the earlier poems' theological resonances following Eliot's 'conversion' both to the Anglican Church and to British citizenship in 1927. In turn, *Ash-Wednesday* helped establish the meditative mode in which Eliot would compose his major sequence of the late 1930s and early 1940s, the *Four Quartets* (1943), of which two parts, 'Burnt Norton' and 'East Coker', date primarily from the 1930s.

Hybrid Forms

However, Eliot's expanding venture into verse drama and parallel willingness to countenance a sort of propagandistic or tendentious verse are organically connected with broad emerging literary tendencies in the 1930s, such as the hybrid verse/prose 'epic' forms and lyric/discursive/dramatic modes explored by key figures such as W. H. Auden, Christopher Isherwood, Stephen Spender, Cecil Day-Lewis, Louis MacNeice, David Jones (in his mythopoetic First World War 'memoir' *In Parenthesis*, 1937); the right-wing poetic satires of Wyndham Lewis (*One-Way Song*, 1933) and Roy Campbell (*The Georgiad*, 1931; *Flowering Rifle*, 1939); and the British prose poetry influenced by surrealism and documentary tendencies, including works by Humphrey Jennings, Len Lye, Charles Madge, Hugh Sykes Davies, and David Gascoyne. Notably, in his 1960 foreword for the reissue of Lewis's *One-Way Song*, Eliot emphasised that Lewis's satire might be thought of as 'verse' even if not 'poetry',[12] and that it 'cannot be fully understood without some knowledge of Wyndham Lewis's prose work', specifically:

> *The Wild Body* for style and for powers of visual observation and description; the *Childermass*, for powers of visual imagination and fantastic invention; *Time and Western Man* for philosophical criticism; and *Paleface* or *The Writer and the Absolute* for polemical criticism of contemporary fiction.[13]

Such versified, hybrid discourse as Lewis's *One-Way Song* is anything but the 'autotelic' poetry that Eliot, and later his followers among the American New Critics, fostered through their other critical writings and that Eliot had sought, in other moments, himself to write.[14]

The decade of the 1930s commenced with the publication of two landmark works of the modernist novel: Virginia Woolf's most stylistically and formally challenging novel, *The Waves* (1931), and Wyndham Lewis's satiric apocalypse, *The Apes of God* (1930). Woolf's novel in particular would seem to be vulnerable to the charge that it is a rarified, detached work of verbal art, far removed from the pressing concerns of a Britain already deep in economic depression and on the brink of a parliamentary crisis by the time of its publication. Although indeed her deeply felt political concerns, especially those concerning masculinity and its relation to war and imperialism, are woven into the fabric of Woolf's text (see, for example, Judy Suh's chapter in this volume), they are at the same time filtered through layers of lyrical style, complexly orchestrated time, and chorally arranged character and narration. Bearing out its dominant *aesthetic* intention is Woolf's suggestion in diary entries from 1927 and 1928 that her then work in progress could be thought of as a 'play-poem',[15] with connotations not only of the children's *games* in the book but also of the interwoven *dramatic* soliloquys of the narration and Woolf's music-like *performance* of the character voices. Woolf's Bernard, the writer-character and master orchestrator of the voices in the book, acts as the registrant of the shocks and differences of the characters of the book as well as the unifying force holding them together in the ebb and flow of the narrative. However, when he speaks in his own name, he often unwittingly reveals the claustrophobic narrowness of the 'world' he encompasses in his consciousness, as in this passage:

> 'It was different once,' said Bernard. 'Once we could break the current as we chose. How many telephone calls, how many post cards, are now needed to cut this hole through which we come together, united, at Hampton Court? How swift life runs from January to December! [. . .] We have to leap like fish, high in the air, in order to catch the train from Waterloo. And however high we leap we fall back again into the stream. I shall never now take ship for the South Sea Islands. A journey to Rome is the limit of my travelling. I have sons and daughters. I am wedged into my place in the puzzle.'[16]

Bernard laments how much arrangement it takes to get together with his friends; the swiftness of life's journey; the crowds in a London train station; the relinquishment of romantic adventures dreamed in youth and their replacement by stock tourist vacations. Different readers may well be more or less emotionally moved by Woolf's mediated attention to these commonplace tugs and pushes of desire and regret. But Woolf's prose, in its framing of these emotional currents, also bears a double-edge irony, reflecting back the narrow, privileged ambit of Bernard's thoughts and concerns.

Woolf's rival and sometimes 'enemy' Wyndham Lewis certainly felt this to be the case, and said so in the context of his broader diagnosis of modernism's malaise in the early 1930s in his critical study *Men Without*

Art. Along with polemical sallies against Ernest Hemingway, William Faulkner, T. S. Eliot, I. A. Richards, Henry James, and others, Lewis assailed Woolf and her Bloomsbury circle of friends as a narrow clique self-promoting works that represented a half-closed clique's-eye view:

> For fifteen years I have subsisted in this to me suffocating atmosphere. I have felt very much a fish out of water, very alien to all the standards that I saw being built up around me. I have defended myself as best I could against the influence of what I felt to be a tyrannical inverted orthodoxy-in-the-making. With the minimum of duplicity I have held my own: I have constantly assailed the swarms of infatuated builders. So, having found myself in a peculiarly isolated position, I had begun to take for granted that these habits of mind had come to stay [...]. But it seems [...] [t]here is [...] a good chance that a reversal of these values – the values of decay – is at hand.[17]

In fact, although Woolf's focus and ideological perspective were the antipodes of Lewis's, her literary direction in the 1930s was, surprisingly, less divergent. Her next major books following *The Waves* (excepting *Flush* and two essay volumes) were *The Years* (1937) and *Three Guineas* (1938), which began conjointly as a hybrid 'novel-essay' form only later teased apart into a voluminous realist novel and a book-length essay. Woolf's original conception can be seen in the uncompleted manuscript, published in 1977 as *The Pargiters*. Yet, far from being as original an experiment as Woolf herself believed, she was reflecting, through her own writing practice, a much broader tendency towards essayism – a hybrid mixture of narrative and discursive writing – in the modern European novel. In the German-speaking world, the interwar writing of Thomas Mann, Robert Musil, and Hermann Broch pointed strongly in this direction; so too did the later, ideologically charged novels and travel essays of D. H. Lawrence such as *Women in Love* (1920), *Aaron's Rod* (1922), *Kangaroo* (1923), *The Plumed Serpent* (1926), and *Mornings in Mexico* (1927), as well as, notably, Wyndham Lewis's entire written corpus of the 1920s. In the first half of the 1920s, accordingly, Lewis composed a huge manuscript of mixed fictional, critical, polemical, and philosophical prose, which he subsequently broke up and published as separate books, with a rough, often-breached generic distinction drawn between fictional-satiric works such as *The Childermass* (1928) and *The Apes of God* (1930) and works of critical exposition and polemic such as *The Art of Being Ruled* (1926), *The Lion and the Fox* (1927), and *Time and Western Man* (1927).

Throughout the 1930s, Lewis's essayistic and polemical prose continued at a torrential pace, alternating with his more careful narrative
treatments of the same topics in novels such as *Snooty Baronet* (1932)
and *The Revenge for Love* (1937) and non-fiction writing such as the
satirically tinged travel book *Filibusters in Barbary* (1932) and the autobiography and war memoir *Blasting and Bombardiering* (1937). Yet, in
his fictions, he consistently embedded ideas and arguments in the
narrative structure and created characters who mouthed positions very
close to those argued out in his critical prose; and in his discursive
works, through the occasional use of explicit characters in dialogue and
a wide range of exaggerated masks and voices, Lewis dramatised his
arguments with roles and sketchy characters. Despite the emphatic look
backwards that Lewis's *The Apes of God* makes thematically to the
fashionable modernists of the preceding decades, we might provoca-
tively view it less as the antithetical 'contemporary' of Woolf's lyrical
high modernist novel *The Waves* and instead as an anachronistically
early complement to Woolf's discursive essayistic-fictional pair of the
later 1930s, *The Years* and *Three Guineas*. In these books, Woolf's
distinctive ventriloquism is no less ostentatious than Lewis's boisterous
'broadcasting' in *The Apes of God*.

In *The Years*, thus, following a passage in which Peggy's aunt
Eleanor apparently sees a picture of Adolf Hitler (unnamed but easily
inferred) and spontaneously curses, Woolf provides interpretative
commentary through the inner thought and direct speech of the
two women, who, despite their generational and intellectual differences, momentarily unite in their passionate recoil from the mascu-
linist values that lead to militarism and oppression (a crux of *Three
Guineas*'s political argument):

> It was the force that she had put into the words that impressed her, not the
> words. It was as if she still believed with passion—she, old Eleanor—in the
> things that man had destroyed. A wonderful generation, she thought, as
> they drove off. Believers...
> 'You see,' Eleanor interrupted, as if she wanted to explain her words, 'it
> means the end of everything we cared for.'
> 'Freedom?' said Peggy perfunctorily.
> 'Yes,' said Eleanor. 'Freedom and justice.'[18]

Lewis, in a facetious conversation between his broadcasting mimic Horace
Zagreus and the 'Keins' about Proust, is even more blatant about letting his
characters bear the burden of dramatising an essayistic, critical argument.

This passage could easily have appeared in any of Lewis's own critical writings, despite being pronounced by one of his master-apes:

> *Fiction*, as we call it, is indeed no misnomer, since it is generally an untruthful picture. In its more high-brow forms it is in fact the *private news-sheet*, the big 'Gossip'-book—the expansion of a Society newspaper-paragraph—of the Reigning Order. And the Reigning Order is the people with the pelf and the circle of those they patronize, and today it is the High Bohemia of the Ritzes and Rivieras. And the 'great novels' of this time are *dramatised social news-sheets* of that particular Social World.[19]

An analogous hybrid of discursive argument with fictional, lyrical, and dramatic modes marks the experiments of T. S. Eliot in such works of the early to mid-1930s as the fragment of *Sweeney Agonistes* (1932), the pageant play *The Rock* (1934), and the verse drama *Murder in the Cathedral* (1935), which in turn should be seen in the larger context of mixed mode texts such as W. H. Auden's *The Orators* (1932); Auden's three co-authored plays with Christopher Isherwood, *The Dog Beneath the Skin* (1935), *The Ascent of F6* (1936), and *On the Frontier* (1938); Louis MacNeice's eclogues (1933–7); Cecil Day-Lewis's *Noah and the Waters* (1936); and Stephen Spender's *Trial of a Judge* (1938). The most striking instance of this mixed generic idiom is, perhaps, *The Rock*, which was instrumentally intended for performance in May and June 1934 to help finance new churches in London. In a prefacing note, Eliot takes claim to be the author only of the 'words', while the pageant scenario was written by E. Martin Browne. Eliot's words, however, are markedly heterogeneous, as Jed Esty points out in his study of various representations and uses of the pageant play genre in 1930s literature, from John Cowper Powys and T. S. Eliot to E. M. Forster, Charles Williams, and Virginia Woolf. As Esty writes:

> The text features a rather motley assortment of styles, ranging from some recognizably elegant and hieratic modernist poetry to some embarrassingly crude dramatic scenes in prose. To read the book of words today is to encounter a fascinating mixture of high and low cultural registers from the 1930s; Eliot manages to combine stock pageantry devices with popular ballet, pantomime, music-hall ditties, radical oratory, Latin liturgy, and Brechtian chants.[20]

This description could easily apply to several of the other works of the younger generation of poets as well, for example Auden's radical montage of ode and other lyric forms, diary, verse letter, oratory, and aphorism in *The Orators* or the melancholy pyrotechnics of MacNeice's 1933 'An Eclogue for Christmas':

> Jazz-weary of years of drums and Hawaiian guitar,
> Pivoting on the parquet I seem to have moved far
> From bombs and mud and gas, have stuttered on my feet
> Cinched to the streamlined and butter-smooth trulls of the élite,
> The lights irritating and gyrating and rotating in gauze—
> Pomade-dazzle, a slick beauty of gewgaws—[21]

Similarly, in these mixed-genre works, the caricature-like reduction and satiric exaggeration of gesture, voice, figure, and character place the work of this younger generation in proximity to that of Eliot and Wyndham Lewis. In a review of *Sweeney Agonistes* from 1932, Michael Roberts, a strong advocate of Auden, Day-Lewis, and Spender, affirmatively characterised Eliot's play as 'a puppet-show: the characters move mechanically and sing or speak in mechanical rhythms, falling readily into patterns: duets, quartets and dialogues with chorus.'[22] So too, for instance, Auden and Isherwood's *The Dog Beneath the Skin*, in which the play's overall satiric intent is especially evident in the campy songs that alternate with prose passages and that are patterned into mechanical exchanges between the chorus and various type-characters:

> If Chanel gowns have a train this year,
>   If Morris cars fit a self-changing gear,
> If Lord Peter Whimsey
>   Misses an obvious clue,
> If Wallace Beery
> Should act a fairy
>   And Chaplin the Wandering Jew;
> The reason is
>   Just simply this:
> They're in the racket, too![23]

A singular work that employs the mixed-genre mode in a very different way is the Welsh poet and engraver David Jones's extraordinary First World War poem-memoir *In Parenthesis* (1937). It also bears the inspiration of Eliot's writings but is more indebted to the intertextual innovations and mythopoetic conception of history of *The Waste Land* than to Eliot's essaying in the verse dramas of the early 1930s; in a preface to the 1961 edition to the book, Eliot himself also points to affinities between the work of Jones and that of Ezra Pound and James Joyce.[24] The late publication of *In Parenthesis* with respect to the spate

of war memoirs and novels that appeared beginning in the later 1920s –
a belatedness shared by Wyndham Lewis's memoir *Blasting and
Bombardiering* (1937) – and its situation of the First World War within
a vast tableau of Roman, Welsh, and British history and legend unmoor
the historical event of the Great War from its temporal limitation and
render it perpetually anachronistic or timeless. As Jones put it in his
preface:

> This writing is called 'In Parenthesis' because I have written it in a kind of
> space between – I don't know between quite what – but as you turn aside to
> do something; and because for us amateur soldiers [. . .] the war itself was
> a parenthesis – how glad we thought we were to step outside its brackets at
> the end of '18 – and also because our curious type of existence here is
> altogether in parenthesis.[25]

Jones's book alternates between block prose passages, sometimes prosaic
and descriptive or straightforwardly narrative, at other times highly lyrical
and allusive, and passages of broken free verse. There are also points at
which a kind of phenomenological fidelity to the event and its perception
blurs the boundary between verse and prose:

> Echoes that make you sit up and take notice tumbled to and
> fro the hollow in emptied hard collapse, quite other than the
> sustained,
> boomed-out
>   boom-oom, boom-oom
> and the felt recoil,
> shocked up from the trained muzzles which sway their sylvan
> masquerade with each discharge.[26]

The book crescendos to a moving, mythopoetic ending, in which, following a deadly skirmish with the Germans in the Mametz Woods at the First
Battle of the Somme, the Queen of the Woods gathers the dead to her and
gives them flowers. 'Dai' Jones thus registers his own close brush with
death, and alludes to his return to be the elegiac voice of mourning and
commemoration for the many from both sides who were so 'gathered'
that day.

Visionary Poetics

The most significant manifestation of renewed modernist impulse in the
British 1930s, however, came from poets inspired by visionary poetics
deriving from surrealism, D. H. Lawrence's spiritual apocalypticism, and

romantic poetry, including Herbert Read, Humphrey Jennings, Len Lye, and Charles Madge to David Gascoyne, Dylan Thomas, George Barker, and Hugh Sykes Davies. One important area of experimentation was with prose poem and lyrical prose forms. Herbert Read, in his utopian philosophical novel *The Green Child* (1935), narrates the adventures of a young man who leaves his village in England and, after various seafaring adventures, becomes the accidental president of a Latin American nation, a kind of benevolent dictator who has minimised the machinery of the state through a rational social order. Faking his death, he returns to his home town, where he renews a relation to a strange creature who had intruded upon his childhood, the survivor of a pair of green children 'who were lightly clothed in a green web-like material of obscure manufacture' and 'further distinguished by the extraordinary quality of their flesh, which was of a green, semi-translucent texture, perhaps more like the flesh of a cactus plant than anything else, but of course much more delicate and sensitive'.[27] He finds himself first returning to the underground cave world from which these nature-children had original come, eventually going through an initiation and spiritual purification towards an enlightened death and transfiguration, along with his love-partner Siloën, into a crystal monument:

> The two bodies were laid side by side in the same trough, and these two who had been separated in life grew together in death, and became part of the same crystal harmony. The tresses of Siloën's hair, floating in the liquid in which they were immersed, spread like a tracery of stone across Olivero's breast, twined inextricably in the coral intricacy of his beard.[28]

In a similar fantastical impulse, Hugh Sykes Davies's short novel *Petron* (1935) created his eponymous character from a series of fable- or dreamlike short episodes strung together in an associative narrative:

> It was quite without malice or intent to wound that Petron, the gentlest of men, happened to step on a toadstool in a meadow. Indeed it was purely accidental, and for the moment he was not even aware that he had done it, passing on out of the field to a lane. But hardly had he gone a score of paces when he heard a rending groan behind him, and turning his head saw an idiot rising from the earth where the toadstool had been. Once again poor Petron is involved in a distressing procession, himself walking briskly down the road, the idiot following with curious inarticulate cries. As he moved, his lower jaw, which hung down between his knees, bumped and banged on the road like a loose stick behind a cart, or broken harness on a runaway horse.

From time to time he would spit out broken pieces of tooth, and tatters of flesh which the stones tore from his lips and chin.[29]

Whereas Read and Davies incorporated these lyrical prose tableaux into larger narrative designs, other writers such as Gascoyne, Madge, Jennings, and Lye created verbal image-objects, through enigmatic descriptions or decontextualised narratives, analogous to documentary images or the reports of everyday of the kind sent in to the Mass Observation project that Madge and Jennings along with Tom Harrisson had founded in 1937. Thus Jennings in 1936, from a group of prose texts entitled 'Reports':

> When the horse is impassioned with love, desire or appetite, he shows his teeth, twinkles his coloured eyes, and seems to laugh.
> He shows them also when he is angry and would bite; and volumes of smoke come from his ears.
> He sometimes puts his tongue out to lick. His mouth consists of the two rays of the eternal twins, cool as a sea breeze.[30]

And Gascoyne, from his 1937 poem 'Three Verbal Objects':

> Vast expanses of devastated territory, jagged skyline, wooden scaffoldings 140 foot high and blazing like giant torches – young women and little old children lying murdered in disordered heaps – abandoned gun-carriages, drifts of snow lying melting in the sun here and there among the ruins. . .[31]

Surrealist and related visionary tendencies also lent an innovatory push to the verse lyric of the period. Most notable was the poetry of Dylan Thomas, whose rhapsodic voice evolved over the 1930s towards the hermetic density of lyrics included in his popular *Twenty-Five Poems* (1936) and *The Map of Love* (1939), such as 'Because the Pleasure-Bird Whistles':

> Because the pleasure-bird whistles after the hot wires,
> Shall the blind horse sing sweeter?
> Convenient bird and beast lie lodged to suffer
> The supper and knives of a mood.[32]

Bearing some affinities to surrealism, George Barker also emphasised his connections with the British Romantic visionary tradition, especially William Blake and Percy Shelley, in poems such as 'Vision of England '38', included in his 1940 volume *Lament and Triumph*. His most ambitious, albeit problematic, work of the period is the long poem *Calamiterror* (1937), which expresses Barker's inner apocalypse in the face of the death of his son and the recent bombings in Spain. We might understand the poem as a spontaneously unleashed psychic abreaction of traumatic events, lending words their 'calamity' and 'terror' in nightmarish condensations of images:

> I see the swan's breast run like the pelican's red
> To feed the crowded myriad her human,
> I see the large parasites that dilate like leech
> Torn, with war and agony, from my mother world's front.
> But the whippoorwill wends his way through the Wyoming woods
> When the leopard, lying low, awaits, or the lion
> Roars. And my mother world, with bomb holes in her bosom.
> Goes gradually on, with the myriad of me at her breast.[33]

Calamiterror is one of the most linguistically daring if controversial poems of the 1930s, merging poetic and political passion in a unique visionary idiom. Its frequent outbursts of bathos, however, led critic A. T. Tolley to pronounce that it 'must be one of the worst poems of the decade, if only because it is so extravagantly bad and at such length'.[34]

David Gascoyne, a key participant in the British surrealist movement, and a knowledgeable chronicler of French surrealist poetry and art, brought surrealist visionary techniques to bear on his metaphysical and political concerns in his 1930s poetry. Through their rhythmic momentum, their end-stopped and unpunctuated lineation, and their relentless conjoining of words in irrational associations, Gascoyne's surrealist poems present a world turned topsy-turvy by the sudden suspension of the normal order, as in these lines from 'The Rites of Hysteria' (1935):

> Now the beckoning nudity of diseases putrifies the saloon
> The severed limbs of the galaxy wriggle like chambermaids
> The sewing-machine on the pillar condenses the windmill's halo
> Which poisoned the last infanta by placing a tooth in her ear[35]

Following Breton's surrealist imperative to 'tend desperately towards' the limits where existing reality and the activity of the mind converge,[36] and at the same time profoundly anti-fascist and committed to proletarian revolution, Gascoyne could wishfully convince himself at the moment that these commitments might together spark an all-consuming, apocalyptic Revolution that would sweep away both social and spiritual limitations on human experience.

Notes

1. W. H. Auden, 'Poetry and Film', in W. H. Auden and Christopher Isherwood, *Plays and Other Dramatic Writings, 1928–1938*, ed. by Edward Mendelson (Princeton: Princeton University Press, 1988), p. 511.
2. Ibid.
3. W. H. Auden, 'Letter to Lord Byron', in *The English Auden: Poems, Essays and Dramatic Writings, 1927–1939*, ed. by Edward Mendelson (London: Faber and Faber, 1977), p. 178.
4. Ibid., p. 198.
5. Ibid.
6. George Orwell, 'Inside the Whale', *in The Collected Essays, Journalism and Letters: Volume One*, ed. by Sonia Orwell and Ian Angus (London: Secker and Warburg, 1968), p. 493.
7. Ibid., p. 509.
8. Ibid., p. 527.
9. Wyndham Lewis, *Men Without Art*, ed. by Seamus Cooney (Santa Rosa: Black Sparrow Press, 1987), p. 234.
10. T. S. Eliot, 'Last Words', *The Criterion*, 18.71 (January 1939), pp. 269–75 (p. 271).
11. Ibid., p. 274.
12. T. S. Eliot, 'Foreword', to Wyndham Lewis, *One-Way Song* (London: Methuen, 1960), p. 9.
13. Ibid., p. 8.
14. See T. S. Eliot's 1923 essay 'The Function of Criticism', in *Selected Prose of T. S. Eliot*, ed. by Frank Kermode (New York: Farrar Straus Giroux, 1975), p. 69, for Eliot's use of this term.
15. See, for example, the entries of 18 June 1927 and 7 November 1928 in *The Diary of Virginia Woolf, Volume Three: 1925–30*, ed. by Anne Olivier Bell (San Diego: Harcourt Brace, 1980), pp. 139, 203.
16. Virginia Woolf, *The Waves* (San Diego: Harcourt, 1959), p. 216.
17. Lewis, *Men Without Art*, p. 140.
18. Virginia Woolf, *The Years* (New York: Harcourt, Brace, 1965), pp. 331–2.
19. Wyndham Lewis, *The Apes of God* (Santa Barbara: Black Sparrow, 1984), p. 262.
20. Jed Esty, *A Shrinking Island: Modernism and National Culture in England* (Princeton: Princeton University Press, 2003), p. 71.
21. Louis MacNeice, 'An Eclogue for Christmas', in *Collected Poems* (London: Faber and Faber, 1979), p. 33.
22. Michael Roberts, 'Sweeney Agonistes', in *Selected Poems and Prose*, ed. by Frederick Grubb (Manchester: Carcanet, 1980), p. 72.
23. Auden and Isherwood, *Plays and Other Dramatic Writings*, p. 211.
24. T. S. Eliot, 'A Note of Introduction', to David Jones, *In Parenthesis* (New York: New York Review Books, 2003), p. viii.

25. Jones, preface to *In Parenthesis*, p. xv.
26. Ibid., p. 141.
27. Herbert Read, *The Green Child* (New York: New Directions, 1935), p. 26.
28. Ibid., pp. 193–4.
29. Hugh Sykes Davies, *Petron* (London: J. M. Dent, 1935), p. 20.
30. Humphrey Jennings, 'Reports', in *On The Thirteenth Stroke of Midnight: Surrealist Poetry in Britain*, ed. by Michel Remy (Manchester: Carcanet, 2013), p. 112.
31. David Gascoyne, 'Three Verbal Objects', in *New Collected Poems, 1929–1995*, ed. by Roger Scott (London: Enitharmon Press, 2014), p. 105.
32. Dylan Thomas, 'Because the Pleasure-Bird Whistles', in *The Collected Poems of Dylan Thomas, 1934–1952* (New York: New Directions, 1971), p. 86.
33. George Barker, 'Calamiterror', in *Collected Poems*, ed. by Robert Fraser (London: Faber and Faber, 1987), p. 61.
34. A. T. Tolley, *The Poetry of the Thirties* (New York: St Martin's Press, 1975), p. 246.
35. Gascoyne, *New Collected Poems*, p. 68.
36. David Gascoyne, *A Short Survey of Surrealism* (London: Enitharmon, 2003), p. 71.

CHAPTER 7

Communism and the Working Class

John Connor

In 1940, George Orwell wrote a profile of the novelist Henry Miller, praising him as a prose-stylist and psychologist of the 'ordinary man', praising him above all as a 'creative writer' in what has ceased to be 'a writer's world'. For 'what is quite obviously happening', Orwell declared, 'is the break-up of *laissez faire* capitalism', 'the destruction of liberalism' and of 'literature as we know it'. In this end-times scenario, Miller is shown clinging to the 'melting iceberg' of liberal humanism, elaborating his own 'subjective truth' in his own inimitable style, indifferent to the world. As a foil, Orwell introduces the communist 'propagandists' and 'cocksure partisans' of the next generation. In 'Auden and Spender and the rest of them', Orwell identifies the same abdication of critical and creative integrity, the same signs of early-stage 'totalitarianism'. Fortunately, beyond the party-political lockstep of the 1930s Left intelligentsia and the radical passivity of Miller, there is a third way forward. Orwell's own concession to the crisis of the times, a life of reluctant social consciousness and jealous independence, suggests a solution to the problem of comportment in this coming 'age of totalitarian dictatorships'.[1]

After the war, Orwell's artful self-fashioning would furnish the Cold War West with the writer it required: the revolutionary personality who would side with no party or state, bleak liberalism's secular saint.[2] Canonisation conferred authority on his portrait of the fashionable leftism of the 1930s, and for those so minded its emphases and omissions could pass as truth. In concert with the decade-end palinodes and organised renditions of the communist god that failed, Orwell's dark suggestions of Party manipulation and 'control' of 1930s British literature supplied a screen memory to forestall any more patient reckoning with the decade's cultural politics.[3] Left literature was simply 'DUCKSPEAK', Orwell's term of art in *Nineteen Eighty-Four* (1949) for the rote rendition of 'Ingsoc' or English socialist opinion.[4] And, indeed, without a positive conception of culture in service to a social movement, of art flowering in a moment of insurgency, the literature of political immediacy becomes the 'quacking' of Orwell's caustic conceit. So it is as a literary movement, a national cultural upsurge within an international formation, that this chapter surveys the communist and working-class writing of the 1930s, and by doing so hopes to cast a clearer light on the truth of Orwell's claim about the relationship of politics and letters. For the forged autonomies of nineteenth-century civilisation *were* in crisis. Politics *was* invading literature, and not only as content but in its structuring conditions of practice.

Politics and Letters

From the fallout of the First World War, amid the slow and uneven transfer of economic and political power from the empires of old Europe to the USA and USSR, new techniques of national projection emerged to manage and mitigate this process of realignment. The French were early pioneers, but the Soviet Union soon outstripped its Western counterparts in the deployment of writers and intellectuals as adjuncts of foreign policy to influence public opinion abroad. By the time Britain and America established cultural diplomacy programmes in the mid-to-late 1930s, the Soviet state presided over a global infrastructure for the promotion, translation, and dissemination of communist culture. Moscow was the lodestar of a literary universe that aspired to rival and ultimately replace the literary culture of capitalism.[5] Only by combining forces in the cultural Cold War did the old- and new-world West succeed in containing the spread of Soviet literary space, using its own array of conferences, publishing houses, and magazines to court and reward foreign writers in defence of capitalist democracy. No writer would in fact owe more to this new model of promotion than Orwell himself, his post-war fiction serialised, translated, adapted, and distributed around the world in the West's now braided fight against communism and colonial independence.[6]

   This power of the Soviet Union to organise and amplify the demands of working people for cultural enfranchisement helps explain the proliferation of communist and working-class writing in Britain. Though there did exist domestic precedent and a middle-class public briefly interested to read and commercial publishers to print the attitudes and experiences of the unemployed and working poor, 1930s Britain found itself a node in a global movement of proletarian and revolutionary writers that took inspiration, and sometimes instruction, from Moscow. The study of mid-century Left literature must therefore be alive to the dynamics of Soviet-sphere cultural production.

At the simplest level, this can mean tallying artistic forms to the so-called Party 'line'. The line set strategy for national sections of the Communist International (Comintern), the 'World Party' established in 1919 to coordinate the international communist movement. It tailored tactics to an assessment of the relative strength and stability of capitalism, the present prospects for revolution, and the needs of Soviet national security. Authoritative and binding, the line was also subject to change. Two main lines have bearing on the 1930s. The 'New Line', formally established in February 1928, announced that post-war capitalism was entering a 'Third Period' of crisis and instability and that the time was ripe for renewed revolutionary agitation. Former allies on the Left – including 'reformist' trade unions, the parliamentary Labour Party, and the broad mass of liberal social democrats – were now denounced for impeding the proletariat on its path to power and branded capitalist collaborators; the struggle was to be fought 'class against class', as much with reactionary elements within the working class as with the bourgeoisie. Signs of a turning away from this ultra-Left sectarian policy, not least within the Soviet Union itself, could be seen from 1932, but it was only midway through 1935, at the Seventh World Congress of the Comintern, that the *new* new line was unveiled: a Popular Front to reunite communists with the wider Left in the fight against global fascism.

In many accounts, the Popular Front represents the heyday of communist influence in Britain, a major boost in Party membership and high cultural visibility the reward for easing off the revolutionary rhetoric and rallying instead behind the defence of culture and civil liberties. Thereafter, the signing of the Nazi–Soviet Non-Aggression Pact in August 1939 and the re-signification of the coming war as no longer a just crusade against fascism but a senseless reversion to inter-imperial rivalry caused widespread Party-line whiplash and some high-profile defections, following as it did upon reports of the Purges and of Moscow's interference in the Spanish Civil War. Simply in numerical terms, however, the damage this about-turn caused was limited. Hitler's invasion of the USSR in June 1941 allowed British communists once again to rally to the war effort. Party membership, which had fallen below 3,000 in 1930, and risen to 18,000 in 1938, peaked at 56,000 in December 1942 in a surge of pro-Soviet sentiment during the Battle of Stalingrad.

Third Period Proletarianism

On the cultural front, changes in the political line had consequence for who made art for whom and what that art communicated. Thus, to the

'Third Period' analysis of capitalist crisis and revolutionary opportunity corresponds the Stalinist 'cultural revolution', the mass mobilisation of worker-writers in the years of the first Five Year Plan and the rise of the Russian Association of Proletarian Writers (or RAPP). In the Soviet Union and abroad, these years fostered a proletarian avant-garde, militantly working class, sectarian, and iconoclastic. The period favoured 'short, immediate, flexible, agitational forms' such as the literary and dramatic 'sketch', and, while the '"big form"' (novel) retained all its nineteenth-century prestige, it was allowed that working its bourgeois conventions into 'harmony with the class content of the proletariat' would take time.[7]

This class content was crucial. As Karl Radek explained at the 1934 Soviet Writers' Congress, the communication of proletarian and peasant experience, of solidarity in the struggle, was the currency of international communist literature. The Soviet Union would export its stories of the construction works, its heroes of the Red Army and the Arctic exploration missions, its millions of everyday men and women becoming class-conscious fighters for socialism, and it looked to import stories from abroad. 'Our workers are thirsting' for narratives of the anti-fascist underground in Germany and the revolutionary struggle in China, he continued: 'help us to show how the French, how the English worker lives – the foreign worker whom we regard as our brother but whom we now see but dimly, as through a mist.'[8]

And so, in Britain, the call went out. With its cover illustration of 'Rinkus', a Soviet metalworker and worker-correspondent captioned as one of the two million 'embryo artists and thinkers' 'building the mass culture of the classless society at the bench', *Forge* (two issues, 1932) asked its readers to send in sketches, suggesting that year's Hunger March as a subject.[9] *Storm* (four issues, 1933) sought to generate forceful 'Stories of the Struggle', with editorials calling on 'every factory' to mobilise 'its worker-correspondent, its cartoonist and its photographer' to supply short pieces and join active debates.[10] A typical sketch recounts a rally in support of the 1932 Burnley Weavers' Strike, as deputations from around the country descend on the mill town in a show of labour solidarity. Salford has sent its 'Red Megaphones', an affiliate of the Workers' Theatre Movement (WTM), who lead the crowd in 'singing revolutionary songs' from the back of a lorry while playing a 'game of "tag"' with the local policeman. 'They wait until he is near and then start off – but only fifty yards further down [. . .]. Again he goes for them and again they move out of reach.' Finally, in a symbol of the larger struggle, the copper admits defeat. For the Burnley workers 'know how to fight', and 'if all Britain follows [their] example, nothing can hold us down!'[11]

For the seventeen-year-old Ewan MacColl, the 'big meeting' at Burnley that summer was the 'peak' of his work with the WTM. By then, Burnley was a town under siege, the roads and railway lines closed, protestors coming in off the moors having to slip in undetected or fight their way through the police cordon to join their comrades, all 150,000 of them, in the town centre. 'There we were with our gleaming megaphones' on a makeshift stage erected atop of four sixteen-wheeler trucks, he recalled. 'And it was a thrilling thing to stand' up there 'and sing and perform, for your own people.' 'Crude? Yes, but as honest as we knew how to be.'[12]

Compared with other countries, Britain's Third Period culture flourished rather in spite of than because of the Communist Party of Great Britain (CPGB). By August 1930, its membership had collapsed to a mere 2,350 (a third of them unemployed), and to many in both the leadership and the rank-and-file, art was an irrelevance next to the necessity of rebuilding the movement. In the early 1930s, initiatives to form groups for revolutionary writers and intellectuals would frequently be shot down or see 'the Party centre nip[. . .] the whole scheme in the bud'. 'There can be no proletarian art until after the revolution', Billy Holt was told: 'To the factories – the masses! That's our job now.'[13]

For Edward Upward, 'bourgeois born' and anxious 'to be a good communist', this raised the question: 'Is it necessary for me to write at all?' 'The fight for communism must be my fight', he reasoned, 'but the fight alone would be a mechanical duty.' How then to justify 'the writing that is both my life for the fight and a mirror of the fight. The enthusiasm without which the fight would be a heavy machine, without initiative, and the fight without which there could be no enthusiasm'? How 'to be a person, a creator, as well as a rank-and-filer', 'an individual' as well as 'a cog'?[14] *Journey to the Border* (1938, begun 1932), his masterwork of the decade, concludes with its middle-class hero resolving to do only 'what the workers would require him to do for the movement'.[15]

In the face of CPGB suspicion of the arts, exposure to the wider Comintern cultural world assumed greater importance. Upward pored over Soviet novels in translation and the pages of *International Literature* to triangulate a style adequate to his understanding of the British struggle, his bourgeois social location, and his exacting standard of practice.[16] The WTM developed contacts in Germany, America, and the Soviet Union and attended international conferences, even competing in the 1933 Moscow Theatre Olympiad. This international orientation was not simply a compensation for national lack; participation in Soviet literary space signified and reinforced an emerging literary solidarity between peasant, proletarian, and revolutionary writers around the world, the realisation of 'something like a Litintern', as Anatoly Lunacharsky had first floated the idea in 1921, not just as an institution or set of networks, journals, and conferences but as an ethos.[17]

Thus the African-American poet and novelist Richard Wright described the 'realm of revolutionary expression' he encountered through the John Reed Club of Chicago: 'here at last . . . was where Negro experience could find a home, a functioning value and role'. In all the communist literary magazines he read, he heard the same 'passionate call for the experiences of the disinherited', and 'feeling for the first time that I could speak to listening ears, I wrote [. . .]'. What he wrote was widely translated and reached ears around the world. 'Who had ever, in all human history, offered to young writers an audience so vast? True, our royalties were small or less than small, but that did not matter.'[18]

British proletarian writing travelled likewise. *Hunger and Love* (1931), Lionel Britton's novel of poverty in pre-war London and of the working-class life of the mind, circulated in America to great praise; a reviewer in the influential American periodical *New Masses* claimed that 'every one interested in revolutionary writing, or writing of any social significance whatever, would want to read it'.[19] The journal *International Literature* also allowed writers such as Harold Heslop to reach readers in other countries, in Heslop's case with a story about mining and militancy in the north-east of England in the February 1933 issue. And both Britton and Heslop had notable success in the Soviet Union. Here, the print runs for Heslop's second and third novels ran to 100,000 copies and the magazine that reissued his first novel, *Under the Sway of Coal*, had a readership of half a million.

Third Period Anti-Colonialism

At its founding in 1919, the Comintern had promised the 'colonial slaves of Africa and Asia' that the 'hour of proletarian dictatorship in Europe' would strike for them as their own hour of 'emancipation'.[20] Lenin's identification of imperialism as the highest stage of capitalism assumed that the two struggles would count as one, but in practice the anti-colonial struggle frequently fell out of focus. The Third Period, however, saw attention return. At the Sixth Congress of the Comintern in 1928, Western communists were instructed to advance the national self-determination of the

American and Global South and to eradicate 'white chauvinism' from their ranks.[21] Africa now emerged alongside the American Black Belt as a major target of communist agitation, with the Red International of Trade Unions (or Profintern) launching a Negro Workers section to braid the fights against colonialism and racialised labour exploitation. The Trinidadian George Padmore led the section at the height of its influence and edited its newspaper, the *Negro Worker*. Smuggled by sailors of colour to ports and cities around the world, the paper carried articles on current affairs and poetry by the likes of Langston Hughes, Claude McKay, and the white socialite turned anti-racism activist Nancy Cunard.

Cunard's membership of the Negro Welfare Association (NWA) and leading role on the London Scottsboro Defence Committee crossed her path with Padmore's and together they collaborated on the single most remarkable document of British Third Period cultural politics. An explosive combination of cosmopolitan modernism and Black Atlantic Communism, Cunard's 850-page *Negro* anthology (1934) assembles images as well as poetry and prose by 'some 150 voices of both races – for the recording of the struggles and achievements, the persecutions and the revolts against them, of the Negro peoples'.[22] At its margins the anthology is surprisingly heterodox – as, for example, in René Crevel's reflections on black female sexuality, or Ezra Pound's homage to Frobenius – and Judy Suh's chapter in this *Companion* explores how this 'necessarily fragmentary' work functions as a 'critique of British imperialism'. But the routine denunciations of black establishment politicians as reformist 'Uncle Toms', incitements to Afrodiasporic insurrection, and genuflections to the Soviet Union as the first post-racial society signal a clear fidelity to the Party line.

Negro devotes much of its section on Europe to anatomising the 'Colour Bar', the system of race-based discrimination in employment and provision of services. An article from the *Negro Worker* notes that 'race prejudice' is 'so widespread in England' that it targets not only the 'Negro, Arab and Indian seamen' whose presence had sparked race riots in 1919 but also 'coloured intellectuals' and professionals.[23] This violence in Britain's seaports is recalled at the start of Roland Ederisu Sawyer's co-authored 'cross between a novel and an essay', *Colour Bar* (1940).[24] A Sierra Leonean sailor active with the Coloured Seaman's Association and the NWA, Sawyer joined the CPGB in 1934, but his novel is not, as one might expect, a tale of the Red and Black Atlantics but the Bildungsroman of an African student in London, his exposure to different kinds of racism, and his eventual conversion to communism.

It is his presence at a pageant organised by the London District Communist Party that finally wins Kofi to the cause. A co-production of scriptwriter Montagu Slater and composer Alan Bush with André van Gyseghem directing, *Heirs to the Charter* (1939) positions the Party as the direct descendant of the wave of working-class militancy that produced the People's Conventions and petitions to Parliament of 1839 and 1848. The pageant's first act ends with Marx, in London, drafting the *Communist Manifesto* (copies for sale in the interval), the second with scenes from the life of Harry Pollitt and his apotheosis on stage as the present Party leader; and it is this narrative trajectory that reassures Kofi of the English people's 'great and noble' character, 'when once they understand clearly what they ought to do'. 'That night,' he explains in the novel, 'I understood the correctness of the Communist approach to social problems, their stern call for struggle and sacrifice, their sunny faith in the future' premised on a deep understanding of the contingency of social forms. Racism may be inherent to capitalist imperialism, he reasons, but neither is for that reason eternal: alter the mode of production and 'you can alter human nature'.[25]

Popular Front England

The latest in a line of Left appropriations of the Edwardian pageant revival, *Heirs to the Charter* exemplifies the shift from 'Third Period' to 'Popular Front' cultural production. Instead of a tiny troupe of working-class actors, acting on their own initiative and performing on an improvised stage sketches tightly tailored to a scene of industrial self-defence – as at Burnley in 1932 – we have an official Party production, professionally run with a core of semi-professional actors, performed across four platforms in the massive ice-hockey arena at Earl's Court, its dynamic, spot-lit cuts and mass processions from stage to stage designed to conjure the epic scale and grandeur of the national-popular past.

Soviet-sphere cultural politics had been turning in this direction since the liquidation in April 1932 of the proletarian writers' association RAPP and the debut in May of 'socialist realism' as the cultural ideal of Stalinism. Broadcast to the world in August 1934 at the Soviet Writers' Congress, the new aesthetic came coupled with criticism of the proletarian avant-garde for its narrow scope and lack of 'craftsmanship'.[26] Rather than break with bourgeois literature and standards of practice, it was now the communist writer's 'duty' to learn from 'the treasury of past literature' and 'the great living masters'; leading speeches called for 'creative fusion' between proletarian and progressive bourgeois writers.[27] It remained for the seventh and final Congress of the Comintern in August 1935 to supply the anti-fascist inflection, declaring that only a politics of broad democratic alliance, uniting Left elements of the 'working intelligentsia' with the revolutionary proletariat, peasantry, and urban petty bourgeoisie, could put an end to this 'putrefaction of capitalism'.[28]

In Britain, this spirit of rapprochement encouraged many middle-class intellectuals to take out Community Party cards, including the poets Valentine Ackland, Cecil Day-Lewis, Edgell Rickword, and Randall Swingler, the novelists Jack Lindsay and Sylvia Townsend Warner, and the novelist and critic Christopher Caudwell. 'I join . . . the Communist Party' ran the *Daily Worker* headline when Stephen Spender took the plunge in February 1937.[29] The drama is all in the ellipsis: the hesitation and delay, the build-up of suspense, the unimaginable or inevitable conclusion. 'Going over' to socialism, crossing the frontier, trusting oneself to the rising revolutionary tide: metaphors of commitment loom large in the literature of those writers, especially of the Auden group, who most flirted with and feared the surrender of their private selves to the proletarian and people's 'we'.[30] The recruitment of famous poets like Spender and Day-Lewis allowed the CPGB to boast 'of the growing army of [. . .] writers, artists and intellectuals, who are taking their stand with the working class in the issues of our epoch', but the fact that they largely opted out of its dominant artistic forms makes even such pro-Communist writing as Day-Lewis's long-poem *Noah and the Waters* (1936) or Spender's popular polemic *Forward from Liberalism* (1937) relatively eccentric.[31] The work of lesser-known figures like Lindsay, Rickword, and Swingler more closely reflects the genres and styles of the new Party line.

In his main speech to the 1935 Congress, Comintern General Secretary Georgi Dimitrov urged the need for 'clear, popular arguments' to combat fascism. Attributing its rise to communism's failure to channel the legitimate 'national pride' of the people to more progressive ends, Dimitrov instructed scientific socialism to adopt a 'national form'. Communism must '"acclimatise itself" in each country', he said, strike down 'deep roots' in the native soil; above all, communists must work to reclaim the national story, linking the 'present struggle' with the people's 'revolutionary traditions and past'.[32] The pageant was one of these national forms, the historical novel another. As Jack Lindsay explained in 1937, with 'fascism raising everywhere demagogic cries of reactionary nationalism, there is no task more important for the Communists in each country than to make it clear that they stand for the true completion of the national destiny [. . .]. And what can do it better than adequate historical novels?'[33] Matching prescription to practice, Lindsay produced in quick succession a trilogy of novels – *1649* (1938), chronicling a year of the English Revolution, *Lost Birthright* (1939) on the 'Wilkes and Liberty' riots of the 1760s, and *Men of Forty-Eight* (written 1939–40; published 1948), dealing with English Chartism and the revolutions abroad. The genre drew contributions from across the cultural front, including James Barke, Simon Blumenfeld, Roger Dataller, D. J. Hall, Harold Heslop, Jack Jones, Naomi Mitchison, Iris Morley, Charles Poulsen, John Cowper Powys, Montagu Slater, Gwyn Thomas, Geoffrey Trease, and Sylvia Townsend Warner. As Marina MacKay's chapter in this volume attests, the historical novel was 'one of the major literary modes of a thoroughly unsettled decade', and its 'revolutionary' form was adopted by writers not only in Britain but around the world as a means to repossess the national-popular past.

In Britain, this people's history produced radical interventions in the cultural record. Edgell Rickword's 'Culture, Progress and the English Tradition' (1937), and the *Handbook of Freedom* anthology (1939) he co-edited with Lindsay, traced a literary history from below, juxtaposing elite and popular literature and showing art alive to its political moment.[34] 'We were trained too long', wrote Alick West in the *Daily Worker*, 'to think that Shelley only heard the skylark and the wind, and to ignore that in their song he also heard the voice of freedom.' For a century, his poems were used 'to kill poetry', to turn it into a fetish of formal perfection cut off from the world. But 'today' 'the spirit of his poetry is awake'. Shelley's 'love of freedom' has become 'the common quality of so many daily lives' and literature is again 'being read and written as he read and wrote'. Once more, there are 'radiant spirits' to serve as 'standard-bearers in the van of Change' and to write 'for freedom wherever the fight [blazes] up'.[35]

Randall Swingler recalled Shelley's praise of poets as the 'trumpets which sing to battle', together with the 'condition' Ralph Fox appended to the line – that the poet also be 'a soldier in that battle' – on the first anniversary of Fox's death in the Spanish Civil War. 'There are many poets', continued Swingler, 'fighting as soldiers in the battle, both in China and Spain, and their works [are] "trumpets" to sharpen our consciousness of the nature and necessity of the fight.'[36] This was the editorial to a special issue of *Left Review* on 'Modern China' in which the poet Wang Lixi explained the importance of 'armed resistance to Japan' and playwright Yao Hsin-nung mapped the rise of radical literary groups in China. Wang had adopted the first name Shelley during his years of exile in England and like Fox he died a soldier in a war, leading the Battlefield Interview Group of the All-China Resistance Association of Writers on a mission to the Henan Front in 1939.

Fox's classic study, *The Novel and the People* (published posthumously in 1937), defined the English 'cultural heritage' as both a 'spiritual community binding together the living and the dead' and a reminder that our 'national interest' lies always in supporting 'movements for democracy and national liberty' abroad. Linking anti-colonialism and cultural defence, Fox hailed the 'reinforcement of imagination' that would surely follow the liberation of Africa, India, and the Middle East.[37] This fantasy of a new world literature born of the synthesis of revolutionary nationalism and socialist internationalism reflects the central tenet of Dimitrov's Popular Front programme, that '*National forms* of the proletarian class struggle' need not contradict international solidarity.[38]

Work and Play

The rhetorical shift to a politics of unity brought an end to the militant proletarianism and exuberant revolutionism of the Third Period, but not to the problematic of labour, which remained central to the Popular Front imaginary and to its national and cultural turns. 'We that love England have our pride in her; / aye, love of England is the tale we tell. / We mix with her in toil,' wrote Lindsay in the dedicatory poem of his historical novel *1649*.[39] The England that is ours, he wrote in the mass declamation, 'not English?' (1936), is sprung 'from the earth of action' and 'the loyalty learned / in mine and factory'. It is a 'compact linking us to past and future', a pledge that one day the workers will 'take the world that they have made! / unseal the horns of plenty [and] join once more / the severed ends of work and play [. . .]'.[40] And it is this capitalist division between labour and leisure, including as it also does the expropriation of mental as well as manual labour, its idealisation in art and functionalisation in the modern entertainment industries, that lies at the heart of the Popular Front cultural theory elaborated in works like Christopher Caudwell's *Illusion and Reality* (1937), Lindsay's *Short History of Culture* (1939), and George Thomson's *Marxism and Poetry* (1945).

Of these writers, it is Christopher Caudwell who casts the longest shadow. Like Fox, another casualty of the Spanish Civil War, killed in the first day's fighting at Jarama, Caudwell bequeathed to the British Left an extraordinary body of work in publisher's proofs and manuscript, some of it polished, a lot of it not, and all of it written in the white heat of discovery. If he was known at all at the time of his death it was as a writer of aeronautical textbooks and popular crime fiction; his reputation as a theorist rests exclusively on material posthumously published and on its subsequent contestation in two high-profile arguments in British Marxism. At the height of the intellectual Cold War, the 1951 'Caudwell Controversy' saw the CPGB turn on one of its own, repudiating what it claimed to be idealist and deviationist tendencies in his thinking; twenty years later, it was Caudwell's vulgar materialism that now riled a New Left intent on marking its break from the Old. In retrospect, it is Caudwell's identification of the prefigurative power of culture, its capacity to generate and educate desire, that aligns this largely self-taught British intellectual with the best impulses of mid-century Marxism in Europe and elsewhere.

'Labour as the basis of culture! What a crass idea that sounds the first time one hears it, being accustomed to the notion of our cultivated people that freedom *from* work is the necessary first condition for exercising artistic or intellectual talent,' Edgell Rickword had written.[41] Cross perhaps, but, as the decade went on, this idea began to wear away at the moral invisibility of the worker and the immaterial fetish forms of the market, troubling the false antinomies – art and politics, spirit and matter, privileged self and unrecognised other – of liberal social thought. This revalorisation of labour provides a framework for the prominence in the 1930s of worker-writers, not all of whom conceived literature as a weapon in the fight for socialism or had their work promoted by the Left, but who all demanded recognition and cultural justice for their works and days.

Simon Blumenfeld spoke the decade's common sense when he hailed the proletarian writer as 'the voice of the inarticulate', a mouthpiece for 'the struggling, dark consciousness of the broad masses'.[42] But even Leslie Halward – remembered as wholly 'unpolitical' by his friend Walter Allen, 'as much likely [...] to vote Conservative as Labour' – embraced the label of proletarian writer and dated his literary emancipation to his decision to 'write in my own language about my own people'.[43] In story collections like *To Tea on Sunday* (1936) and *The Money's All Right* (1938) Halward is happy to explain the unfamiliar techniques of the plastering trade, but it is the artist's craft that has his whole attention, delivering his celebrated economy of description and amply rounded characters. Not for nothing did E. M. Forster describe Halward as the only working-class writer who ever made 'the working class come alive' for him.[44] There is no vanguard sensibility here, no political didacticism or narrative arc of insurgency, but Halward's commercially successful stories share in the moral economy of the Litintern, the global Left's commitment to the *self*-representation of working-class place and labour.

In this, the CPGB must be given its due: though forever far from becoming a ruling force in society, a minority formation even within the British labour movement, the Party became a central feature of cultural life in the 1930s. *Pace* Orwell, the Party never could 'control' English literature, but some of its arguments did enter the cultural mainstream. The literary class war of the 1930s empowered a generation of plebeian writers who when they graduated into radio and television passed their fictional East Ends and Coronation Streets on into the national imaginary, no longer as 'special areas' or exotic otherworlds but as authentic sites of a more inclusive, social-democratic Britain.[45] And though the Soviet orientation must implicate British communist writers in some relation to violence and atrocity, the commitment can perhaps more charitably be framed as a question about the nature and necessity of capitalist modernity. The turbulence of the 1930s gave this question resonance, and catalysed a culture that was at once a structure of participation in the production and consumption of art and a way of being in and imagining the world differently.

Notes

1. George Orwell, 'Inside the Whale', in *The Collected Essays, Journalism and Letters: Volume One*, ed. by Sonia Orwell and Ian Angus (London: Secker and Warburg, 1968), pp. 497, 500–1, 525–7.
2. See John Rodden, *The Politics of Literary Reputation: The Making and Claiming of 'St George' Orwell* (Oxford: Oxford University Press, 1991).
3. Orwell, 'Inside the Whale', p. 512; see E. P. Thompson, 'Outside the Whale', in *Out of Apathy*, ed. by E. P. Thompson (London: Stevens, 1960), pp. 160–1.
4. George Orwell, *Nineteen Eighty-Four* (London: Penguin, 2000), pp. 57, 322.
5. See Katerina Clark, *Moscow, The Fourth Rome: Stalinism, Cosmopolitanism and the Evolution of Soviet Culture, 1931–1941* (Cambridge, MA: Harvard University Press, 2011).
6. See Andrew Rubin, *Archives of Authority: Empire, Culture, and the Cold War* (Princeton: Princeton University Press, 2012), pp. 24–46. On the concept of literary space, see Pascale Casanova, *The World Republic of Letters*, trans. M. B. DeBevoise (Cambridge, MA: Harvard University Press, 2004).
7. 'Resolution on Political and Creative Questions of International Proletarian and Revolutionary Literature', *Literature of the World Revolution* (1931), Special Number, 'Reports, Resolutions, Debates of the Second International Conference of Revolutionary Writers', pp. 87–8. For a masterful survey of Soviet-sphere aesthetic ideologies and artistic forms, see Michael Denning, 'The Novelists' International', in *Culture in the Age of Three Worlds* (London: Verso, 2004), pp. 51–72.
8. Karl Radek, 'Contemporary World Literature and the Tasks of Proletarian Art', in *Problems of Soviet Literature*, ed. by H. G. Scott (London: Martin Lawrence, 1935), p. 159.
9. Dick Beech, 'P.B.S. From Within and Without, by the Secretary', *Forge*, 2 (1932), p. 11.

10. Such a call is issued in *Storm*, 1.2 (1933), p. 32. Copies of the magazine and other material can be found in the Security Service Personal File of the magazine's editor, George Douglas Jefferies, PRO KV2/2806, The National Archives. On *Storm*, see James Smith, 'The Radical Literary Magazine of the 1930s and British Government Surveillance: The Case of *Storm* Magazine', *Literature & History*, 19.2 (2010), 69–86.

11. 'Solidarity. A Lancashire Miner's Impressions of the Burnley Weavers' Strike', *Storm*, 1.1 (1933), pp. 11–13.

12. Ewan MacColl, 'Grass Roots of Theatre Workshop', *Theatre Quarterly*, 3.9 (1973), 60; Ewan MacColl, 'Theatre of Action', in *Theatres of the Left, 1880–1935: Workers' Theatre Movements in Britain and America*, ed. by Raphael Samuel, Ewan MacColl, and Stuart Cosgrove (London: Routledge and Kegan Paul, 1985), p. 238.

13. Rajani Palme Dutt, 'Intellectuals and Communism', *Communist Review* (September 1932), p. 425; William Holt, *I Haven't Unpacked. An Autobiography* (London: George G. Harrap & Co., 1939), p. 209.

14. Edward Upward, Journal 1931–4, Supplementary Papers of Edward Upward, Add. MS 89002/1/3, British Library. I am grateful to Kathy Allinson and Janet Upward for permission to quote from this document.

15. Edward Upward, 'Journey to the Border', in *The Railway Accident and Other Stories* (Harmondsworth: Penguin, 1972), p. 220.

16. See Glyn Salton-Cox, 'Literary Praxis Beyond the Melodramas of Commitment: Edward Upward, Soviet Aesthetics and Leftist Self-Fashioning', *Comparative Literature*, 65.4 (2013), 408–28.

17. Cited in David Pike, *German Writers in Soviet Exile, 1933–1945* (Chapel Hill: University of North Carolina Press, 1982), p. 28.

18. Richard Wright, *Later Works: Black Boy (American Hunger), The Outsider* (New York: Library of America, 1991), pp. 302–3; 328.

19. Clinton Simpson, 'A Young Proletarian', *New Masses*, May 1932, p. 26.

20. Leo Trotsky, 'Manifesto of the Communist International of the Proletariat of the Entire World', 6 March 1919, in *The Communist International, 1919–1943: Documents: Volume One*, ed. by Jane Degras (Oxford: Oxford University Press, 1956), p. 43.

21. *The Revolutionary Movement in the Colonies* (New York: Workers Library Publishers, 1929), p. 57.

22. Nancy Cunard, 'Foreword', in *Negro: An Anthology*, ed. by Nancy Cunard (London: Wishart, 1934), p. iii.

23. 'Race Prejudice in England', in *Negro*, p. 555.

24. Ederisu Sawyer and Anne M. Bagshaw, *Colour Bar* (London: [privately printed], 1940), pp. 38–9.

25. Ibid., p. 95.

26. Andrei Zhdanov, 'Soviet Literature – The Richest in Ideas, the Most Advanced Literature', in *Problems of Soviet Aesthetics*, p. 23; Radek, 'Contemporary World Literature', p. 161.

27. Radek, 'Contemporary World Literature', pp. 146, 139–40.

28. Georgi Dimitrov, *The Working Class Against Fascism* (London: Martin Lawrence, 1935), pp. 28, 69, 72.

29. Stephen Spender, 'I Join the … Communist Party', *Daily Worker*, 19 February 1937, p. 4.

30. See Valentine Cunningham, *British Writers of the Thirties* (Oxford: Oxford University Press, 1988), pp. 211–225.

31. Spender, 'I Join the … Communist Party', p. 4.

32. Dimitrov, *The Working Class Against Fascism*, p. 69.

33. Jack Lindsay, 'The Historical Novel', *New Masses*, 12 January 1937, pp. 15–16.

34. Edgell Rickword, 'Culture, Progress and English Tradition', in *The Mind in Chains: Socialism and the Cultural Revolution*, ed. by Cecil Day-Lewis (London: Frederick Muller, 1937), pp. 236–57. See Ben Harker, '"Communism is English": Edgell Rickword, Jack Lindsay and the Cultural Politics of the Popular Front', *Literature & History*, 20.2 (2011), 23–40.

35. Alick West, 'The Spirit of Shelley is AWAKE Today', *Daily Worker*, 8 July 1937, p. 4.

36. Randall Swingler, 'Two Anniversaries', *Left Review*, 3.12 (January 1938), p. 702.

37. Ralph Fox, *The Novel and the People*, 2nd ed. (London: Cobbett, 1944), pp. 141, 148, 153–4.

38. Dimitrov, *The Working Class Against Fascism*, p. 71.

39. Jack Lindsay, 'To Marley Denwood', *1649: A Novel of a Year* (London: Methuen, 1938), p. v.

40. Jack Lindsay, 'not english? a Reminder for May Day', *Left Review*, 2.8 (May 1936), p. 357.

41. Rickword, 'Culture, Progress', p. 245

42. Simon Blumenfeld, 'Controversy', *Left Review*, 1.3 (December 1934), p. 80.

43. Walter Allen, *As I Walked Down New Grub Street: Memories of a Writing Life* (Chicago: University of Chicago Press, 1981), p. 69; Leslie Halward, *Let Me Tell You* (London: Michael Joseph, 1938), p. 226.

44. Quoted in John Lehmann, *I Am My Brother* (London: Longmans, 1960), pp. 101–2.

45. Andy Croft comments on the preservation in post-war British soap of a kind of 'anglicised social romantic realism' in 'Authors Take Sides: Writers and the Communist Party, 1920–56', in *Opening the Books: Essays on the Social and Cultural History of British Communism*, ed. by Geoff Andrews, Nina Fishman, and Kevin Morgan (London: Pluto, 1995), p. 84.

CHAPTER 8

Empire

Judy Suh

Throughout the 1930s, old and new forms of media continued to uphold the centrality of imperialism in British nationalism. Adventure stories featuring imperial benevolence and derring-do written in the previous century by Henry Rider Haggard, Robert Louis Stevenson, Rudyard Kipling, and G. A. Henty remained popular cultural touchstones.[1] Popular radio programmes such as the BBC's Empire Day and Christmas broadcasts reflected a view of the Empire 'as a topic of central concern to national life, one which could be turned to nationalist, moral, and quasi-religious ends'.[2] And, at the movies, this decade was the heyday of imperial adventure films, such as *Sanders of the River* (1935), *King Solomon's Mines* (1937), *The Drum* (1938), and *Gunga Din* (1939).[3]

Perhaps with a view towards this persistence, C. L. R. James warned in 1933 that 'empires prod their citizens into violence and sow the seeds of their own dissolution. Yet though the writing on the walls stretched from Burma to Cyprus, there are those who will not read.'[4] Despite its standing in popular culture and its immense colonial holdings, the British Empire was indeed in the midst of precipitous decline. The Indian National Congress began the decade by declaring independence in 1930, and concluded it with a successful record of mass civil disobedience and a number of key electoral footholds. In 1931, the Imperial Parliament relinquished its legislative authority over the 'White Dominions', which had been lobbying for the autonomous implementation of foreign policy since the end of the First World War. In the Middle East, insurgent forces had challenged British control almost from the moment of its inception after the war. Iraq ended its status as a British mandate when it was accepted into the League of Nations as an independent nation in 1932. Moreover, the worldwide Depression was aggravating already intolerable working conditions and workers' debt all over the Empire. Workers' revolts led the charge against the British and French Empires in Africa and the Caribbean throughout the decade.

This chapter presents literary challenges to imperial beliefs and practices in the 1930s by some key authors who saw the writing on the walls. In their important redefinitions of late modernism, Jed Esty, Laura Winkiel, Kristin Bluemel, and Jane Marcus have explored literary responses to the contraction of British global supremacy.[5] In the process, they have brought a stronger light to the profound concern with anti-colonialism in Britain within the wider turn to politics in literature of the decade. They have also created stronger links between this body of literature and the cultural critiques that emerged more frequently and sharply alongside large-scale immigration and anti-colonial revolutions after the Second World War. The authors discussed in this chapter share insight into the cultural implications of imperial decline, but each wrote with different targets in mind and from experiences enabled by their specific locations in and migrations across the Empire.

Virginia Woolf and Nancy Cunard, the most privileged of the authors here, call attention to the psychological and economic dependence of the British ruling classes on the imperial subjugation of others. Like some other key voices at the time, they strategically compared the Empire to other racist ideologies widely acknowledged by the British left as unjust, namely continental fascism and the racial segregation in the American South.[6] A related approach was taken by a group of prominent writers born in British colonies and deeply familiar with methods of colonial rule. George Orwell, Rumer Godden, and Jean Rhys sketch the colonial governing classes and their interactions with colonised subjects to demonstrate the impossibility of justice in colonial systems. Finally, Olivia Manning, Mulk Raj Anand, and C. L. R James explored the emergence of leaders and intellectuals amongst the colonised as a vital and at times troubling element of revolution.

Views from the Metropolis

Both Virginia Woolf and Nancy Cunard spent much of the 1930s working tirelessly against imperialism and fascism. Woolf's *Three Guineas* (1938) and her posthumously published *Between the Acts* (1941) have retained their reputation as powerful critiques of fascist and imperialist patriarchies. Cunard often lent her skills directly to anti-fascist activism, even reporting from the front lines of the Spanish Civil War. Both also supported anti-imperialist ideas through their publishing and editing. In the 1930s, Woolf's Hogarth Press published some of the most important anti-colonial intellectuals of the interwar period, including C. L. R. James.[7]

Cunard poured much of her time and money into the mammoth project of compiling and editing *Negro* (1934), her most important contribution to anti-colonial critique. These writers had economic and social resources unavailable to most of the writers discussed in this chapter, but a great deal of their professional lives in this decade were dedicated to undermining the prevailing imperial consensus from within the powerful metropolitan perspectives enabled by their privilege.

Virginia Woolf's *The Waves* (1931) features interior monologues in the voices of six friends from their childhood to senescence. Considered by many to be her most experimental, the novel allows seemingly unfettered access to the characters' interior lives and psychological states. Persistent images of the Empire's heroic myths weave themselves into their conscious and unconscious desires. On one hand, Woolf demonstrates the attractions of imperial aesthetics and the difficulty of transcending them for the upper class in the geographical centres of power. Binding the characters together is love for their heroic friend Percival who in early adulthood departs for India to begin a brilliant career. His death soon after his departure enables him to act as a screen for his friends' subsequent colonial fantasies in which they project onto him an unfulfilled 'rapture of benignity' and thus vicariously bolster their own self-regard.[8] Bernard imagines Percival selflessly 'applying the standards of the West' in India so that 'the Oriental problem is solved'.[9] Far from exclusively male, imperial fantasies are also prevalent in the women's visions of the nation. As an adult, Jinny imagines her role in the Empire as both spectator and active participant, comparing everyday London street life to a victorious military procession. She imagines herself taking part in the march triumphing over 'savages in loin-cloths' with 'patent-leather shoes, my handkerchief that is but a film of gauze, my reddened lips and my finely pencilled eyebrows'.[10] Her dress and makeup act as a kind of uniform and warpaint; women too are interpellated by the imperial process.

On the other hand, these fantasies of imperial benevolence and conquest are also shown to facilitate war and fascism. The 'boasting boys' who follow Percival at school are militaristic bullies who exacerbate Louis's sense of colonial shame; they 'laugh at my neatness, at my Australian accent'.[11] Louis nonetheless envies their ability to conform: 'How majestic is their order, how beautiful is their obedience! [...] Peeping from behind a curtain, I note the simultaneity of their movements with delight.'[12] Woolf's critique of imperialism depended on her ability to perceive the stunning pageantry as well as the brutality of Empire from the inside and the outside.

For some critics, Woolf left much of imperial discourse far too intact. To Urmila Seshagiri, for instance, her novels despite their anti-imperialism 'often reproduce a wide range of assumptions about nonwhite otherness'.[13] By directing her critique primarily at delusional fantasies and destructive desires of imperial culture, however, Woolf created a significant field for anti-imperial thinking in Britain: the scrutiny of individual desire and psyche within and alongside state, military, and economic imperial apparatuses.

In contrast to Woolf's subtle approach, Cunard often takes direct aim and adopts an accusatory tone towards the problem of Empire. At the beginning of the decade, she had famously rebelled against her socialite mother's racism in a pamphlet, 'Black Man and White Ladyship' (1931). Vilified by many for her interracial affair with the African-American jazz pianist and composer Henry Crowder, the lengths to which she was willing to go to confront the British ruling class in which she was raised were quite a departure from Woolf's comparatively sympathetic critique. In an entry in her *Negro: An Anthology* (1934), for instance, Cunard wonders, 'how much longer the roguery, insolence, and domination of the whites must last'.[14]

With more than 220 entries comprising 855 pages, Cunard's *Negro* sought to represent African and African diasporic histories and cultures, arts, and politics through personal and expository essays, short memoirs, ethnographies, tables and statistics, musical scores, poems, photographs and illustrations, advertisements, and press clippings. Its reputation has fluctuated through the decades. The anthology, necessarily fragmentary in its drive for a comprehensive look at a centuries-long and worldwide diaspora, inevitably led to inconsistent messaging given the number of contributors. The value of *Negro* for the critique of British imperialism emerges not in the lines of argumentation, which often contradict each other, but in the patterns to be perceived in the unexpected similarities or disparities between entries.

A group of press clippings on racism in Britain, for example, focusses on the Liverpool race riots of 1919, in which white Britons vandalised property and assaulted blacks as well as whites perceived to be their friends or relatives. A pattern emerges in which interracial sexuality is shown to incite white violence. In other words, a racist discourse of sexuality violently demarcated the proper place of blacks. In this section, the widespread leftist assumption of a gap between racist practices in the colonies and liberal practices in England is obliterated. The imperial obsession with interracial sexuality extended to the conditions of the text's production as well. Cunard also included newspaper and periodical clippings that attempted to paint Cunard herself 'as an English heiress slumming in search of sex with black men'.[15] Maureen Moynagh writes that Cunard 'continually risks a rehearsal of the imperial script' by implying a 'place outside of imperial constructions of whiteness in her political identification with black struggles'.[16] As this section proves, however, Cunard was fighting in her own defence as well.

In perhaps the most confrontational pieces on British imperialism, Johnstone (Jomo) Kenyatta and George Padmore analyse British strategies of imperial rule that were prevalent throughout Africa and beyond. They thereby challenge the tendency to understand Africa in an ahistorical vacuum and as exceptionally primitive. In his piece on Kenya, Kenyatta (who would later serve as its first president) notes the prevalence of divide and rule, heavily restricted voting, and forced labour. Padmore notes these same strategies in South Africa and further compares them with those in India and Ireland. Both entries place African colonies in a global context with an eye towards national liberation movements across the entire Empire.

It is because of *Negro*'s sometimes contradictory juxtapositions, and not in spite of them, that the work has undergone a critical revival in recent years. The anthology, sometimes regarded in the context of the Harlem Renaissance as a 'somewhat belated [...] act' of 'racial rebellion',[17] might now be regarded as speaking meaningfully to a postcolonial future. In Laura Winkiel's assessment, the anthology 'anticipates the postcolonial era of colonial national sovereignty'.[18]

Views from the Margins

The next set of writers were born into colonial governing-class families in the Caribbean, India, and Burma, and so had a direct vantage point on the effects of colonial rule on the coloniser as well as on colonised subjects and subjugated cultures. All convey a mixture of sympathy with the colonised, on one hand, and a profound discomfort with the customs of the colonisers with which they were so intimate. A pervasive sense of alienation accounts for their shared focus on marginalised figures of colonial society to explore contact zones where Europeans and colonised subjects came into conflict as well as affection.

Born and raised in Dominica in a family with British slaveholding roots, Jean Rhys nonetheless felt like an outsider amongst whites, especially after emigrating by herself from the Caribbean to England as a teenager.

Portions of her direct experience of racial alienation surface in *Voyage in the Dark* (1934). Like Rhys, the protagonist Anna is a poor white Dominican Creole who immigrates to England. The novel underplays plot to focus on character and interiority, giving the reader access to unusual and unstable viewpoints, and thus to constantly shifting sources of irony.

Far from improving her situation in England, Anna becomes increasingly desperate and exploited over the course of the novel. First employed as a chorus girl, she soon quits her job to live as a kept woman and finally becomes a prostitute in London. From her first-person perspective, England appears irredeemably bleak and conformist. Looking out from a train car, she thinks, 'this is London – hundreds thousands of white people white people rushing along and the dark houses all alike frowning down one after the other all alike all stuck together'.[19] Such vividly drawn moments of the immigrant's disillusionment regarding the 'Mother Country' have led Kenneth Ramchand to describe the novel as the Caribbean's 'first negritude novel'.[20] Anna's uneasiness in the imperial metropolis is racialised by the English and tinged by shame. As her friend Maudie explains to others regarding Anna's strangeness, 'She was born in the West Indies or somewhere, weren't you, kid? The girls call her the Hottentot. Isn't it a shame?'[21] Her stepmother Hester also locates Anna on a precarious racial boundary: 'I tried to teach you to talk like a lady and behave like a lady and not like a nigger and of course I couldn't do it.'[22] In these hostile inscriptions of otherness, Rhys offers a vision of shared interests between poor women across races and proposes a shared defiance of metropolitan values.

Anna's memories of Dominica provide a provisional challenge to urban England, a critique deepened by sensuous images of home. In its first half, the novel represents Dominica in utopic contrast: 'the smells of frangipani and lime juice and cinnamon and cloves, and sweets made of ginger and syrup'.[23] Her positive memories are dominated by her servant Francine, who represents to Anna the warmth missing from the English: 'I was happy because Francine was there, and I watched her hand waving the fan backwards and forwards and the beads of sweat that rolled from underneath her handkerchief.'[24] Yet those 'beads of sweat' trouble Anna's memories, which increasingly acknowledge differentials of power between women across a racial divide as the novel proceeds.

The fact of Francine's servitude and the inequality at the core of their relationship thus haunt Anna's dreams of home. In a memory that crops up later in the text, Anna describes an unannounced visit to Francine's house:

> the kitchen was horrible. There was no chimney and it was always full of
> charcoal-smoke. Francine was there, washing up. Her eyes were red with the
> smoke and watering. Her face was quite wet. She wiped her eyes with the
> back of her hand and looked sideways at me.[25]

Descriptions of Francine therefore yield telling details that repeatedly
point to the faultiness of Anna's nostalgic imagination. The visibility of
exploitation haunts her memories as the novel begins to form continuity rather than discontinuity between Dominica and the imperial
metropolis in their transformation of women into exchangeable com-
modities. The memory of violent colonial exploitation indicts the will
to forget that can result from the desire for harmony between the
coloniser and colonised. Anna's poignant longing for direct lines of
solidarity between the colonised and whites alienated by Empire,
however, remains a key for understanding the novel's innovative play
with time and memory.

Rumer Godden grew up in the small town of Narayanganj as the
daughter of an English steamer company manager. Like Rhys, Godden
diverges from realism as she emphasises history and memory in colonial
contact zones. During the 1930s, she set two of her novels in India: *The
Lady and the Unicorn* (1937) and *Black Narcissus* (1939). *The Lady and the
Unicorn* depicts 'half-caste' Anglo-Indians as discarded victims of Empire;
the men cannot get work, and the women are systematically seduced and
abandoned. Set largely in a decaying Calcutta boarding house, *The Lady
and the Unicorn* explores the psychological, social, and economic consequences of these colonial sexual customs. Rosa Lemarchant falls in love
with an upper-class Englishman, Stephen Bright, who in defiance of his
compatriots considers marrying her. But aside from Stephen's disapprov-
ing relatives, he is put off by Rosa's inauthenticity: 'You talk of going home
to England, when the only home you have is here in India. It's such
a sham.'[26] In the background, Godden interweaves a peculiar supernatural
plot in which the ghost of Rosa's eighteenth-century French ancestor,
Rosabelle LeViste, relives family betrayal and her own history of abandon-
ment on the estate grounds, foretelling Rosa's similar fate to those who are
capable of seeing her weeping. Not until Stephen is engaged to an
Englishwoman and revisits Rosa's house, now razed to make room for
a Paramount movie theatre, can Stephen see Rosabelle's ghost. Not altogether successfully integrated, the ghost story and the family history enable
some themes that found better realisation in her next novel, *Black
Narcissus*, which explores the power of hidden histories, the haunting of
decadent spaces, and the repetition of individual histories under the

Empire's racial regime. These themes indirectly challenge the justification of Empire as a motor of progress.

The bestselling *Black Narcissus* reflects the growth of European women's roles in twentieth-century imperialism and simultaneously 'exposes the colonial presence as a dangerous illusion'.[27] At the invitation of an Indian general, a group of Anglican nuns, led by the wilful Anglo-Irish Sister Clodagh, arrives in the Himalayas to establish a girls' school and medical clinic at a palace that once housed a harem. From the moment of their arrival, the house and its surroundings appear to resist the nuns' goals of improvement. Instead of reproducing the order's values, the nuns succumb to disruptions of the idealised coloniser–colonised relationship. The natives, far from grateful, remain largely indifferent to their ministrations and eventually become actively hostile. The nuns' mission fails before a year has passed and they leave with a sense of their insignificance: 'The servants would have gone back to their homes and soon they would forget the Leminis except in tales to tell their children.'[28]

In these novels, Godden unblinkingly posits the irreversible breakdown of colonial self-justification, traces the fissures in imperial hegemony, and questions the power of mere individuals to change a futile (from her perspective not wholly corrupt) imperial system in South Asia. Her aesthetic, however, brims with mysticism, and even the bizarre and supernatural. Decidedly anti-realist, the decadence created by these Romantic flourishes suggests a heady mix of dread and nostalgia that must have emerged as a structure of feeling in those colonisers able to see the unmistakable verge of revolt.

On the other end of the stylistic spectrum, George Orwell, strongly associated with social realism since his first book, *Down and Out in Paris and London* (1933), set some of his earliest writing in British-ruled Asia. Born in Bengal, Orwell was the son of an official in the Indian Civil Service and a mother whose family were involved in business and investments in Burma. In the 1930s, he wrote some powerful works drawing on his experience as an imperial police officer in Burma, including the non-fiction essays 'Shooting an Elephant' (1936) and 'A Hanging' (1931), and the novel *Burmese Days* (1934–5). In this novel, John Flory, a timber merchant, despises the racism of the European Club, yet he finds that he cannot discard club life for fear of the loneliness that overcomes him throughout the novel. He attempts to begin a new life in the colony by courting a new arrival, Elizabeth Lackersteen, but he is thrust out of the social order of the club by the humiliating revelation of his Burmese mistress and eventually commits suicide. Elizabeth, who regards Burma as an opportunity to climb back into the upper-middle-class life she'd lost when her father died, marries another club member and comes to epitomise the imperious memsahib.

The bleak outlook of Orwell's novel accords with a belief in the intransigence of white supremacy. The extremism of imperial ideology is epitomised by the character Ellis, who 'hated [Orientals] with a bitter, restless loathing as of something evil or unclean',[29] and by Westfield, who longs for Burmese rebellion so that the natives might be suppressed with impunity.[30] After Ellis attacks a Burmese teenager with his cane, the club closes ranks: 'None of them thought to blame Ellis, the sole cause of this affair; their common peril seemed, indeed, to draw them closer together for the while.'[31] Here, Orwell depicts a form of totalitarian conformity that he would later satirise scathingly in *Nineteen Eighty-Four* (1949). In *Burmese Days*, as his characterisation of the club demonstrates, he was already tuned into racist imperialism as a source of fascist totalitarian thought.

Nevertheless, Orwell's defiance of imperial racism did not translate into a defence of anti-colonial nationalisms. The Burmese revolts in the novel lack any legitimacy. The first revolt is a ruse, the machinations of a corrupt Burmese magistrate. The second revolt is described as a genuine reaction to Ellis's attack, but the narrator nonetheless qualifies its validity: 'The Burmans seemed to have no plan beyond flinging stones, yelling and hammering at the walls.'[32] These mindless Burmese crowds are reminiscent of those that torment the narrator of Orwell's non-fiction essay 'Shooting an Elephant', where a similar ambivalence is the prevailing affect of a voice that is contemptuous simultaneously of the Burmese and of the imperial machine that he is serving as a British police officer. Unable to regard the Burmese as fully human, the narrator describes them metonymically on one hand ('grey, cowed faces', 'scarred buttocks', and 'teeth bared and grinning') and as grouped in unthinking, prodding masses on the other.[33] Protest against the colonial system did not necessarily entail support for anti-colonial revolt; Orwell provides evidence of and even reinforces the vast distance between these two positions. His failure to find legitimacy in anti-colonial nationalisms, in Kristin Bluemel's estimation, was a consequence of his belief – made explicit in 'his correspondence, war-diary, and journalism' – that Indian anti-colonial movements were comprised of 'power hungry nationalists or duped victims'.[34] He was perhaps unable to imagine anti-colonial movements leading to legitimate stable forms of political agency.

Across a wide range of narrative styles, Rhys, Godden, and Orwell present various levels of colonial self-irony. Their works also invoke a deep ambivalence towards anti-colonial revolts that they had witnessed in the past and undoubtedly expected in the future.

Views from the Revolution

Whereas the previous set of authors found revolt difficult to inscribe in their works, Mulk Raj Anand, Olivia Manning, and C. L. R. James dove in to draw the decade not so much as a period of imperial decline as one of revolution and proto-revolution. These writers analyse the relevance of narrative to anti-colonial politics and draw robust pictures of the processes of revolution.

Before entering the doctoral programme in philosophy at University College London in 1925, Anand was twice imprisoned in India for anti-colonial activism. Deeply committed to Indian nationalism and Marxism, he spent time in Gandhi's Sabarmati Ashram, where he was encouraged to write in the service of national liberation. Once in London, his writing impressed his wide and illustrious literary network. The foreword to *Untouchable* (1935) was written by E. M. Forster and he was included in the *New Series* anthology published by the Hogarth Press, where he also worked as a proofreader. Along with R. K. Narayan and Raja Rao, he is considered a founder of Indo-English fiction, which first flourished in this decade.[35]

Anand's adherence to humanism inspired him to incorporate what had previously been taboo – as he put it, 'The poverty, the dirt and squalor of the lower depths'.[36] This concern is especially clear in *Untouchable*, which brazenly tackled the taboo subject of human waste within a critique of the caste system. While the protagonist Bakhu never comes to a clear understanding of what is driving his exploitation as a Dalit latrine cleaner, he nonetheless begins to detach himself from his fetishisation of British customs and is exposed to a nationalist critique of untouchability in the form of a mass gathering addressed by Gandhi at the novel's conclusion.

In *The Village* (1939), the protagonist Lalu Singh, the son of an impoverished Sikh peasant, is a fuller realisation of the humanist individualism inherent in Anand's mapping of genuine freedom. Lalu is critical of the religion that mires his family in superstition and the systems of trade and exploitation that have sunk his village in 'slow decay' and 'general decrepitude'.[37] That his rebellion eventually leads him to fight in the First World War as cannon fodder does not diminish his continual struggle against the forces – both Indian and British – that efface his humanity. Even in *Two Leaves and a Bud* (1937), Anand's most direct indictment of

the British Empire, in which the protagonist Gangu and other workers at
a British-run tea plantation are so continually subjected to degradation that
the imperial system appears impervious to human intervention, Anand
inscribes two British characters (John de la Havre and Barbara Croft-
Cooke) who are critical of British rule, again attesting to the significance
of individualism in socialist critique.

Anand's humanism thus calls attention to the limits of the classic
European realist novel in depicting the effects of colonialism and the
caste system. Both *Coolie* and *Untouchable* feature wandering young male
protagonists who are clearly rejoinders to Rudyard Kipling's *Kim* (1901), in
which the young male protagonist exuberantly wanders across India eventually to serve the Empire as a spy. The poignancy of Munoo's story in part
is created not only by the contrast between his fate and Kim's but also by
the similarity of their outlooks and youthful energy: 'He was wonder-
struck at the baby railway, which he had seen standing at Kalka station,
ascending the gigantic heights with strange puffs such as a toddling child
utters when he first learns to walk.'[38] This account of childlike excitement
might have been written by Kipling; the resonance between the texts points
to Munoo's wasted potential. In his memoir of interwar Bloomsbury,
Anand recalls his desire to 'rewrite Kipling's *Kim* [. . .] from the opposite
point of view', finding the novel too much of 'a fairy tale' about a 'little
hero of the Empire – a fantasy boy'.[39] The realism of his novels was aimed
squarely at narratives of imperial fantasy. Each of these works is also deeply
invested in the process of laying down the groundwork for nationalist
revolution. All contain key scenes in which the protagonists attend political
gatherings or meetings to capture the intellectual and rhetorical labour
involved in building a revolutionary consensus.

Although Anand later bristled against the categorisation of his works as
social realism, which he dismissed as tending towards an over-reliance on
facts and crude characterisation,[40] his works of the 1930s can nevertheless
be read as participating in the socialist revival and redirection of realism in
the mid-twentieth century, and creating within it an important anti-
colonial turn.

Like Anand, Olivia Manning also focussed on the behind-the-scenes
work of building anti-colonial revolution. In her sceptical estimation, the
previous decade's anti-colonialism in Ireland was necessary but prone to
appropriation by self-regarding masculinists. Manning's *Balkan Trilogy*
and *Levant Trilogy* (published over the period 1960–1980) famously
captured nuances of British imperial contraction at mid-century, but
her less frequently read novel *The Wind Changes* (1937) initiated her grasp

of this theme decades earlier. The loose plot unfurls a love triangle set in Ireland in the week leading up to the 1921 truce that established the Irish Free State and its Dominion status in the British Empire. Elizabeth, a would-be painter from Northern Ireland, is at first attached to Arion, an English writer and anti-colonial sympathiser. She then attaches herself to Arion's mentee, Sean Murtough, an Irish revolutionary leader who is drawing secret plans to bring Riordan, a hero of the 1916 Easter Uprising, out of hiding to reinvigorate the revolution. Passively searching for ways to develop her fledgling adulthood, Elizabeth often invites herself to meetings and inadvertently gains access to secret political information in the process. When Sean and his circle are arrested, it is up to Elizabeth to find Riordan in the Aran Islands and warn him to stay away from Dublin. She finds the much-vaunted Riordan a disappointment as a potential hero. When she returns to Dublin, she discovers that a truce has been declared, Sean has died in prison of pneumonia, and Arion is about to leave Dublin.

The narrator deflates both British military and Irish revolutionary displays of masculinity. The British occupation is represented by a maniacal war-minded Black and Tan, Wheeler, who declares that he was 'gloriously happy' during the First World War and hopes 'to prolong my happiness' in Ireland.[41] Manning also implies a fascist aesthetic in his belief that 'war is no more than an excuse for exercising the perfection of discipline and the beauty of well-drilled men'.[42] The Irish revolutionaries are taken to task as well, particularly for their impulsive veneration of barely secular political martyrs: 'In Ireland a leader was indeed a leader – to be worshipped in life and canonized after death.'[43] Sean's obsession with his own death and possible future martyrdom is narrated as a self-obsessed means to cope with the grinding daily reminders of personal failure. When we finally meet Riordan, the legendary veteran of 1916, we see him through Elizabeth's disappointed perspective: 'No revelation here, no hope of mutation.'[44] Riordan's ordinariness empties the masculine myths of war.

Like Woolf, Manning builds scepticism towards the worship of leaders in the age of European fascism and charismatic politics. Her often-noted ironic distance is exercised on both sides of the colonial divide, however, and with an intimacy in which history is 'deliberately rendered in terms personal, casual, very nearly unhistoric'.[45] She explores with a clear eye the deeply personal and sometimes ignoble motives behind political action, taking aim at the affects and postures demanded by twentieth-century colonialism *and* anti-colonialism. Her anti-heroic mode of inquiry thus continued a critical legacy shared by contemporary Irish and Anglo-Irish writers such as Sean O'Casey, Elizabeth Bowen, and W. B. Yeats.

Meanwhile, one of the twentieth century's most powerful and original Marxist thinkers immigrated to England from the Caribbean. In 1932, C. L. R. James left a teaching position at the Government College in Trinidad to write in London and stayed for more than seven years. There, he would produce the best work of a long and prolific career. In contrast to Rhys, a fellow Caribbean immigrant, James was impressed by London's cosmopolitanism, expressions of gender equality and freedom for women, and vast opportunities for intellectual and political life. Far from alienated, then, James felt very much at home. It was in London rather than in the Caribbean that the literary West Indian Renaissance began with the publication of James's novel *Minty Alley* (1936) and his pamphlet 'The Case for West Indian Self-Government' (1933), both originally drafted in Trinidad.[46]

Partly autobiographical, *Minty Alley* is set in the slums of Port of Spain and features a middle-class protagonist, Mr Haynes, who moves into a neighbourhood where he vicariously experiences working-class dilemmas and witnesses the residents' conflicts that, although on the surface feature sexual intrigues and jealousy, yield a set of questions concerning skin colour and class that also emerged in James's historical writing as a key colonial problem.[47] The trajectory of *Minty Alley* increasingly imbricates Mr Haynes into the neighbourhood: 'He was one of them now, sharer of joys and troubles.'[48] The characters, mostly working-class women, also present strategies of survival and enjoyment in the midst of poverty to the middle-class intellectual Haynes.

The relationship between intellectuals and masses appears a central concern throughout James's entire oeuvre, and most acutely in his masterpiece, *The Black Jacobins* (1938), a history of the Haitian slave revolt. The book emphasises the agency of the masses in the making of history and inquired into the intellectual's relationship to the masses. The revolutionary leader Toussaint L'Ouverture is pictured as failing to trust the former slaves enough to break away from the French, leaving him with a set of mutually exclusive goals: on one hand, exalting French civilisation, and, on the other, building an independent social and military structure among the enslaved. L'Ouverture explains nothing to the masses of his reasoning in staying loyal to the French and becomes a despot in the process.[49] James's play *Toussaint L'Ouverture* (1936), produced at the Westminster Theatre in London, was based on the same subject as *The Black Jacobins* with the star Paul Robeson playing the tragic lead role. Both works also sought to challenge fascism as an extension of the anti-imperial project.[50]

In L'Ouverture's quandaries and revolutionary struggle, James referred not only to the history of anti-colonialism but also to the liberation movements in the present and future. He thereby challenged the twentieth-century imperial discourse of development, which had reworked the nineteenth-century imperial language of 'progress' to characterise colonised spaces and subjects as primitive and backward. In his work, African and Caribbean histories appear as harbingers of the democratic future rather than as vestiges of a retrograde past.[51] While some might have considered the labour strikes in 1930s Trinidad to be minor backwater events, he analysed them convincingly in *Toussaint L'Ouverture* and *A History of Negro Revolt* (1938) as the vanguard of liberation movements: 'these workers have almost at a single bound placed themselves in the forefront of the international working-class movement'.[52] This multidimensional historical sense also enabled his work to speak to multiple global locations through the illumination of a local event.

James's sense of his own intellectual heritage also carried the same cosmopolitan outlook, namely he created effective materialist critiques of British imperialism while embracing the critical lessons of modern British culture and education. Edward Said notes that James refused to consider himself an outsider to Europe: 'James stubbornly supported the Western heritage at the same time that he belonged to the insurrectionary anti-imperialist moment.'[53] In the reading practices that his work demanded, James's work is quintessentially contrapuntal, 'reaffirm[ing] the historical experience of imperialism as a matter first of interdependent histories, overlapping domains'.[54]

The decade has been regarded by many literary critics as a reaction against the experimental modes of high modernism that marked the 1920s. Samuel Hynes, in his classic study *The Auden Generation*, mapped the 1930s turn to documentary and social realism on one hand and surrealism or expressionism on the other as artists and writers searched for ways to cope with the advent of fascism and economic depression. The decade seemed to call for works that could ostensibly better respond in a new era of mass politics and economic catastrophe.[55] In much British fiction and non-fiction inquiring into the British Empire, however, there is a notable blending of high modernist and documentary technique rather than a disavowal of interiority. The combination enables views of complex individual motive and ethical dilemma with regard to imperial history. It also enables clear views of the historical and political forces at work in these dilemmas, as well as of collective (rather than individual) subjects characteristic of documentary.

In terms of tone, these writers are remarkably ambivalent. While all tend towards a deflation of imperial heroism increasingly regarded as a national myth, there are also notable attempts to salvage or elegise other elements of post-Enlightenment British literary or political traditions. It is more than possible that their intersecting literary and political networks enabled these writers to feed each other's critiques. In addition to Cunard's, James's, and Anand's ties to the Hogarth Press, both James and Cunard were involved in the IASB (International African Service Bureau), a pan-African network of intellectuals based in London, and Anand and Orwell would eventually become colleagues at the BBC during the war. Of course, they all share more or less critical views of the Empire whether their focus is on effects in the metropolis, in the colonies, or both. Beyond this broad concern, they share literary attempts to make a postcolonial future emerge by effecting shifts in collective loyalties, deflating imperial tropes and boundaries, and recording or projecting anti-racist feelings and perceptions.

Notes

1. John MacKenzie, *Propaganda and Empire: The Manipulation of British Public Opinion, 1880–1960* (Manchester: Manchester University Press, 1984), pp. 217–20.
2. Ibid., pp. 91–3, 221.
3. See chap. 3, ' Empire, War, and Espionage Films', in Marcia Landy, *British Genres: Cinema and Society, 1930–1960* (Princeton: Princeton University Press, 1991).
4. C. L. R. James, 'The Case for West-Indian Self Government', in *The C. L. R. James Reader*, ed. by Anna Grimshaw (Cambridge, MA: Blackwell, 1992), p. 61.
5. Jed Esty, *A Shrinking Island: Modernism and National Culture in England* (Princeton: Princeton University Press, 2003); Laura Winkiel, *Modernism, Race and Manifestos* (New York: Cambridge University Press, 2011); Kristin Bluemel, *George Orwell and the Radical Eccentrics: Intermodernism in Literary London* (New York: Palgrave, 2004); and Jane Marcus, *Hearts of Darkness: White Women Write Race* (New Brunswick, NJ: Rutgers University Press, 2004).
6. See Stephen Spender, *Forward from Liberalism* (London: Gollancz, 1937), and Stevie Smith, *Over the Frontier* (London: Cape, 1938).
7. Anna Snaith, 'The Hogarth Press and the Networks of Anti-Colonialism', in *Leonard and Virginia Woolf, the Hogarth Press, and the Networks of Modernism*, ed. by Helen Southworth (Edinburgh: Edinburgh University Press, 2010), pp. 103–27.
8. Virginia Woolf, *The Waves* (New York: Harcourt, 1978), p. 137.
9. Ibid., p. 136.

10. Ibid., p. 194.
11. Ibid., p. 20.
12. Ibid., p. 47.
13. Urmila Seshagiri, *Race and the Modernist Imagination* (Ithaca, NY: Cornell University Press, 2010), p. 303.
14. Nancy Cunard, *Negro: An Anthology Made by Nancy Cunard: 1931–1933* (New York: Negro Universities, 1969), p. 450.
15. Ibid., p. 39.
16. Maureen Moynagh, 'Cunard's Lines: Political Tourism and Its Texts', *New Formations*, 34 (1998), 70–90 (p. 71).
17. Michael North, *The Dialect of Modernism: Race, Language, and Twentieth-Century Literature* (New York: Oxford University Press, 1994), p. 194.
18. Winkiel, *Modernism, Race and Manifestos*, p. 190.
19. Jean Rhys, *Voyage in the Dark* (New York: Norton, 1982), p. 17.
20. Kenneth Ramchand, *The West Indian Novel and Its Background* (London: Faber, 1970), p. 90.
21. Rhys, *Voyage*, p. 13.
22. Ibid., p. 65.
23. Ibid., pp. 7–8.
24. Ibid., p. 31.
25. Ibid., p. 72.
26. Rumer Godden, *The Lady and the Unicorn* (London: Virago, 2015), p. 82.
27. Phyllis Lassner, *Colonial Strangers: Women Writing the End of the British Empire* (New Brunswick, NJ: Rutgers University Press, 2004), p. 80.
28. Rumer Godden, *Black Narcissus* (London: Virago, 2013), pp. 256–7.
29. George Orwell, *Burmese Days* (New York: Time, 1962), p. 19.
30. Ibid., p. 16.
31. Ibid., p. 227.
32. Ibid.
33. George Orwell, 'Shooting an Elephant', in *The Collected Essays, Journalism and Letters: Volume One*, ed. by Sonia Orwell and Ian Angus (London: Secker and Warburg, 1968), pp. 236, 238.
34. Bluemel, *George Orwell and the Radical Eccentrics*, p. 160.
35. See Shyam Asnani, 'The Socio-Political Scene of the 1930s: Its Impact on the Indo-English Novel', *Commonwealth Quarterly*, 6.21 (1981), 14–23; and *Leonard and Virginia Woolf*, ed. by Helen Southworth.
36. Mulk Raj Anand, 'Why I Write', in *Indo-English Literature: A Collection of Critical Essays*, ed. by K. K. Sharma (Ghaziabad: Vimal Prakashan, 1977), p. 13.
37. Mulk Raj Anand, *The Village* (London: Cape, 1939), p. 204.
38. Mulk Raj Anand, *Coolie* (New York: Penguin, 1994), p. 256.
39. Mulk Raj Anand, *Conversations in Bloomsbury* (New Delhi: Heinemann, 1981), pp. 52, 21.
40. See Saros Cowasjee, *So Many Freedoms: A Study of the Major Fiction of Mulk Raj Anand* (New Delhi: Oxford University Press, 1977), p. 78.

41. Olivia Manning, *The Wind Changes* (New York: Virago, 1991), p. 159.

42. Ibid., p. 166.

43. Ibid., p. 53.

44. Ibid., p. 302.

45. Harry J. Mooney, Jr., 'Olivia Manning: Witness to History', in *Twentieth-Century Women Novelists*, ed. by Thomas F. Staley (Totowa, NJ: Barnes and Noble, 1982), pp. 39–60 (p. 41).

46. The pamphlet is an excerpt from his larger book on the labour leader and powerful advocate of colonial liberation, Arthur Cipriani, *The Life of Captain Cipriani* (1932). For his account of the West Indian Renaissance, see C. L. R. James, *Beyond a Boundary* (London: Serpent's Tail, 1994), p. 120.

47. See 'The Case for West Indian Self-Government', in *The C. L. R. James Reader*, pp. 49–62, in which the bad faith of the colonial system is visible in the futile social climbing of the mixed race, light-skinned middle classes.

48. C. L. R. James, *Minty Alley* (Jackson: University of Mississippi Press, 1997), p. 153.

49. C. L. R. James, *The Black Jacobins: Toussaint L'Ouverture and the San Domingo Revolution* (New York: Vintage, 1963), p. 284.

50. The play drew the support of the League for the Protection of Ethiopia, in support of the last independent nation in Africa recently colonised by Italy with no substantial blockages offered by the British government. See James's essay 'Abyssinia and the Imperialists' (1936) in *The C. L. R. James Reader*, pp. 63–66, for a direct treatment of these events.

51. See Minkah Makalani, 'An International African Opinion: Amy Ashwood Garvey and C. L. R. James in Black Radical London', in *Escape from New York: The New Negro Renaissance beyond Harlem*, ed. by Davarian L. Baldwin and Minkah Makalani (Minneapolis: University of Minnesota Press, 2013), pp. 77–101; and Winkiel, *Modernism, Race and Manifestos* on the modernism of *Toussaint L'Ouverture*.

52. C. L. R. James, *A History of Negro Revolt* (New York: Haskell, 1969), p. 79.

53. Edward Said, *Culture and Imperialism* (New York: Random House, 1993), p. 248.

54. Ibid., p. 259.

55. Samuel Hynes, *The Auden Generation: Literature and Politics in England in the 1930s* (Princeton: Princeton University Press, 1976).

CHAPTER 9

Travel

Tim Youngs

The end of the First World War and the relaxation of restrictions on travel
that were in place during it produced a sense of release, among other
emotions. Paul Fussell employs an aptly exuberant simile when he refers
to the many writers who were 'propelled on their post-war travels as if by
a wartime spring tightly compressed'.[1] Besides those that will be discussed
in this chapter, Fussell's list of several members of the 'British Literary
Diaspora' who travelled or went to live in exile around the globe includes
Norman Douglas, Lawrence Durrell, V. S. Pritchett, and Robert Graves.
The propulsion that Fussell describes is evident in D. H. Lawrence's
statement in his *Sea and Sardinia* (1921): 'Comes over one an absolute
necessity to move.'[2] This urge to mobility is often accompanied by an
energetic sense of inquiry. Travel writers were curious not only about other
cultures but about themselves and the effects of their own society upon
them. 'It is only when you meet someone of a different culture from
yourself that you begin to realise what your own beliefs really are', pro-
claims George Orwell.[3] On both a national and personal level, much of the
travel writing of the decade is explicitly engaged in self-investigation,
looking inward as well as out.

Several scholars remark upon the importance of travel in the 1930s and
upon the importance of that decade to travel writing, which is the focus of
the present chapter. Here travel writing is understood to be predominantly
first-person, written accounts of travel undertaken by the author.[4] This is
not to say, however, that we should ignore the 1920s. As Fussell puts it,
declining to draw sharp distinctions between the two decades: 'More
important than discriminating [them] from each other is understanding
the whole age's sense of having barely squeaked through one war and its
gradually augmenting awareness of the approaching menace of another.'[5]

The literature of the interwar years is characterised by a concern with
journeys. Samuel Hynes identifies travel as 'the most insistent of 'thirties
metaphors'.[6] Fussell declares that even to survey 'the titles of works

between the wars is to sense their permeation by the "travel" spirit'.[7] David
Farley notes that, 'In addition to the political, industrial, and technological
reasons for the increase in travel, many writers of the time also expressed
psychological motivations for going abroad', stirred by 'feelings of rest-
lessness and anxiety [. . .] prompted by the political situation as well as by
the dire economic conditions of the interwar years'.[8] Philip Dodd suggests
that the travel book is 'the most important literary form of the 1930s',
appearing to be 'the most appropriate form for writers restless with
inherited beliefs, and eager to "explore" and "discover" new allegiances'.[9]
Dodd's comment indicates that it is not simply the prominence of travel
writing in the decade that is worthy of attention but the ways in which the
genre suited and was adapted to contemporary social and political concerns. These included reflections on the war that had ended in 1918, the
Russian Revolution of 1917, the rise of Mussolini, Hitler, and Franco, the
Italian invasion of Abyssinia in October 1935 which led to the second war
between the two countries in 1935–6, the Spanish Civil War that broke out
in 1936, the outbreak of the Sino-Japanese War the following year, and the
apprehension of another world war. Each of these events spawned travel
narratives by journalists, adventurers, and supporters or opponents of
governments, causes, and ideologies.

Along with the anxieties listed above were re-examinations of Britain's
place in the world, in particular concerning its Empire. Not infrequently
those reassessments produced a less disdainful view of other cultures than
had been held before the 1914–18 war. Mabel Steedman introduces her
1939 book on Haiti by insisting 'I have endeavoured to give a true,
accurate, and unbiased account',[10] and concludes by emphasising her
consciousness of 'the tremendous effort, the indomitable will, and the
enormous expenditure of energy that lies behind the rapid, but to the
world, unrealized, progress of the Black Republic'.[11] Encounters and
representations often remained self-serving, however, with some travellers seeking in so-called pre-industrial societies an antidote to the ills of
the West, as D. H. Lawrence had done in the previous decade.
Simultaneously, economic depression and the volatility in social class
relationships, evidenced most dramatically in the General Strike of 1926,
contributed to a national introspection that provoked a new wave of
travel books as social investigation.

All of these factors – conflicts abroad, uncertainty about one's position
in the world, dangerous inequalities at home – fed into a travel writing that
was often questioning of authority, including its own. Orwell, who was
born in 1903, writes in *The Road to Wigan Pier* (1937) of how, at the age of

seventeen or eighteen, 'I was against all authority'. He attributes this
attitude to a revolutionary feeling, shared across 'almost the whole nation',
which was 'a revolt of youth against age, resulting directly from the war'.
The cause, he states, was the sacrifice of the young in that conflict and the
fact that the old had conducted the war 'with supreme incompetence' and
'behaved in a way which [. . .] is horrible to contemplate'.[12]

Orwell looks back at those days from 1937 and finds the spirit of revolt
now quietened. Nevertheless, he presents it as having been pervasive. It
shaped the thinking of his peers and is a part of the more general questioning that informs many of the travel narratives with their critical
attention to how one sees and writes about things. Mocking British
ignorance of Abyssinia and the public's reliance on outdated or irrelevant
information, Evelyn Waugh, having 'secured employment with the only
London newspaper which seemed to be taking a realistic view of the
situation', then has 'an inkling of what later became abundantly clear to
all, that I did not know the first thing about being a war correspondent'.[13]
Peter Fleming, recalling being in Mukden (now Shenyang) days after the
Japanese seizure of Manchuria in 1931, observes: 'one had been hardly any
nearer coming at the truth behind the situation than if one had stayed at
home and read *The Times*'. He concludes that 'The advantages of being On
The Spot are often overestimated'.[14] Serious points about credibility and
credulity are being made here, though they are voiced with a wry humour
and an assured self-deprecation. Modern travel narrators often exhibit this
character, unable to conduct and portray themselves as conventionally
heroic and conscious that the traveller's is but one perspective.

Contemporary intellectual currents and aesthetic innovations encouraged experimentation with point-of-view and voice. The fact that the
interwar years increasingly saw travel 'undertaken specifically for the sake
of writing about it'[15] meant that professional writers drew on their awareness of literary conventions and techniques consciously to manipulate (and
often to confound) readers' expectations. Several of them (including
Auden, Greene, Isherwood, Lawrence, Day-Lewis, MacNeice, and
Waugh) also wrote (or indeed painted) in other genres and were better
known for those works, but for many travel writing was 'an important
complement to their imaginative work'.[16]

Form and Perspective

The travel writing of the 1930s is remarkable for the number of its still
celebrated titles, its innovation, and its self-awareness. In several cases it

evinces a knowing self-criticism about its power structures. According to Stacy Burton, after the First World War, 'writers question the travel narrative's foundational premises, particularly the presumption of narrative authority, far more directly than ever before'. Burton observes that the literary context for this is modernism, 'with its emphasis on the subjectivity, fluidity, and contingency of points of view'.[17] Stan Smith notes that 'The 1920s and '30s were a boom time for travel writing in a specifically Modernist mode'.[18] Whether in identifiably modernist travel texts or in other contemporaneous works that share some of their characteristics, certain features associated with modernism are apparent. Among these are the influence of Freud and psychoanalysis; of new movements in the visual arts, such as cubism; and an engagement with (or a flight from) technology. Graham Greene's *Journey Without Maps* (1936) depends upon the conceit that the author's journey into West Africa is simultaneously a rediscovery of that which his home society has repressed in its members. Signalling his departure from the all-knowing travel narrator, Greene declares: 'It is not the fully conscious mind which chooses West Africa in preference to Switzerland. [. . .] [W]hen I say that to me Africa has always seemed an important image, I suppose that is what I mean, that it has represented more than I could say.'[19]

Several writers of the decade expose the limitations of any one perspective, in contrast to the fixed, certain gaze of so many of their predecessors. Auden and MacNeice's *Letters from Iceland* (1937) presents an assemblage of materials, including poems, letters (in verse and prose), photographs, and statistics. The authors frequently switch from one mode to another, having informed their readers that 'It is a collage that you're going to read'.[20] In his extraordinary *Eimi* (1933), an account of a visit to Soviet Russia, E. E. Cummings breaks up the narrative at sentence and even at word level with seemingly erratic punctuation. Orthography is further disrupted by spellings that exaggerate people's accents. Cummings represents himself in the third person as 'Kem-min-kz', in approximation of his hosts' pronunciation of his name, and subsequently modifies this to 'Kself', thus recasting the relationship between author, narrator, and reader.[21]

A number of writers experienced crises of faith, a reflection of the broader uncertainties of the age. Greene and Waugh both wrestled with their Catholicism. The struggle with belief coincided with a widespread sense that the grand days of exploration were over and that excitement and heroism must now be found in the banal. Steedman, in confirming her choice of Haiti as an exception, regrets that 'these days it is difficult to find any part of the world where, in peace-time, travel is a real adventure'.[22]

Fleming's *Brazilian Adventure* announces its anti-heroic stance in the foreword: 'The hardships and privations which we were called on to endure were of a very minor order, the dangers which we ran were considerably less than those to be encountered on any arterial road during a heat wave.'[23] All is not as it seems, though: Fleming does have an adventure, his narrative culminating in a long boat race. The dismissal of one's own exploits contributes to the construction of a self-deprecating, ironically confident narrator.

The factors above, together with reflections on the effects of new, speedier forms of travel, affect the presentation of the self, the representation of others, and the relationship with one's environment. They all have radical implications for travel writing. Burton goes so far as to assert that modernism:

> calls into question the original premises of the travel genre, particularly its long-standing ambition to describe peoples and places so persuasively that the text is deemed veracious. The twentieth-century traveler thus writes from a precarious, uncertain position [. . .].[24]

The texts' material contexts and their literary form do not exist in isolation from each other. Most critics of travel writing testify to the genre's amorphousness, explaining that it overlaps with and is composed of various types of writing that include letters, the diary, memoir, the essay, scientific report, journalism, and fiction.[25] The often deliberate blurring of these generic boundaries that occurs in the 1920s and 1930s may be read against the background of the threat to international borders affecting countries such as Poland, Abyssinia, Austria, and Czechoslovakia. Auden's early poetry, for example, shows a preoccupation with frontiers, and *Letters from Iceland* contains a reference to the Nazis, as does Greene's *Journey Without Maps*.[26]

The travel books also play with conventions and readers' expectations. In Auden and Isherwood's book of travel to the Sino-Japanese War, *Journey to a War* (1939), a photograph captioned 'Enemy Planes Overhead' has no aeroplanes in it but instead shows two men crouching, one of them in military uniform, looking at an angle into the sky.[27] This mismatch between what the caption leads us to expect and what we can actually see makes us aware of how we are normally led to look. A similar concern shapes the opening of D. H. Lawrence's *Mornings in Mexico* (1927), in which the narrator invites us to consider a town in the south of Mexico, then a house, then a spot on the verandah, and then a person there with a pen and paper. 'We talk so grandly, in capital letters, about Morning in Mexico', writes Lawrence, but 'All it amounts to is one little individual looking at a bit of sky and trees, then looking down at the page of his exercise book.'[28] Greene directs us to think about our perspective as the narrative controls our eye, like a film camera steadily zooming in. The technique encourages us to reassess the confidence we place in authors who claim to present the truth of a country. It is a shame, Lawrence goes on, that when we come across books whose titles suggest a survey of a whole country, or even of a continent, we do not 'immediately visualise a thin or a fat person, in a chair or in bed, dictating to a bob-haired stenographer or making little marks on paper with a fountain pen'.[29] Lawrence urges his readers to think for themselves and not to take at face value what they are told by travel writers who are only individuals occupying a particular space. Yet, in doing so, he establishes his distinctiveness, as travel writers have long done, and invites our trust.

Mornings in Mexico was published in 1927, but outside the calendar there is no sharp turn between one decade and another, and for Lawrence to begin his book like this indicates a break from the bulk of works that have preceded it. Introducing his own travel book on Mexico, *The Lawless Roads*, published twelve years later, Graham Greene writes similarly that 'This is the personal impression of a small part of Mexico at a particular time, the spring of 1938'.[30] In the body of the book itself, Greene considers the difficulty facing writers who want to describe a city: 'Even for an old inhabitant it is impossible: one can present only a simplified plan, taking a house here, a park there as symbols of the whole.' He admits: 'I was taking the tourist view – on the strength of one prosperous town on the highway, on the strength of a happy mood, I was ready to think of Mexico in terms of quiet and gentleness and devotion.'[31]

Robert Byron's *The Road to Oxiana* (1937), the most influential of all travel books of the 1930s – and probably of the twentieth century – likewise displays a playful knowingness about the conventions of the genre. The narrative voice frequently offers sardonic comment on what other writers would do and what readers would expect. For example, describing his visit to the eleventh-century tower Gumbad-i-Kabus in Teheran, Byron writes: 'Superlatives applied by travellers to objects which they have seen, but most people have not, are generally suspect; I know it, having been guilty of them.' The narrator's admission invites us to regard him with suspicion but also to trust him because he has confessed and his exaggerations seem to be in the past. (That the tense does not rule out further complicity enlivens the act of reading.) Furthermore, his statement is contained in a parenthetical interjection in which he interrupts his narrative to tell us:

> re-reading this diary two years later, in as different an environment as possible (Pekin), I still hold the opinion I formed before going to Persia, and confirmed that evening on the steppe: that the Gumbad-i-Kabus ranks with the great buildings of the world.[32]

Readers are likely to be engaged even more by this intrusion of the later self commenting on his earlier impression. Two types of immediacy are at play: that of the narrator of the diary, contemporaneous with the travel; and that of the author, who is closer in time to the reader, and who seems to be reviewing it. Yet, although the notelike and fragmentary nature of the latter has the quality of spontaneity, Byron's book was 'the product of three years of constant writing and revision. Its casualness is an elaborate fiction.'[33]

A Mechanical World

The 1930s belong to what Wyndham Lewis, in his travelogue of North Africa, called 'the Petrol Age'.[34] The deployment of new and recently developed forms of transport, and the corresponding growth of infrastructure that we nowadays take for granted, greatly impacted on people's experiences, sensations, and stories of travel. The start of J. B. Priestley's *English Journey* (1934) sees its author take his first ever ride in a motor coach (into Southampton). Astonished by its 'speed and comfort', he declares: 'I never wish to go any faster.' He and his contemporaries have 'arrived at a time when men have a passion [. . .] for machines' and he is 'glad to have lived in their age'.[35] Priestley also writes that: 'There is in front of us – we are definitely *in for* – an electrified world.' Of 'electrical engineers, motor-car designers, aviators, wireless technicians and the like', he exclaims: 'This is their age and they are completely at home in it, unlike the rest of us, who are desperately trying to make ourselves at home in it.'[36] On the other hand, Orwell, taking a much more negative view, complains: 'It is only in our own age, when mechanisation has finally triumphed, that we can actually *feel* the tendency of the machine to make a fully human life impossible.'[37] While some, like Orwell, decried the machine age and others, like Lawrence, sought on occasion to escape it, Priestley tells a medievalist craftsman friend of his that we should not 'sentimentalise the Middle Ages' but 'take the whole roaring machine-ridden world as it is and make a civilised job of it'. Rather than the machine itself being at fault, 'the real villain' is the 'shoddy, greedy, profit-grabbing, joint-stock-company industrial system we had allowed to dominate us'.[38]

Yet Priestley does not wholly embrace the new automotive age. He remarks that 'To travel swiftly in a closed car, as so many of us do nowadays, is of course to cut oneself off from the [. . .] reality of the regions one passes through', and in a lament that anticipates Fussell's disappointment at the vanishing specialness of travel, he suggests that 'Now that we are whizzed about the world, there is no time for absorbing and adjusting'.[39] This, he speculates, is why there is less variety available to the traveller and why, when we are able to travel at 400 miles per hours, everything will seem uniform, by which time 'there will be movement, but, strictly speaking, no more travel'.[40]

The sense of travel experiences becoming more mundane is felt in the air, too. In 1939, E. Colston Shepherd, the author of *Great Flights*, reminded his readers that forty years previously no one had flown, except for a few people who had ascended in balloons, but that now the aeroplane had become 'a regular vehicle of civilization'. A challenge for those who wanted to cling to the special thrill provided by still new forms of travel was to find how exhilaration could survive familiarity and institutionalisation. When Shepherd writes that 'the hazards remain even in these days of trustworthy engines, of good navigational instruments, and of wireless and meteorological aids', one infers from his comments an almost desperate attempt to preserve the excitement of risk. He seems not entirely reconciled to a world of travel without danger. Trying to come to terms with the fact that 'It is as true in flying as in other things, that the great feats of yesterday become the commonplaces of to-day', he consoles himself with the thought that 'they belong, like all courageous deeds, to the long scroll which proves to each succeeding generation the enduring greatness of the human spirit'.[41]

Shepherd's is not a neutral position for he explicitly identifies those early feats of aviation with maritime endeavour and its role in colonisation. At the same time, he displays an attitude towards gender that regards women travellers as secondary. He states of the pioneers of flight:

> They gambled with their lives as the famous seamen and colonizers gambled with theirs. This was almost entirely the work of men and it opened the way to achievements by women, in what may be called the *consolidating class*, which were so surprising as to partake virtually of the pioneering quality.[42]

That idea of consolidation places women in the second rank. Shepherd's measure of travel having become routine is evident in his disappointment that 'There is little glory to be won, *even by a woman*, in flying alone from England to Australia as Amy Johnson did in 1930'.[43]

A Subjective Colouring

Shepherd's outlook demonstrates that professedly authoritative overviews of others' travels are not in fact impartial. In travelogues themselves, we find many statements that attest to this fact. At times, in *English Journey*, Priestley seems to join certain of his contemporaries in disclaiming authority. Visiting Birmingham and the Black Country to the north and west of it, he writes:

> You have to live some time in these places to understand their peculiar qualities. All I can do is to offer a few sketches, probably not at all accurate nor free from a certain subjective colouring [. . .]. But perhaps that does not matter [. . .].[44]

Priestley's disavowal of objective knowledge is shared by several writers of the interwar years, as is his suggestion that the subjective may prove a more reliable guide. Introducing the self into travel writing is by no means new but the preponderance of professional authors who do so in the 1930s is remarkable. Along with the challenges to authority that I have outlined in this chapter, this emphasis on individual perspective should be seen in the context of the increasing hold of the mechanical and the scientific, for it provides a demonstrably human counterpoint to it.

Priestley proceeds to tell us that although in recent years he has been away from industrial areas, he passed the first nineteen years of his life in 'the industrial West Riding, in the shadow of the tall chimneys'.[45] There is, then, a claim to authority here after all, but it is based on the onlooker's experiences and moods. Priestley's *English Journey* and Orwell's *The Road to Wigan Pier* impress with their swingeing social commentaries which depend on their commanding narrative voice. For all of Priestley's caveats about not presenting as full a picture as he might, both his and Orwell's strident critiques of 1930s England reinstate the travel narrator's authority. Fusing the subjective and the documentary strengthens the power of the texts' critiques.

The Road to Wigan Pier is divided into two parts. The first describes the life of the working class in Wigan and other Northern towns, doing so through the author's experience of travelling and staying among members of it for several months. The second begins with autobiographical memories and reflections, accompanied by and then moving more intently on to

pronouncements on class, economics, the deleterious effects of mechanisation, and nationalism. The second part becomes an extended essay
whose themes are evident in the first, as the conditions that Orwell reveals
lead him to condemn aspects of social and economic policy. The effect is to
challenge the authority of the government and of the ruling classes.

These domestic travelogues do not seem to sit easily with the lack of
confidence in a commanding view that we have observed in some of the
overseas travel narratives. Priestley and Orwell speak truth to power,
exposing inequality, injustice, and poverty. They write with conviction,
employing a documentary mode (including photographs) but with the
added force of witness testimony. Thus, although there appears to be
a difference between the inward-looking state-of-the-nation inspections
of Britain and the outward-looking, overseas-based travel books, both are
born of post-war unease and disillusionment, and they share some of the
same impulses. David Farley notices of those who journeyed abroad that
'Travel writing was often a way for them to recognize and register, through
the examples of foreign peoples and contexts, alternatives to Western
decline and fatigue'.[46]

Priestley and Orwell describe conditions at home that demand remedy.
For example, visiting a derelict shipyard at Hebburn on the Tyne and
observing the 'idle ships' on the river, Priestley is scornful of 'the idiotic
muddle of our times' that has 'these fine big steamers rusting away in rows'
when Britain and other countries have need of one another's goods. The
narrator is scathing about the state of the nation. It is a society with 'a
workshop that has no work [. . .] an industrialism that has lost its industry
[. . .] a money-making machine that has ceased to make money'. At the
coastal colliery town of Seaham Harbour in East Durham, Priestley
informs his readers that 'In these unhappy districts there is a war on, and
the allied enemies are poverty, idleness, ignorance, hopelessness and
misery'.[47]

According to Orwell, the English regard 'Foreign oppression [as]
a much more obvious, understandable evil than economic oppression'
and so 'tamely admit to being robbed in order to keep half a million
worthless idlers in luxury'. Having served in the Indian Imperial Police
after moving to Burma when he left Britain around the age of twenty,
Orwell admits to having been 'part of the actual machinery of despotism'.
When he came home to England on leave in 1927 after five years as 'part of
an oppressive system', he resolved not to go back to it, referring to it as
'evil'. The guilt he wanted to alleviate and his 'hatred of oppression' led his
thoughts towards the English working class because he saw them as

'symbolic victims of injustice', reminding him of the Burmese in Burma. He now realises that 'tyranny and exploitation' exist in England, where the 'submerged working class' endure 'miseries which in their different way were as bad as any oriental ever knows'.[48]

It is this that drives Orwell to spend time living with the working classes in order to try to get to know them and their lives. No matter that he lived in coal-miners' houses for months, shared in his hosts' domestic and social activities, and 'liked them and hoped they liked me', he 'went among them as a foreigner, and both of us were aware of it'. Despite his efforts, the 'accursed itch of class-difference' is always felt.[49]

For other travel writers of the 1930s, overseas countries provide the opportunity to distance themselves less dramatically from their country-men and women and to assert their individuality. Freya Stark seems to exemplify this latter attitude in her *Baghdad Sketches* (1932), when, at a bazaar in Nejf, she muses: 'I like people different, and agree with the man who said that the worst of the human race is the number of duplicates.'[50] Her sentiments appear to reveal a preference for diversity, while also giving licence to her own difference. These reflections are prompted, however, when, 'feeling in love with all the world' at the sight of the lit, busy, colourful bazaar, she is shocked to see 'an old shoemaker cross-legged in his booth staring at me with eyes of concentrated hate'. Stark observes:

> One gets these shocks in Nejf, and it is horrid to be hated all for nothing. And what a strange revelation of self-esteem it is when people only love those who think and feel as they do – an extension of themselves, in fact! Even Christianity does not cure us – since one cannot feel right without assuming that the rest must be wrong.[51]

Stark's manoeuvres in this passage display the complicated situation of post-war British travellers. On the one hand, she demonstrates openness towards other people and other cultures, valuing difference over homo-geneity. On the other hand, her expression of this openness arises from the hostile stare of an old man in the bazaar. Even allowing that the incident happened as described, Stark's account of it contrasts her attractive liberal-ity towards others with the stereotype of the sullen, antagonistic Oriental old man. That she does not exempt Christianity from the intolerance or superiority she condemns serves further to distinguish her as someone operating between cultures.

A similarly mixed picture emerges from the same author's *The Valleys of the Assassins* (1934). In that work, she is moved by the kindness shown her

by Said Ibrahim, 'a charming old man', who sits with her outside at night
to take her mind off 'the discourtesy of our host and to discuss Persian
history'.[52] His considerateness and companionship lead her to state:

> If I were asked to enumerate the pleasures of travel, this would be one of the
> greatest among them – that so often and so unexpectedly you meet the best
> in human nature, and seeing it so by surprise and often with a most
> improbable background, you come, with a sense of pleasant thankfulness,
> to realize how widely scattered in the world are goodness and courtesy and
> the love of immaterial things, fair blossoms found in every climate, on every
> soil.[53]

Here we have a telling illustration of the paradoxes produced by the age.
Stark again appears receptive to other cultures. She seems to avoid stereo-
types and to take genuine delight in the company of this thoughtful man.
The experience affirms her commitment to the joys and rewards of travel.
Good, welcoming, kind people are to be found the world over. But that
this should come as any surprise at all can be due only to the existence of
negative preconceptions. True, she counters these, but in doing so she
attests to their hold.

The embrace of the foreign sees the traveller appearing to loosen his or her
affiliation to Britain. In addition to the criticism of conditions in and policies
of one's own country, there is a feeling that it may no longer be enough to be
defined by nationality. Travel abroad and an open curiosity about other
cultures draw this out. In *Sea and Sardinia*, D. H. Lawrence finds himself
subject to complaints about the price of coal, which is expensive for Italians
because of Britain's (and the USA's) high exchange rates. Lawrence insists: 'I
am not England. I am not the British Isles on two legs.'[54] It is quite obvious
that there is more to Lawrence's protestation than the immediate context.
And in the final chapter, acknowledging that the Italians are 'not to blame
for their spite' against England, which has for so long assumed the role of
leading nation and has now led them into a mess, Lawrence writes:

> for all that, I must insist that I am a single human being, an individual, not
> a mere national unit, a mere chip of l'Inghilterra or la Germania. I am not
> a chip of any nasty old block. I am myself.[55]

While Lawrence's sentiments speak much of his belief in individualism,
they illustrate the unease about national identity felt by many travellers
between the wars. They point also to the increasing subjectivity of travel
writing in the twentieth century which would intensify in the decades after
the Second World War but probably never reach the heights of Rebecca
West's monumental *Black Lamb and Grey Falcon* (1941). That work's more

than 1,000 pages combine a powerfully intelligent, engagingly witty, and markedly female narrative voice with detailed (if disputed) historical, geographical, and cultural information; political and philosophical reflection; and critical observations on gender. In it, West tells her husband that she hates the stinking corpses of empires that smell so much she doubts they can ever have been healthy. Challenged by him to admit that there is 'a certain magnificence about a great empire in being', she responds: 'Of course there is [. . .] but the hideousness outweighs the beauty.'[56]

Like any literary or historical survey, the outline offered in this chapter is necessarily by way of a sketch. An approach focussed on particular regions, modes of transport, or motive for travelling will yield titles not mentioned here, some well-noticed at the time. For their significance and enduring influence, however, the texts discussed here are notable. They self-consciously review the role of the traveller and ways of writing about the journey. In many respects, despite their sometimes slipping into attitudes and disparaging comments more redolent of late nineteenth-century imperialism, they show a formal innovation and a critical seriousness about contexts, perspectives, and methods that have rarely been seen since.

Notes

1. Paul Fussell, *Abroad: British Literary Traveling Between the Wars* (New York: Oxford University Press, 1980), p. 11.
2. D. H. Lawrence, *Sea and Sardinia* (Harmondsworth: Penguin, 1944), p. 7.
3. George Orwell, *The Road to Wigan Pier*, with a foreword by Victor Gollancz (London: Victor Gollancz, 1937), p. 197.
4. In common with the other contributions to this volume, this chapter concentrates on British writing. For studies of 1930s travel writing from elsewhere in Europe, see, for example, *Cultural Encounters: European Travel Writing in the 1930s*, ed. by Charles Burdett and Derek Duncan (New York: Berghahn, 2002), and Charles Burdett, *Journeys Through Fascism: Italian Travel Writing Between the Wars* (New York: Berghahn, 2007).
5. Fussell, *Abroad*, pp. vii–viii.
6. Samuel Hynes, *The Auden Generation: Literature and Politics in England in the 1930s* (London: Pimlico, 1992), p. 229.
7. Fussell, *Abroad*, p. 53.
8. David Farley, 'Modernist Travel Writing', in *The Routledge Companion to Travel Writing*, ed. by Carl Thompson (London: Routledge, 2016), pp. 276–87 (p. 279).
9. Philip Dodd, 'The Views of Travellers: Travel Writing in the 1930s', *Prose Studies*, 5.1 (1982), 127–38 (p. 128).

10. Mabel Steedman, *Unknown to the World: Haiti* (London: Hurst and Blackett, 1939), p. 9.
11. Ibid., p. 254.
12. Orwell, *Wigan Pier*, pp. 172, 170.
13. Evelyn Waugh, *Waugh in Abyssinia* (London: Penguin, 1986), p. 40.
14. Peter Fleming, *Brazilian Adventure* (Harmondsworth: Penguin, 1957), p. 79.
15. Helen Carr, 'Modernism and Travel (1880–1940)', in *The Cambridge Companion to Travel Writing*, ed. by Peter Hulme and Tim Youngs (Cambridge: Cambridge University Press, 2002), pp. 70–86 (p. 74).
16. Farley, 'Modernist Travel Writing', p. 278. See, for example, Christopher Isherwood's novel *Goodbye to Berlin* (1939) with its famous opening description of the first-person narrator as a camera.
17. Stacy Burton, *Travel Narrative and the Ends of Modernity* (New York: Cambridge University Press, 2014), p. 30.
18. Stan Smith, 'Burbank with a Baedeker: Modernism's Grand Tours', *Studies in Travel Writing*, 8.1 (2004), 1–18 (p. 2).
19. Graham Greene, *Journey Without Maps* (London: William Heinemann, 1936), p. 9.
20. W. H. Auden and Louis MacNeice, *Letters from Iceland* (London: Faber and Faber, 1937), p. 21.
21. E. E. Cummings, *Eimi* (New York: Covici, Friede, 1933), pp. 89, 289.
22. Steedman, *Unknown to the World*, p. 10.
23. Fleming, *Brazilian Adventure*, p. 9.
24. Burton, *Travel Narrative*, pp. 33–4.
25. See, for example, Tim Youngs, *The Cambridge Introduction to Travel Writing* (New York: Cambridge University Press, 2013), Chapter One.
26. See Tim Youngs, 'Auden's Travel Writings', in *The Cambridge Companion to W. H. Auden*, ed. by Stan Smith (Cambridge University Press, 2004), pp. 68–81.
27. W. H. Auden and Christopher Isherwood, *Journey to a War* (New York: Random House, 1939); see 'Picture Commentary'.
28. D. H. Lawrence, *Mornings in Mexico* (London: Martin Secker, 1927), p. 9.
29. Ibid., p. 9.
30. Graham Greene, 'Author's Note', *The Lawless Roads* (London: Longmans, Green and Co., 1939), p. 5.
31. Greene, *The Lawless Roads*, pp. 69, 42.
32. Robert Byron, *The Road to Oxiana* (London: Penguin, 1992), p. 231.
33. Jonathan Raban, 'The Journey and the Book', in *For Love and Money: Writing, Reading, Travelling, 1969–1987* (London: Collins Harvill, 1987), pp. 253–60 (p. 255).
34. Wyndham Lewis, *Filibusters in Barbary* (London: Grayson and Grayson, 1932), p. 115.
35. J. B. Priestley, *English Journey* (London: William Heinemann, 1934), pp. 3, 14.
36. Ibid., pp. 217, 216.
37. Orwell, *Wigan Pier*, p. 233.

38. Priestley, *English Journey*, p. 64.
39. Ibid., pp. 151, 152.
40. Ibid., p. 152.
41. E. Colston Shepherd, *Great Flights* (London: Adam and Charles Black, 1939), pp. 2, 4, 6.
42. Ibid., pp. 8–9 (my emphasis).
43. Ibid., p. 6 (my emphasis).
44. Priestley, *English Journey*, p. 110.
45. Ibid.
46. Farley, 'Modernist Travel Writing', p. 279.
47. Priestley, *English Journey*, pp. 316, 306, 325.
48. Orwell, *Wigan Pier*, pp. 176, 177, 179, 180–1.
49. Ibid., p. 188.
50. Freya Stark, *Baghdad Sketches* (London: John Murray, 1937), p. 268.
51. Ibid.
52. Freya Stark, *The Valleys of the Assassins and Other Persian Travels* (London: John Murray, 1934), p. 327.
53. Ibid.
54. Lawrence, *Sea and Sardinia*, p. 50.
55. Ibid., p. 185.
56. Rebecca West, *Black Lamb and Grey Falcon: The Record of a Journey through Yugoslavia Made in 1937, Volume One* (London: Macmillan, 1942), p. 287.

CHAPTER 10

The Regional and the Rural

Kristin Bluemel

The outpouring of novels about regional and rural Britain that peaked in the 1930s had as its context a more broadly social cult of the countryside that generated all kinds of extravagant proclamations about the powers of rural life to define an urban nation and global empire. Among the most notorious of these statements was Prime Minister Stanley Baldwin's toast to members of the Royal Society of St George, a group devoted to advancing English patriotism, at their annual meeting at London's grand Hotel Cecil on 6 May 1924. A celebration of England and Englishness, this toast was not only an exercise in exclusionary nationalism, one that discounted the nations and regions of Wales, Scotland, and Northern Ireland, but also an exercise in exclusionary natural and cultural geography, one that promoted images of a single, privileged rural region of England to represent the nation at large:

> The sounds of England, the tinkle of the hammer on the anvil in the country smithy, the corncrake on a dewy morning, the sound of the scythe against the whetstone, and the sight of a plough team coming over the brow of a hill, the sight that has been seen in England since England was a land, and may be seen in England long after the Empire has perished and every works in England has ceased to function, for centuries the one eternal sight of England.[1]

These words are both symptom and cause of the confusion that social historian Alun Howkins describes over the tendency in interwar England to conflate images of the south of England with the English nation itself. Howkins directs our attention to the political, linguistic, economic, and cultural limitations imposed or encouraged by a national ideal shrunk in the 1930s to fit a 'ruralist version of a specifically English culture', providing some context for Baldwin's ecstatic vision of corncrakes and plough teams.[2] He also helps us understand the relation of speeches about regional and rural life to the ephemeral but once ubiquitous novels, travel books, memoirs, and periodicals that were published in the 1930s that took the subject of non-metropolitan places and peoples as their specific concern. As Tim Youngs describes in his chapter in this volume, many 1930s writers took as their subjects people in British regions who regarded them as 'foreigner[s]'.[3] This chapter in contrast considers 1930s writers who take as their subjects people in rural places who regard them – and whom they regard – as part of the same story of region and nation.

A 'flood' of print materials contributed to the 'battles for the country-side' that John Lowerson describes in an early account of the social conflicts that racked rural Britain in the 1930s.[4] Manufactured with new mass printing technologies and distributed by new mass media delivery systems, everything from novels to travel guides to picture books and pamphlets exhorted readers to head out of cities, into the countryside, if not to a villa, then to a garden suburb or weekend retreat.[5] Social historian Howard Newby emphasises in his *Country Life* that these newly rural citizens were 'knowledgeable about the aesthetic appreciation of land-scapes' but were 'woefully ignorant about agriculture and the economic basis of life in the countryside'. He, like Lowerson, blames a 'plethora' of books, pamphlets, and magazines for creating a rural population that enjoyed the countryside as a 'cultural and aesthetic matter' rather than through direct personal experience.[6] Hiking, cycling, gardening, golf, tennis, rambling – all were seen as rejuvenating for individuals and 'the race'. While the landed gentry were in retreat from rural lands, their social stature diminished along with their post-war incomes and properties, and working-class people were newly active in rural spaces and vocal about claiming their right to access them,[7] it was primarily the prosperous middle-class workers of the urban south-east who were busy resettling the country lands in the interwar years. Whether clerks, councillors, or their wives, these new rural residents were very interested in spending some of their white-collar earnings on books about those who came before them and earned their living from the land. By 1932, they represented a happy turning point in the fortunes of agricultural areas: before that year, rural society, like farming, was in decline; after it, rural society and farming show signs of recovery.[8] Sales of books about rural life, including the bestsellers *Farmer's Glory* (1932) by Wiltshire farmer A. G. Street and the trilogy *Corduroy* (1930), *Silver Ley* (1931), and *The Cherry Tree* (1932) by Suffolk farmer Adrian Bell, similarly grew and prospered.

Rural literature of Britain such as that by Street or Bell is a subset of British regional literature and regional literature is a subset of national literature. This chapter examines some of the most widely read and most intensely beloved of rural regional novels, lying at the intersection of these three literary traditions: those by H. E. Bates about the Midlands, Winifred Holtby about coastal Yorkshire, Richard Llewellyn about South Wales, and Lewis Grassic Gibbon about the Mearns of Scotland. All these writers do powerful cultural and aesthetic work contesting the south-east England rural ideal maintained by a 1930s print culture fixated on thatched roofs, village greens, and hedgerows. Their rural regional writing differs from other kinds of 1930s literature, including 'highbrow' late modernist novels and 'lowbrow' mass-marketed country propaganda, by making land instead of landscape the focus of our gaze. And this gaze belongs to a rural worker, not rural visitor, someone whose vision of the land is not determined by aesthetic categories or distances but rather by economic or cultural demands and priorities. These priorities are often best communicated when the narrator shares the perspective of a character walking across land, the perspective of the hero or heroine on foot. Instead of the modernist *flâneur* looking at his reflection in windows or the urban motorist looking at rural scenes selected by fragmented images in guidebooks, readers adopt the continuous gaze of the rural worker survey-ing the land slowly. Recent theorisations of romantic moderns, the com-modified authentic, and rural modernity, discussed at the conclusion of this chapter, invite comparative literary readings of these rural regional characters into the mainstream of critical discourse about twentieth-century British literature and national self-fashioning.

Decline and Regeneration

In one of the few full studies of the regional novel to emerge within the last twenty years, K. D. M. Snell explains that '"regional" [. . .] is not the same as "national", but it does not exclude that: the term includes regional writing within the four countries of the British Isles'.[9] Raymond Williams, in a nearly contemporary essay on 'Region and Class in the Novel', argues that we know what the regional novel is at the point when we know certain other regions – for example, the Home Counties or the regions of London – are *not* seen as regional. For Williams, the regional novel is an ideologically motivated expression of historically specific social conditions that render 'the life and people of certain favoured regions [. . .] as essentially general, even perhaps normal, while the life and people of certain other regions, however interestingly and affectionately presented, are, well, regional'.[10] One implication of Williams's argument is that all rural novels are regional novels, even as all regional novels are not rural novels. Another implication is that all novels featuring rural settings and communities are not necessarily rural novels. For example, Steven Matthews, in 'English Regional Fiction and National Culture', includes 1930s rural novelists Francis Brett Young, Phyllis Bentley, and Winifred Holtby in a lineage founded on the work of the Brontës, George Eliot, Thomas Hardy, and Arnold Bennett, but excludes Woolf and other figures typically regarded as modernist who appear in several recent studies of regional literature.[11] He follows in the path of Phyllis Bentley, whose 1941 study of *The English Regional Novel* also creates a regional literary history that excludes metropolitan-based writers like Woolf or Yeats.[12] Both Matthews and Bentley comment on the realist approach of regional writers, who tend to be conservative in their use of 'chronological third-person narratives' just as they are conservative in their vision of a past that is 'more coherent and full of potential than the present'.[13]

Pursuing a more limited history of *The Rural Tradition in the English Novel 1900–1939*, Glen Cavaliero examines all the most popular 1930s writers who contributed to the rural realist tradition; in addition to the writers already mentioned, he directs readers to works by E. C. Booth, T. H. White, Kenneth Grahame, Eden Phillpotts, Hugh Walpole, Sheila Kaye-Smith, Llewelyn Powys, Mary Webb, E. H. Young, Constance Holme, and T. F. Powys.[14] Cavaliero seems uneasy making claims about the value of those writers' aesthetic contributions even as he is in no doubt about their cultural power. Marion Shaw chides Cavaliero for offering no definition of the rural novel but rather an apology. She places the rural novel firmly in the tradition of the regional novel, remarking that both 'enjoyed a popular, "middle-brow" following' that kept the traditional novel alive amid a dominant modernist movement.[15] Her genealogy of the rural novel, like Stevens's of the regional novel, extends the legacies of Emily Brontë and Thomas Hardy into the 1930s. And, like this chapter, hers cites changes in interwar social formations and institutions in order to explain the hold of the rural novelists on the popular imagination.

This chapter develops previous work on 1930s rural and regional novels by focussing on the language of seeing and looking that characterises not only how critics describe novels – in terms of landscape and scene – but also how authors structure readers' vision of rural and regional geographies. In short, it makes the difference between land and landscape central to its investigation of rural regional novels of the 1930s. How are we taught to see the land? As an artist would, as landscape? Or as a farmer would, as land? What perspectives are we adopting, guided by agreeable, sympathetic first-person or invisible third-person narrators who ask us to assimilate our vision to theirs? Do we see from above, as from the top level of a motor bus, as from an aeroplane or balloon? Or are we taught to see the rural topography from eye level, as would a farmer walking the land or a schoolteacher walking to work?

For purposes of this chapter about fictions that reflected and shaped the 1930s cult of the countryside, the most representative regional rural novels are those whose narrators primarily ask us to regard rural places as land, as something vital, dynamic, and changing – alternately dangerous and generous, something to be lived on and from which to derive one's living. This distinguishes the rural novel from novels that are set in rural places but whose characters regard the rural as landscape, something remote that can be viewed from a distance, aestheticised, stabilised, and appreciated. Rural novels primarily represent a countryside of production, rather than a countryside that offers itself up for consumption, visual or otherwise.

Rural Novelists and Novels

H. E. Bates may be the 'quintessential rural writer' of the 1930s,[16] but, in the words of Dominic Head, he 'presents a genuine conundrum to the literary historian' for his visibility as an especially prolific contributor to diverse genres of mid-century English literature – in addition to his five 1930s novels, he was a celebrated short story writer – and his near total critical neglect.[17] While his 'associat[ion] with rural regional writing' is secure,[18] knowledge about the circumstances informing this status or theorising its influence is scant. According to Bates's biographer Dean Baldwin, Bates was born in Rushden, Northamptonshire, in 1905, winning in 1916 a free place at Kettering Grammar School, working for a time as a journalist until launching in 1926 his career as a novelist.[19]

A number of Bates's most original novels were published in the 1930s. They are well represented by *The Poacher* (1935), which describes through the fate of one family the social and economic transformations experienced in rural Northamptonshire between 1880 and 1920. The novel's heroes are a father and son, Buck and Luke Bishop, shoemakers by day, poachers by night. These men are always moving over the land by foot, and Bates's multiplication of simple verbs of walking, climbing, and running effectively connects the lived experience of rural outlaws' work to the geography of the land. This effect is achieved most memorably in a poaching expedition that leads to Buck's death from a keeper's gunshot. His entry into the darkened parkland symbolises the dangers and oppressions and fear of rural life as well as its possibilities for independent thought, self-direction, of freedom from routine and machine.

> The first sounds brought them to a sudden standstill again, listening. They did not speak. They were sounds which normally they would have dismissed unconsciously, as part of the silence and the darkness, but in a strange place the sounds too were strange, and they stood for a moment arrested in half-alarm before walking on again. They had walked the ten miles from Nenweald under cover of darkness, by the little by-roads, missing the villages, bringing nothing with them except an ash stick, a mouthful of bread and cheese which they had already eaten as they walked along. Bishop had decided that they might enter the park on the south side and cross it diagonally, going northwards, making an exploration. [. . .]
> The feet of the men were soundless. They were walking now, due northward, the stars by the Plough very brilliant to the right of the great house.[20]

The four repetitions of the verb 'walk' packed into these few sentences, coupled with Bates's thematising of sound and silence, create for readers a rhythm that links Bates's repeating verbs to the imagined sounds that guide and arrest his characters' movement over the land. The men's ghostly experience of walking through the silent, starlit parkland is humanised by Buck's geographical thinking, his locating of himself in space as though on a map: entering on the south, moving north, following the Plough. Here, we encounter all Bates's peculiar qualities as a writer of rural regional novels: his creation of a specific and realistic countryside in a time–space continuum, the representation of workers walking over the land, the situating and describing of local land within the world through reference to the points of the compass that organise all tracked human passage over the earth.

The Poacher does not present an idealised landscape such as those associated with the 1930s travel brochures and railway posters, but, in its focus on the past, on what has been lost rather than what might be gained, its readers could choose to ignore its more sobering ideological pronouncements on the human encounters characteristic of rural life. In contrast, the Yorkshire writer, socialist, and feminist Winifred Holtby represents the losses of a traditional patriarchal rural society as gains for modern rural women. While readers do witness the passing of a familiar and in some ways noble way of life, they are not led to regret its disappearance as they would in reading a Bates or Street or Bell novel. Especially in Holtby's celebrated *South Riding* (1936), the transformation of rural Yorkshire land and communities by modern economics and politics is largely positive, as it permits rural girls and women to escape lives of poverty, drudgery, or anonymity.[21]

Born in 1898 in Rudstone, Yorkshire, to a wealthy farming family, Holtby's mother, Alice, was the first alderwoman on the East Riding County Council and the model for the wise, charismatic, and maternal Alderman Mrs Beddows in *South Riding*. The novel's other powerful female character is the heroine, Sarah Burton, a tiny red-haired school-teacher, daughter of a blacksmith and district nurse native to South Riding. Sarah comes up from London to assume the position of Head Mistress of the girls' high school of Kiplington. *South Riding* has attracted critical attention for building its feminist plot out of the 'drama of English local government'.[22] Endorsed as a 'highly regional novel' by Bentley, it is also recognised by Shaw as a rural novel, an important one insofar as it refuses to 'endorse the pervasive belief that the real England is a rural one, and that there is a deep continuity between ancient rural practices and the current needs of society'.[23] It is also one of the few to represent a rural slum – the Shacks – made up of derelict caravans and inhabited by Sarah Burton's most promising young scholar, Lydia Holly, as well as the more familiar scenes of a rural estate owned by a gentleman farmer, Robert Carne, who Sarah falls in love with. By the end of the novel, both slum and estate are charted for destruction. Carne's end comes during a walk along a cliff path on a stormy afternoon as he is contemplating the horizon: 'he had little love for the unquiet water, but to his right lay the element that he had always trusted. The land stretched dark and unbroken to the sunset.'[24] The walker in this case is not the farmer but rather the farmer's horse who rears and plunges with Carne into the waves below. The horse's body is found but Carne's is not, his disappearance thought a possible suicide. It is not until many months later that Lydia Holly and her four siblings discover his decaying corpse in a salt marsh as they are taking a picnic walk to the Leame foreshore. Horrified, 'they ran away, away from that monstrosity mourned by wheeling sea birds that circled and screamed above it. Panting, running, sobbing, their picnic ruined, the Holly children ran.'[25] No distanced perspective of land or sea is possible and, as with Luke Bishop in *The Poacher*, the Holly children make a decisive contribution to the rural novel through their movement over the land. Their walking and then their 'panting, running, sobbing' link them to other rural characters whose bodies register the effects of a specific geography on breath and gait, who know and appreciate the land in sometimes fearful, always material, rather than distanced or aesthetic, ways.

Committed to political more than geographical concerns, *South Riding* affirms the importance of local government, women's professional work, and girls' education as themes for what Holtby described in a letter to Phyllis Bentley as her 'arcadian novel'.[26] Despite the fact that Holtby subtitled her novel 'An English Landscape', her feminist version of a progressive rural modernity in Yorkshire challenges the politics of rural nostalgia endorsed by conservative ruralists like Stanley Baldwin. It also challenges the politics of Welsh writer Richard Llewellyn, whose deeply elegiac version of a destructive rural modernity helped make *How Green Was My Valley* (1939) an instant bestseller.[27] This novel offers no redemption through progressive politics, no way out from complete destruction by industrialised mining practices that have turned a green valley black and will literally bury the home of the narrator, Huw Morgan, in a giant heap of slag.

Llewellyn's narrator is the youngest son in a family of nine children, all of whom are dead or have disappeared when, at age sixty-two, he begins his tale. We may not understand how vulnerable his narrative position is until we read, at the beginning of Chapter 9, 'The slag heap moves, pressing on, down and down, over and all round this house which was my father's and my mother's and now is mine. Soon, perhaps in an hour, the house will be buried.'[28] Such bleak vision ironically uses a classic pastoral stance – the wise man surveying and judging rural folk – with a narrative about pastoral annihilation. Only in memory do pastoral method and scenery come together, as Huw imagines and recreates innumerable childhood walks up the mountain with his father. Intensifying the elegiac pastoral effect, the ageing Huw remembers remembering these walks as he also remembers his father's death in his arms due to a mining accident: 'I shut my eyes and thought of him at my side, my hand in his, trying to match his stride as I walked with him up the mountain above us.'[29]

All the descriptions of Huw's walks with his father up the mountain to Chapel or with his brothers to union meetings take him through a lush countryside that has earned Llewellyn a reputation as a rural writer. It is Huw's walks down into the mountain, as a miner, that have earned Llewellyn a reputation as a regional writer, one who contends with the historical shift in the early twentieth century from a Welsh mining community supported by local owners, self-governing workers, and sustainable practices of pick and shovel to one of large mining conglomerates, wage reductions, violent labour disputes, and gross abuse of the surrounding land. Llewellyn's personal claim to represent the Welsh region is tenuous, however. Chris Hopkins explains that the novel 'seems to be a text from within Wales, since it represents Welsh speech' but that this 'seems' is the key word, since the novel was not written in any Welsh-English variety nor was it written by someone from or in Wales.[30] Richard Llewellyn was really named Vivian Lloyd and when he began the novel, he had not been to Wales. Hopkins does not dismiss the novel's 'Welsh resonances' on these grounds but rather points out that its 'mythic nature' is valuable because it 'tells us something of how Wales was read from England'.[31]

Hopkins emphasises that, in the 1930s, the market for Welsh fiction – typically written in English and published in London – was partly a product of a 'new market for working-class writing and writing about working-class experience but also a new market [...] about the regions of England, and about the other nations of Great Britain'.[32] The reception of working-class fiction as regional fiction resulted in the curious pattern observed in *How Green Was My Valley* of authors promoting a regional and working-class outsider hero who is also representative of the nation. For English-language Welsh regional fiction this dynamic is complicated politically and socially by the fact that Wales is both part of England, governed from London, and with Scotland and Ireland maintaining a separate national identity.[33] It is both region and nation but not simply region or nation. Geographically speaking, one could assert that the same contradictory dynamic is true of all rural regional novels in the 1930s; they both are and are not of the nation. For enthusiasts and romantics like Stanley Baldwin, rural England is all England; for sentimental pastoralists like Llewellyn, rural Wales is totally other, complete to itself and doomed in its isolation from the modern nation by a gulf of time and space that no modernising technology can overcome even as modern technology has brought an end to the region's life as a viable autonomous human place.

Lewis Grassic Gibbon's trilogy of early twentieth-century Scottish rural life, *A Scots Quair*, avoids Llewellyn's enclosure of a rural region in an inaccessible past but risks popular failure in doing so.[34] The first instalment, *Sunset Song* (1932), was an immediate bestseller. Published in England but set in the Mearns of Scotland during the years between 1911 and the early 1920s, it tells of Christine 'Chris' Guthrie's coming of age on a small farm called Blawearie located in the farming village of Kinraddie. Both Blawearie and Kinraddie are imaginary places, but it is well known that Gibbon (the pen name of James Leslie Mitchell) built them out of his memories of the land and peoples in and near his childhood home of Arbuthnott.[35] The second instalment, *Cloud Howe*, is not an assuredly rural novel as it is set in the fictional town of Segget, with its mills and labour disputes, and with a plot that revolves around the Kirk and its minister, Robert Colquohoun, whom Chris has married. Even less so is

Grey Granite a rural novel, as it is set in the busy and sometimes violent streets of 'Duncairn toun', an 'imaginary city' of the Depression which Gibbon explains in a 'Cautionary Note' was alternately mistaken in the press for Dundee, Aberdeen, and Edinburgh.[36]

Attention to the human and natural geography of farming areas and more particularly the language of maps – or in Gibbon's case, inclusion of hand-drawn maps themselves – emphasises the continuities between Gibbon's novel of rural Scottish life and the representation of rural life in novels by English regional writers celebrated by Bentley, Cavaliero, Snell, and Matthews. Similarly, Gibbon's stylised English, which incorporates Scots vocabulary into a standard English syntax, recalls the dialect writing of Bates or Holtby and most obviously Richard Llewellyn. Also like the other rural writers discussed in this chapter, Gibbon tends to associate the best of a remembered rural regional life, the rural life that will come to an end with the devastations of the First World War, with characters who walk (or run) over the land, who see it with the eyes of agricultural workers rather than artists or tourists. For example, the first chapter of *Sunset Song* begins with Chris Guthrie lying atop a hill above Blawearie next to the Druids' Standing Stones, escaping her farm labours for a few precious moments. She is looking down on the June moors, thinking about her family's ties to Kinraddie lands, and before that to the lands of the more northern village of Echt where her mother and father first met and settled and where she was born. She recalls her mother's words, '*There's no land like Aberdeen or folk so fine as them that bide by the Don*' and again, in a quoted speech of her mother's that establishes as the most acute site of nostalgia the time before the time of the novel, the land before the land of the novel, '*Oh, Chris, my lass, there are better things than your books or studies or loving or bedding, there's the countryside your own, you its* [sic]*, in the days when you're neither bairn nor woman*'. The past and tradition are important to all the characters' experiences in a countryside that has seen 'the Last of the Peasants, the last of the Old Scots folk',[37] but something more complicated than nostalgia characterises Chris's relation to the changing land. In what could be described as a modernist ruralist epiphany, we read:

> And then a queer thought came to her there in the drooked fields, that nothing endured at all, nothing but the land she passed across, [...] the land was forever, it moved and changed below you, but was forever, you were close to it and it to you, not at a bleak remove it held you and hurted you. [...]
>
> She walked, weeping then, stricken and frightened because of that knowledge that had come on her, she could never leave it, this life of toiling days and the needs of beasts and the smoke of wood fires [...].[38]

Unlike more familiar, less regional, more assuredly national modernist novels of consciousness, Chris Guthrie's thought is explicitly tied to her walks up the land. Over the course of the trilogy, Chris's name may change from Guthrie to Tavendale, to Colquohoun, to Ogilvie, but her walks up hills serve as a consistent structuring device, beginning virtually every chapter of each novel in *A Scots Quair*. In addition to her walks up to the Standing Stones above Blawearie, she walks to the ruins of Kaimes above Segget, the stairs of Windmill Place in Duncairn, and, finally, in the novel's last pages, to the summit of Barmekin above Echt. These walks also function as a kind of narrative code guiding readers how to interpret the value and meaning of Chris's heightened moments of consciousness. Walks up imply escape for reflection, escape from work and trouble, a chance for renewal and adjustment. Walks down, which initiate the two middle chapters of *Grey Granite*, imply descent, entrapment, stagnation. When, at the end of the trilogy, 'Chris Ogilvie made her way up the track',[39] readers should know this is a positive change, even as Chris's return to the house of her childhood, her mother's lands where she can hope to find '*the countryside your own*', cannot bring back the people or language or culture of *Sunset Song*. Too much time has passed. *Grey Granite*'s ambivalent ending leaves Chris in a rural place with fields and croft, but the trees are gone as a result of First World War clearcutting, and all social and economic relations have changed because of global incursions on a small farming community.

Modernism, Modernity, Rural Modernity

A Scots Quair is regarded by critics as a problem trilogy. In part, this is a problem of nostalgia, as critics trained to value a modernist aesthetic cannot quite endorse either the popularity of *Sunset Song*'s ruralism or the unpopularity of the other two novels' modernism. But it is also a problem of narrative geography. Chris with her married names of Colquohoun and Ogilvie no longer seems a rural figure, walking for work, ploughing, seeding, and harvesting as Chris Guthrie and Chris Tavendale did. Rather, she seems akin to urban characters we encounter in modernist novels, walking up city pavements, achieving a view. She has always had an ability to see the land as landscape, inviting us into her stream of consciousness inspired by her aesthetic gaze. But, unlike her gaze in *Sunset Song*, that in *Cloud Howe* and *Grey Granite* is separated from the land as a source of livelihood. In effect, we have lost our rural regional novel but are not sure how to describe what we have gained.

A number of scholars have proposed new vocabularies and conceptual frameworks that promise to address this critical confusion. While more a storyteller than theorist, Alexandra Harris in *Romantic Moderns* provides evidence that 1930s English art was not a fragmented and antagonistic battleground divided by highbrow, middlebrow, and lowbrow forces but a field united by artists' shared commitment to a modern and modernist romanticism. She associates the romantic moderns with expressions of and affection for 'the particular' or 'the crowded, detailed, old-fashioned and whimsical'.[40] Literary critic Elizabeth Outka provides a more fully theorised account of how to understand the literature that fed the cult of the countryside in an increasingly commercialised, mass-marketed, and democratic 1930s culture. Outka introduces the concept of 'the commodified authentic', a 'phenomenon' she associates with British modernity and modernism and that she argues was responsible for generating 'hybrid' products and places indebted equally to ideals of authenticity and artifice.[41] Among the most compelling of those appeals to authenticity were 'nostalgic evocations of an English rural past',[42] appeals packaged and delivered in forms ranging from model towns and garden cities to modernist texts like Virginia Woolf's *To the Lighthouse* (1927) and George Bernard Shaw's *Major Barbara* (first performed in 1905). They might also include the latter novels of Lewis Grassic Gibbon (which were written in Welwyn Garden City, outside of London).

Art historian Rosemary Shirley's notion of rural modernity is perhaps the most flexible theorisation of contexts that can invigorate the study of rural and regional British novels. Her book attempts 'to perambulate the margins of ideas of the rural, the everyday and modernity [...] reactivating the rural as a site of modernity'. While Shirley builds her theory out of the visual materials of the last one hundred years of everyday British life, her insistence that 'the "countryside" [is] a populated place with lived rhythms and routines, rather than a "landscape" which is primarily to be looked at or visited' best supports the definitions and conceptions of rural regional literature advanced by this chapter.[43] For Shirley, and perhaps for all scholars dwelling on the contradictions of rural and regional values and places in 1930s Britain, the critical problem of accounting for the hybrid nature of twentieth-century rural–regional places or cultural objects can be solved by replacing the word 'rural', 'loaded as it is with the pressures of the picturesque and the peaceful', with the term 'non-metropolitan'. Shirley argues that describing places or cultural objects as non-metropolitan helps us see how these places and objects 'themselves complicate the established polarities of the country and the city'.[44] While the potentially distinct histories of production and consumption of rural and regional novels must be part of any revised 1930s literary and cultural history, the possibility of studying them as part of a more broadly understood experience of rural modernity holds promise for scholars of rural and regional literature. Not only could adoption of a theory of rural modernity minimise confusions over the status of novels like *A Scots Quair* but it could also support a more sophisticated, more densely contextualised criticism on relations between rural and regional literary traditions, bringing new attention to non-metropolitan arts and places as those arts and places redefine the history of 1930s literature itself.

Notes

1. Stanley Baldwin, 'England Is the Country, and the Country Is England', in *Writing Englishness 1900–1950: An Introductory Sourcebook on National Identity*, ed. by Judy Giles and Tim Middleton (New York and Abingdon: Routledge, 1995), p. 101.
2. Alun Howkins, 'The Discovery of Rural England', in *Englishness: Politics and Culture 1880–1920*, ed. by Robert Colls and Philip Dodd (London: Croom Helm, 1986), pp. 62–88 (p. 63).
3. Rather notoriously, George Orwell wrote in *The Road to Wigan Pier* that he 'went among them [the residents of Wigan] as a foreigner, and both of us were aware of it'. For further discussion, see Tim Youngs's preceding chapter on 'Travel' in this *Companion*.
4. John Lowerson, 'Battles for the Countryside', in *Class, Culture, and Social Change: A New View of the 1930s*, ed. by Frank Gloversmith (Sussex: Harvester, 1980), pp. 258–80 (p. 262).
5. Ibid., pp. 260–2.
6. Howard Newby, *Country Life: A Social History of Rural England* (London: Weidenfeld and Nicolson, 1987), p. 175.
7. For data on regional variations in 'aristocratic flight', see Alun Howkins, 'Landowners and Farmers', in Alun Howkins, *The Death of Rural England: A Social History of the Countryside since 1900* (London: Routledge, 2003), pp. 55–76. For a brief history of working-class rural activism, see Lowerson, 'Battles for the Countryside', pp. 68–77.
8. Alun Howkins, 'Death and Rebirth?: English Rural Society, 1920-1940', in *The English Countryside Between the Wars*, ed. by Paul Brassley, Jeremy Burchardt, and Lynne Thompson (Woodbridge: Boydell Press, 2006), pp. 10–25 (pp. 22–3).
9. K. D. M. Snell, 'The Regional Novel: Themes for Interdisciplinary Research', in *The Regional Novel in Britain and Ireland, 1800–1990*, ed. by K. D. M. Snell (Cambridge: Cambridge University Press, 1998), pp. 1–53 (p. 2).

10. Raymond Williams, 'Region and Class in the Novel', in *Writing in Society* (London: Verso, 1985), pp. 229–38 (p. 230).

11. Steven Matthews, 'English Regional Fiction and National Culture', in *The Reinvention of the British and Irish Novel, 1880–1940*, ed. by Patrick Parrinder and Andrzej Gasiorek (Oxford: Oxford University Press, 2011), pp. 506–21. For examples of other recent studies, see *Regional Modernisms*, ed. by Neal Alexander and James Moran (Edinburgh: Edinburgh University Press, 2013), and Alexander Davis and Lee Jenkins's *Locations of Literary Modernism: Region and Nation in British and American Modernist Poetry* (Cambridge: Cambridge University Press, 2000).

12. Phyllis Bentley, *The English Regional Novel*, P. E. N. Books (London: George Allen and Unwin, 1941).

13. Matthews, 'English Regional Fiction', p. 507.

14. Glenn Cavaliero, *The Rural Tradition in the English Novel 1900–1939* (Totowa, NJ: Rowman and Littlefield, 1977). See also W. J. Keith's *Regions of the Imagination: The Development of British Rural Fiction* (Toronto: University of Toronto Press, 1988), for a study focussed on nineteenth-century antecedents to the 1930s rural regional novel.

15. Marion Shaw, 'Cold Comfort Times: Women Writers in the Interwar Period', in *The English Countryside Between the Wars*, ed. by Paul Brassley, Jeremy Burchardt, and Lynne Thompson (Woodbridge: Boydell Press, 2006), pp. 73–86 (pp. 74, 77).

16. Ibid., p. 78.

17. Bates was discovered by Edward Garnett, the reader for Jonathan Cape who also edited D. H. Lawrence, Joseph Conrad, and W. H. Hudson. Received in this company, the prolific and popular Bates could not live up to expectations. See Dominic Head, 'H. E. Bates, Regionalism and Late Modernism', in *The Legacies of Modernism: Historicising Postwar and Contemporary Fiction*, ed. by David James (Cambridge: Cambridge University Press, 2012), pp. 40–52 (p. 40).

18. Head, 'H. E. Bates', p. 42.

19. Dean Baldwin, 'H.E. Bates: *The Poacher*', in *Recharting the Thirties*, ed. by Patrick Quinn (Selinsgrove: Susquehanna University Press; London: Associated University Presses, 1996), pp. 124–133 (p. 124).

20. H. E. Bates, *The Poacher* (London: Breslich & Foss and Robinson Publishing, 1984), p. 65.

21. Winifred Holtby, *South Riding: An English Landscape* (Glasgow: Fontana Books, 1954).

22. Winifred Holtby, 'Prefatory Letter to Alderman Mrs. Holtby', in Holtby, *South Riding*, p. 5.

23. Bentley, *The English Regional Novel*, p. 40; Shaw, 'Cold Comfort Times', p. 85.

24. Holtby, *South Riding*, pp. 430–1.

25. Ibid., p. 485.

26. Quoted in Marion Shaw, *The Clear Stream: A Life of Winifred Holtby* (London: Virago Press, 1999), p. 233.

27. Richard Llewellyn, *How Green Was My Valley* (New York: Scribner Paperback, 1997).

28. Ibid., p. 101.

29. Ibid., p. 492.

30. Chris Hopkins, *English Fiction in the 1930s: Language, Genre, History* (London: Continuum, 2006), pp. 71–2.

31. Ibid., p. 72.

32. Ibid., p. 61.

33. Ibid., p. 62.

34. Lewis Grassic Gibbon, *A Scots Quair* (Edinburgh: Polygon, 2006).

35. Ian Campbell, 'Introduction to the Trilogy', in Grassic Gibbon, *A Scots Quair*, p. xiii.

36. Gibbon, *A Scots Quair*, p. 482.

37. Ibid., pp. 37, 254.

38. Ibid., p. 123.

39. Ibid., p. 632.

40. Alexandra Harris, *Romantic Moderns: English Writers, Artists, and the Imagination* (London: Thames and Hudson, 2010), pp. 10, 14.

41. Elizabeth Outka, *Consuming Traditions: Modernity, Modernism, and the Commodified Authentic* (Oxford: Oxford University Press, 2009), pp. 4–5.

42. Ibid., p. 4.

43. Rosemary Shirley, *Rural Modernity, Everyday Life and Visual Culture* (Farnham and Burlington: Ashgate Publishing, 2015), p. 3.

44. Ibid., p. 6.

CHAPTER II

The Queer 1930s

Glyn Salton-Cox

It is today often presumed – by, for instance, the *Oxford English Dictionary* – that the term 'queer' only began to be reclaimed with pride in the 1980s.[1] But as queer historians have long recognised, this is in fact inaccurate, for a more or less defiant use of this term as a self-descriptor dates at least as far back as 1939, to Christopher Isherwood's *Berlin Stories*.[2] It is, therefore, not so much an anachronism as a historical imperative to affirm the 1930s as queer. Indeed, given the prominence of a particular group of left-wing writers, including Isherwood himself, W. H. Auden, and Stephen Spender, the 1930s have often been categorised as a 'pink decade': as, in other words, foundational for twentieth-century queer literature, politics, and culture in Britain. The period's queer writing, however, extends far beyond these most celebrated writers – to lesser-known male writers such as William Plomer and J. R. Ackerley, and unjustly neglected women including Katharine Burdekin, Valentine Ackland, and Sylvia Townsend Warner.

As discussed in the Introduction to this volume, in conventional historical terms 'the thirties' is usually seen as beginning with the Wall Street Crash in October 1929 and ending with the outbreak of the Second World War in September 1939. For queer literary history, however, we might see the signal events bookending the decade as the obscenity trial of Radclyffe Hall's lesbian novel *The Well of Loneliness* (1928) in November 1928 and the departure of W. H. Auden and Christopher Isherwood for the United States in January 1939. But these too can be misleading. For while both events were indeed salient moments, focussing too exclusively on a particular interpretation of their importance also sets up problematic ways of reading queer writing of the period. The censorship of *Well* might lead one to an overemphasis on the closet and repression as fundamental structuring principles; while Auden and Isherwood's departure on the eve of war could create a tendency to see queer experience as incompatible with serious political engagement. In what follows, I will probe the weaknesses of an over-reliance on these two modes of understanding the queer 1930s, charting the ways in which diverse writers produced a lively body of work that is as at least as much defiantly political as it is at times subtly coded.[3]

To stress this over-reliance is not to deny the important role repression has played, nor to occlude the complexities and difficulties encountered in attempts to articulate queer politics with other forms of political engagement. Indeed, Michel Foucault's famous critique of the repression thesis in *History of Sexuality, Volume 1* does not, as is sometimes supposed, completely do away with the concept but rather seeks to frame it within a wider narrative of what he calls the 'deployment of sexuality'.[4] While for many repression – the refusal, denial, interdiction, or forbidding of certain modes of sexual expression – is the basic oppressive dynamic of modern sexuality, for Foucault it is better seen as but one strategy in a series of productive movements by which sexuality and power are intertwined. Foucault, for instance, interrogates the intricate ways in which adolescent sexuality was policed in the eighteenth and nineteenth centuries not only by forbidding such practices as masturbation and homosexuality but also, and more importantly, by actually producing intricate and lengthy discourses about the proper uses of the body. In other words, it is not fundamentally silence but rather incessant speech, a 'discursive explosion', which constitutes the ways sexuality is managed and produced by power.[5] But it would be a mistake to jump from this insight to a denial of the importance of repression. Rather, both refusal and regulated disclosure operate dialectically to produce the distinctive textures of modern sexuality, in a particularly salient fashion when it comes to non-normative practices and desires.

The decency trial of *The Well of Loneliness* and its effect on modernist literary history is a paradigmatic instance of this interrelationship between different modes of disciplining and managing queer sexuality and the variegated resistances they call forth. Hall's novel is a disarmingly frank, despairing portrayal of a lesbian woman, seen in contemporary sexological terms as an 'invert', or woman with a male spirit.[6] Forthrightly intended to incite public sympathy for 'inversion', Hall's novel was quickly seized on by the right-wing tabloid newspaper *The Sunday Express*. The paper ran a luridly homophobic campaign to have the book banned on grounds of indecency, which succeeded despite little public outcry about the novel. (Previously considered a widespread 'moral panic', Laura Doan has convincingly demonstrated that *The Express's* position was actually quite marginal, with few reviewers or readers expressing disgust at Hall's novel.)[7] The trial sparked a counter-campaign boasting many prominent modernist writers, including E. M. Forster and Virginia Woolf, who published a number of articles and letters to the press and offered themselves as witnesses in the obscenity trial. It might be tempting to see this event as a fairly straightforward instance of repression, whereby the literary expression of queer sexuality is stifled and censored by the state. This interpretation could be bolstered by the fact that Forster and Woolf, despite publicly opposing the ban on anti-censorship grounds, were themselves evasive about their queerness when in the public gaze; as Jodie Medd has shown in *Lesbian Scandal and the Culture of Modernism*, both writers were fearful of the personal revelations the trial could possibly bring and were relieved when they were not called as witnesses.[8] But Medd's study also compellingly argues that the trial and its attendant anxieties were also *productive* of certain allusive modes through which Woolf came to discuss gender and sexuality, as she deployed the case of *The Well of Loneliness* in subtle ways at certain points in her work following the trial, including the review essay 'Geraldine and Jane' (1929) and *The Waves* (1931).[9] And, although Forster disassociated himself from homosexuality in a later article in *Nineteenth Century and After*, and was to forbid the publication of his homosexual novel *Maurice* until after his death in 1970, he returned to the novel's manuscript in the early 1930s, rewriting certain scenes with greater candour, a decision that critics have also attributed to the *Chatterley* trial.[10]

It is with these two modernist forbears to the queer 1930s that this chapter will begin, before turning to the famous 'Auden gang' of radical writers who are often seen as defining the decade's literary history, and whom I read as crucially informed by the sexual-political culture of Weimar Berlin. I will then examine several lesser-known but equally important queer women writers, including Sylvia Townsend Warner, her partner Valentine Ackland, and Katharine Burdekin. In conclusion, I will consider the afterlife of the queer 1930s in post-war Britain, complicating usual accounts by considering the figure of the 'respectable homosexual' with reference to Dorothy Strachey's 1949 lesbian novel *Olivia* and to the Auden group's continuing influence.

Why Shouldn't It Date?

The figures known collectively as the Bloomsbury Group have long been central to debates over the politics of modernism, particularly as regards queer sexuality. There is no space here to rehearse these debates in detail, except to note that it is hard to disentangle the group's political virtues, such as they were, from their vices. Our concern is with how Bloomsbury was involved with a series of negotiations over the terms of private and public that were to be drawn on and transformed by 1930s writers, a question that is given particular salience given the strong material links between Bloomsbury publishing networks and the emergence of the Auden group – the group's central promoter and publisher, John Lehmann, was employed by the Woolfs as an assistant and then a director of the Hogarth Press, and published works by Isherwood, Auden, and Spender both at the Hogarth Press and in his magazine *New Writing*.[11]

Woolf's 1928 novel *Orlando* is in many ways a characteristic product of Bloomsbury sexual politics. Highly allusive, reflexive, and ironised, the novel is a fantastical 'Biography' of the eponymous 350-year-old nobleman who transforms into a woman in the eighteenth century during a heavily Orientalised stint in Constantinople. The protagonist of *Orlando* is based on Woolf's friend and sometime lover Vita Sackville-West; the novel constantly alludes to, but never directly represents, queer sexuality in its subtle attention to the slippages of desire and gender performance inherent in Orlando's transition from man to woman. Literary history is a central thematic concern of the narrative, as Orlando constantly returns to a long poem they had been writing since adolescence, and meets a variety of notable writers and critics. Offering a thoroughgoing critique of the concept of stable gender and sexual identity (Orlando has 'a great variety of selves to call upon, far more than we have been able to find room for'), and always drawing away from fully positioning this critique as queer ('some [selves] are too wildly ridiculous to be mentioned in print at all'), it would be misplaced to argue that the novel fails to fully disclose its queerness, seeing as a major part of Woolf's project is the dissolution of identity itself.[12] And yet, the novel's insistence on the centrality of elite coterie sociality to queer self-expression – Orlando is constantly mixing with different noble circles and bourgeois literary cliques – remains problematic and indeed paradigmatic for the limits of Bloomsbury's privatising sense of sexual radicalism.

The production, circulation, and reception of Forster's *Maurice* (1971) also serve as an important case study in this regard; as an explicitly homosexual text that itself only reached a coterie audience during the period, we might call it the obverse to Woolf's novel. Forster wrote a draft of the manuscript in 1913–14, revised it in 1932, but felt it was not publishable during his lifetime, no doubt influenced by the *Well of Loneliness* trial and of other texts, including James Hanley's 1931 novel *Boy*. Hanley's novel was prosecuted for obscenity in 1935; this was another successful prosecution, resulting in a fine, despite the support of Forster, who defended the novel and became Hanley's friend. Forster was in a long-term partnership with a police constable, Bob Buckingham, and his novel features a romance between an upper-middle-class man, Maurice Hall, and a gamekeeper, Alec Scudder. Maurice describes Alec as 'a find in a thousand, the longed-for dream', and their relationship is represented as offering a much more fulfilling and fully sexual pairing than that Maurice experienced with the uptight fellow bourgeois Clive.[13] The major inspiration for the novel's presentation of cross-class intimacy was the relationship between the radical queer socialist Edward Carpenter and his working-class lover George Merrill, whom Forster had visited in 1912. Forster showed a draft of *Maurice* to Isherwood in 1933, and, anxious to see how a younger queer writer would view the novel, asked him whether it would 'date', to which Isherwood replied 'why *shouldn't* it date?' Echoing this idea, when the novel appeared, it was with a dedication not to an individual but 'to a Happier Year'.[14] A keen admirer of Forster, Isherwood was to oversee the publication of the novel after Forster's death and often cited him as a central influence on his own work.[15]

Maurice is thus significant not only as one of the first major English novels to sympathetically portray homosexuality but also as a pivotal point in a longer history of literary production; like *Orlando*, Forster's novel is a staging post in the development of queer literary history. It is, however, important not to overstate the extent of Bloomsbury influence over queer writers of the 1930s, for despite their links to the earlier group, Isherwood, Spender, and Auden were to work within a very different conception of the relationship between the private and public realms, one in many ways closer to Carpenter's radical queer socialism than to Forster and Woolf's cautious liberal hygiene between public persona and private expression.

Berlin Meant Boys

More than Bloomsbury, or indeed Carpenter, it was in fact the political, cultural, and sexual climate of Weimar Berlin that was to prove decisively formative for the Auden group. Auden, Isherwood, and Spender all visited the city in the early 1930s, with Isherwood staying for an extended period and making Berlin his home from 1931 to 1933.[16] Following the politically abortive but culturally generative revolution of 1918, interwar Germany, particularly Berlin, had become the site of an extensive and fast-paced process of sexual, social, and cultural radicalisation. During this period, Berlin saw the emergence of two interrelated yet distinct radical public spheres, associated on the one hand with queer sexuality and non-normative gender practices and on the other with Marxist radicalism.[17] Both these scenes were absolutely central to the development of Auden's, Spender's, and Isherwood's writing during the 1930s, which is marked by an urgent sense of political engagement.

Auden's 1935 poem 'To a Writer on His Birthday', written for his close friend and sometime sexual partner Isherwood, and subsequently dropped by Auden from his *Collected Poems*, explicitly exhibits an earnest desire for literary production to influence the world in political ways:

> So in this hour of crisis and dismay,
> What better than your strict and adult pen
> Can warn us from the colours and the consolations,
> The showy arid works, reveal
> The squalid shadow of academy and garden,
> Make action urgent and its nature clear?[18]

Here, in some of Auden's most cited lines, Isherwood's political virtues as a novelist are praised in an unmistakably sexual register. While some commentators have complained that the 'nature' of the action compelled is unclear, it seems quite obvious that Auden is punning on the political stakes inherent in Isherwood's documentary prose, and on his own sexual desire for his friend's 'strict and adult pen'. Indeed, earlier in the poem Auden writes with fairly open desire that 'I each meal time with the families [...] Have thought of you, Christopher, and wished beside me / Your squat spruce body and enormous head'.[19] Auden's later decision to excise this poem and others may, then, be thought to reveal a queasiness about both their political and their sexual charge. The salient point is, however, that some of his poems of the period were to exhibit homosexual desire relatively openly, making an over-reliance on the concept of the closet inadequate to describe Auden's work in the 1930s.

In a much-cited notebook entry, Auden was later to write of the 'erotic joy' of collaboration, arguing that 'queers, to whom normal marriage and parenthood are forbidden, are fools if they do not deliberately look for tasks which require collaboration, and the right person with whom to collaborate'.[20] Auden and Isherwood collaborated on three celebrated plays, *The Dog Beneath the Skin* (1935), *The Ascent of F6* (1936), *On the Frontier* (1938), and a travel book, *Journey to a War* (1939). As further discussed by Claire Warden's chapter in this volume, the plays were produced by the leftist theatre company the Group Theatre (run by the homosexual couple Rupert Doone and Robert

Medley), and present an attempt to reach a broader leftist public while simultaneously appealing to a coterie audience. *The Dog Beneath the Skin*, for instance, offers an anti-imperialist critique of British and European militarism, while subtly alluding to Auden and Isherwood's friend, the queer archaeologist Francis Turville-Petre (who was later to be given a more explicit portrait in Isherwood's 1962 novel *Down There on a Visit*). In addition to being important documents of collaboration, the plays thus exhibit a distinct movement away from Bloomsbury divisions of private and public – while not being explicitly 'out' texts according to the terms that have become dominant since the 1970s, they insistently blend queer sociality with broad leftist public address, an intersection given particular salience given the Group Theatre's queer management. The collaborative plays are also influenced by a characteristically Weimar avant-gardist mode in their Brechtian insistence on an urgent didactic political theatre that never seeks to hide its own artifice.[21] The plot of *Dog Beneath The Skin*, for instance, hinges on a transparent comic disguise, frequently broken in absurd ways, while *The Ascent of F6* features a series of scenes of a placid, foolish home audience listening to jingoistic radio shows, thus troping the audience's own putative recognition of their experience's mediation.

Of all the Auden group, Isherwood was perhaps most deeply formed by Weimar Berlin's distinctive crossroads of dissident sex and socialism. While in Berlin he visited and for a time lived next door to the queer sexologist and campaigner Magnus Hirschfeld's Institute for Sexual Research, perhaps the best-known and most important centre for queer life and research in the city. A major influence on Isherwood in Berlin was John Henry Mackay's *The Hustler* (*Der Puppenjunge*, 1926). A landmark early queer novel set in Berlin, *The Hustler* relates the story of the love of a young provincial petit bourgeois man, Hermann, for another recent arrival to Berlin, Gunther, a teenage prostitute. Mackay's novel was given to Isherwood for Christmas in 1930 by Hirschfeld's partner and assistant Karl Giese, and Isherwood went on to provide Hubert Kennedy's 1985 translation of the novel with a blurb, approving Mackay's novel from personal experience: 'It gives a picture of the Berlin sexual underworld early in this century which I know, from my own experience, to be authentic.'[22] As Isherwood was later to assert in his memoir, *Christopher and His Kind* (1976), 'Berlin meant boys' – in particular, working-class boys.[23]

Isherwood not only was influenced by Weimar Berlin's queer scene embodied in Mackay's novel and Hirschfeld's institute but was also in close contact with the communist left in the city.[24] Accounts of Isherwood's work, however, often overlook the extent of his radicalisation during this period, influenced in part by Isherwood's later disclaimers that he was never really invested in leftist politics in Berlin.[25] His *The Berlin Stories* (1939; consisting of the 1935 *Mr Norris Changes Trains* and the 1939 *Goodbye to Berlin*), for instance, set in the city in the early 1930s and charting the rise of Nazism, has all too often been seen as exhibiting an attitude of mere spectorship.[26] In fact, *The Berlin Stories* is deeply politically committed, but, in a spectacular misreading of Isherwood's darkly camp humour, this has missed precisely because of Isherwood's burlesquing tone throughout the narrative, itself part of the text's queer politics properly considered. In other words, the text's wryly comic style in no way invalidates its political bite; indeed, this very style is a coding and instantiation of a politically aware queer readership. And, even as Isherwood depicts Berlin communism with dry wit, *The Berlin Stories* exhibits a clear admiration of and affiliation with leftist communities.

More concerned than Auden or Isherwood with respectability and public success, Stephen Spender has been called 'the fellow-traveller's fellow-traveller', and his journey from sexual and political radicalism to establishment figure, fond husband, and Cold Warrior has often been taken to be characteristic of the Auden group's inability to fully commit politically.[27] While Auden and Isherwood never joined the Communist Party of Great Britain (CPGB), Spender did so very briefly and to much fanfare in 1937, and then made an abrupt about-turn, as he records in his autobiography, *World Within World* (1951), and in his contribution to the virulently anti-communist volume *The God That Failed* (1949).[28] Moreover, Spender went on to edit a magazine funded by the CIA, and, although he vehemently denied that he was aware of this (as does his authorised biographer, John Sutherland), recent scholarship on the relationship between the British secret state and mid-century leftist writers that draws on previously classified MI5 files has revealed that it is extremely likely that Spender in fact knew about the funding.[29] Tellingly, Spender's public recanting of his former communism was accompanied in his autobiography with a statement that his romantic relationships with men were at an end. Once more, however, it is crucial to recognise that even in Spender's case the story is rather more complicated than it may first appear. *World Within World* performs a curious double movement, revealing a great deal about Spender's bisexuality at a time when persecution of queer men was mounting, even as it seeks to safely confine such deviance to the past.

Apparitional Utopias

As feminist critics have pointed out and increasingly corrected, canonical accounts of 1930s literary history have consistently occluded women writers; this applies in particular to queer women, as a double foreclosure has been at work, not only that of the sexist canon but also the principle which Terry Castle has called 'the apparitional lesbian', whereby queer female experience and writing have been systematically erased.[30] The point, however, is not merely to include these writers in new accounts but rather to seriously examine their articulation within and against dominant literary-historical narratives. An important study by Elizabeth English, for instance, seeks to reintegrate the role of genre fiction in accounts of queer women's contribution to interwar literary history. *Lesbian Modernism: Censorship, Sexuality, and Genre Fiction* (2015) aims not only to 'expose buried networks of women working outside the cultural geographical centres of modernism' but also to redefine the canon of lesbian modernism itself through a stress on the period's genre fiction, often overlooked as it does not fit the dominant paradigm of high experimentalism.[31]

One queer writer English examines is Katharine Burdekin, whose work serves to reveal the problematic assumptions of canonical literary history. The 1930s are often defined as 'late modernist', coming as they do after the heyday of such modernist writers as Woolf and James Joyce. And, while this appellation does make sense for a number of figures of the period whose writing registers a sense of bathos after the glories of earlier interwar literary production, it is particularly unsuited to queer leftist writers and to the important future-oriented genres of utopia and dystopia. Burdekin produced several notable utopian and dystopian novels in the 1930s, the best known of which is the dystopian fantasy *Swastika Night* (1937), but which also include the feminist utopia *The End of This Day's Business* (unpublished until 1989), and the gender-queer *Proud Man* (1934). As opposed to Orwell's and Huxley's better-known dystopias, *Swastika Night* speculates on the central role of gender oppression in a putative Nazi victory (even as it also contains some troublingly disgusted glances at queer male desire). *The End of This Day's Business*, meanwhile, imagines a matriarchal future, in which men have been reduced to a childlike status and women rule over a well-managed but troubled world. One of the most striking elements of Burdekin's work is the way in which gender performance is privileged over sexual object choice as an interpretative rubric, revealing the way in which these two differing paradigms overlapped during the 1930s.

Another instance of the ways in which attention to lesbian writers should lead to a thoroughgoing reconceptualisation of the period's literary history can be observed in the figures of Sylvia Townsend Warner and Valentine Ackland. While the Auden group's leftist engagements might appear (unfairly in the case of Isherwood) in hindsight to be perhaps flickering and uneven, Sylvia Townsend Warner's and Valentine Ackland's commitment to communism in the mid-to-late 1930s was implacable; indeed, Warner presciently warned fellow communist Edgell Rickword in 1937 of the possibility of Spender's future treachery.[32] Both women joined the CPGB in the mid-1930s, and became among the most respected Party members in the west of England during the period, coming into close contact and carrying on correspondence with the CPGB's general secretary, Harry Pollitt, among other important figures. Many accounts of these two writers' lives – and, crucially, editions of their works – have, however, worked to erase their communism during the period, with the exception of Wendy Mulford's excellent critical biography.[33] The past few years have seen a resurgence in interest in Warner from feminist and queer scholars producing path-breaking studies of her lesbian fictions. However, this work also tends to ignore or elide her communist commitment.[34] This is a serious omission, for evading the question of such commitment misplaces Warner in terms of dominant literary accounts of the decade. Her unwavering affiliation to communism radically destabilises the usual assumptions about the incompatibility of queer life and left-wing commitment, which typically overemphasise the vacillations of Spender and Auden.

Despite the resurgence of interest in Warner, Ackland has remained an enigmatic figure, more castigated for her poor treatment of Warner than appreciated as an important writer in her own right. The critical failure of Warner and Ackland's jointly authored volume of poetry *Whether a Dove or Seagull* (1933), typically attributed to Ackland's supposedly weaker contributions, can be seen as symptomatic of the ways in which literary collaboration was less available to female writers during the period. Ackland's own work, in fact, deserves more attention: not only her poetry but her leftist journalism, which was at the time widely praised. For instance, the main communist publisher in Britain during the period, Martin Lawrence, published an expanded edition of her columns for *Left Review*, entitled *Country Dealings* (1937). Ackland's idiosyncratically effective perspective in these essays was critically formed by her unconventional gender performance. Somewhat like Stephen Gordon, the protagonist of *The Well of Loneliness*, she sometimes dressed like a country gentleman and at others like a poacher; her investigations into rural injustice were enabled and shaped by this presentation as she was able to interview rural people who were at turns comforted and disquieted by her appearance. Ackland's leftist journalism thus further destabilises dominant perceptions in its imbrication of queer experience and political engagement, not opposed but rather symbiotic in her fearless attacks on rural systems of privilege.

Respectable Futures?

Alongside Spender's Cold War retrenchment, Auden and Isherwood's decision to move to the United States in 1939 has often been taken to reveal the extent to which the Auden group's commitment to radical politics was shaky at best. When the pair left, and remained following the outbreak of war, a variety of voices from both right and left in Britain castigated them for desertion of their home country at its hour of need. Homosexuality was, of course, illegal in Britain until 1967, and, indeed, Isherwood's attempt in 1934 to bring back his German partner Heinz was blocked by customs officials who discovered their correspondence. Moreover, having removed the sodomy statute from its constitution in 1918, Soviet Russia under Stalin reversed this bold move, recriminalising male homosexuality in 1934. If, as Marx famously declared in the *Communist Manifesto*, 'the working men have no country' then this was certainly true of the queer, and Auden and Isherwood's move should not be viewed in terms of an escape or shirking of duty. It is better seen as an example of what we might call a *queer nomadism*, one episode in the series of migrations queer people have made since at least the nineteenth century in the face of repressive legislation and oppressive social forms.

Perhaps the most memorably unfair depiction of Isherwood and Auden's departure for the United States in 1939 comes in Evelyn Waugh's 1942 novel *Put Out More Flags*. Waugh gives the pair the monikers 'Parsnip and Pimpernel', and depicts their departure in a set piece deriding the radical politics of the 1930s. A 'cross, red-headed girl in spectacles from the London School of Economics' remarks that '"What I don't see is how these two can claim to be *Contemporary* if they run away from the biggest event in contemporary history. They were contemporary enough about Spain when no one threatened to come and bomb *them*."'[35] Waugh's novel goes on to narrate the wartime exile of the homosexual aesthete Ambrose Silk, who, in a clear reference to Isherwood, had a lover in Germany named Hans whom, like Isherwood, he tried in vain to save from the Nazis. Waugh continues this emphasis in *Brideshead Revisited*

(1946), in Sebastian Flyte's draft-dodging German lover, described as a 'thoroughly bad hat'.[36] While Alan Sinfield's critique may slightly over-emphasise quite how hateful Waugh's depiction is, it is certainly unfortunate that Waugh's novels have come to play such a prominent part in how interwar queer writers are viewed.[37] In particular, as has been astutely mapped by Sinfield, the stereotype of an effeminate male upper- or upper-middle-class homosexual promoted by Waugh and others such as George Orwell came to dominate post-war conceptions of the literary establishment, set in opposition to the doughty proletarian or lower-middle-class hero of much of the period's writing.

From around the 1950s onwards, however, a new figure emerged in the popular imagination, even as persecution of queers mounted: the 'respectable homosexual', a personage whose entrance on the British scene has undoubtedly influenced and indeed was shaped by the Auden group's growing reputation.[38] The 1957 inquiry into female prostitution and male homosexuality known as the Wolfenden Report recommended the decriminalisation of homosexual acts between consenting males in private, which was then enacted into law in 1967. The Report simultaneously shaped a limited tolerance toward the respectable homosexual and yet multiplied and underscored further sites of abjection (for instance, promiscuous and/or non-normative gender performing homosexual and bisexual men) and erasure (lesbian women, for example, who were not even in the purview of the report). Emerging in response to pervasive fears about the sturdiness of the mid-century family in the face of supposedly rising rates of prostitution and homosexual promiscuity, Wolfenden neutralised the threat of the queer man to the family by domesticating his dangerously public desires and practices.

It is always difficult – indeed perhaps even inadvisable – to gauge the traffic between literary and social history with any precision, but some remarks may be ventured in conclusion. First, it is clear that, as prominent bourgeois male queers, the Auden group were still central cultural figures, more or less respectable homosexuals (or, officially, former bisexual, in the case of Spender, who was rewarded with a knighthood in due course). Tellingly, Auden was to go on in private to refer to his partnership with the American poet and librettist Chester Kallman as a marriage, not only placing him, if uneasily, within a narrative of mid-century respectability but also foreshadowing the dominant concern of mainstream contemporary gay rights. The 1949 publication of Dorothy Strachey's lesbian novel *Olivia* meanwhile complicates the question of the relative visibility of male and female homosexuality in the post-war period. Composed in 1932, and set in the early 1880s, Strachey's novel narrates the sexual awakening of a young woman attending a boarding school in France, and the disruption of two teachers' Boston marriage (the co-habitation of two women traditionally seen in terms that occlude lesbian sexuality) by her more openly articulated desires.

Like Forster's *Maurice*, and the Auden group's various memoirs, Strachey's novel demonstrates the ways in which queer literary history works in complex relays, never simply tracking a progressivist history of so-called social attitudes but rather through a series of complex imbrications between publishing cultures, literary publics, and queer practices and formations. There is no doubt that these texts of the 1930s were produced under conditions of censorship, repression, and vilification; from the perspective of post-Stonewall discourses of disclosure and identity they may initially appear rather tame and closeted. Yet this is surely not the whole story. For such an appearance of mere timidity itself indicates that there still remains much crucial literary-historical work to be done on this insistently pink decade – work that must not only draw on but also contribute to the body of contemporary theoretical knowledge known as queer theory.

Notes

1. *Oxford English Dictionary* [hereafter *OED*], queer, adj. 3.
2. Christopher Isherwood, *The Berlin Stories* (New York: New Directions, 2008), pp. 192–3. The *OED* actually cites a short part of Isherwood's passage but fails to recognise the resignification it enacts when read as a whole.
3. Both these tendencies are in evidence in Valentine Cunningham's *British Writers of the Thirties* (Oxford: Oxford University Press, 1988), a well-known and encyclopaedic study that is, however, very weak on queer writing. Paul Fussell's account of Auden and Isherwood's travel writing is a particularly salient example of the tendency to see these writers' camp style as insufficiently serious: see his *Abroad: British Literary Traveling Between the Wars* (New York and Oxford: Oxford University Press, 1980), pp. 219–20.
4. Michel Foucault, *History of Sexuality, Volume I: An Introduction*, trans. Robert Utley (New York: Vintage, 1990), pp. 75–132.
5. Foucault, *History of Sexuality*, p. 17.
6. Radclyffe Hall, *The Well of Loneliness* (Garden City, NY: The Sun Dial Press, 1928).
7. See Laura Doan, *Fashioning Sapphism: The Origins of a Modern English Lesbian Culture* (New York: Columbia University Press, 2001), pp. 1–30.
8. Jodie Medd, *Lesbian Scandal and the Culture of Modernism* (Cambridge: Cambridge University Press, 2012), pp. 160–76.
9. Medd, *Lesbian Scandal*, pp. 177–91.

10. See Adam Parkes, *Modernism and the Theater of Censorship* (Oxford: Oxford University Press, 1996), p. 210, n. 55.

11. See John Lehmann, *The Whispering Gallery: Autobiography I* (London: Longman, 1955).

12. Virginia Woolf, *Orlando* (New York and London: Harcourt Brace, 1956), p. 309. Moreover, a complaint was in fact made about the text's presentation of gender and sexuality: see Celia Marshik, *British Modernism and Censorship* (Cambridge: Cambridge University Press, 2006), p. 118.

13. E. M. Forster, *Maurice* (New York: Norton, 1971), p. 229.

14. Christopher Isherwood, *Christopher and His Kind* (Minneapolis: University of Minnesota Press, 2001), p. 126, emphasis in original; Forster, *Maurice*, dedication page.

15. See, inter alia, Carola M. Kaplan, '"The Wandering Stopped": An Interview with Christopher Isherwood', in *The Isherwood Century: Essays on the Life and Work of Christopher Isherwood* ed. by James J. Berg and Chris Freeman (Madison: University of Wisconsin Press, 2001), pp. 259–82 (pp. 276–77), and *Christopher and His Kind*, p. 105.

16. See Isherwood, *Christopher and His Kind*; Norman Page, *Auden and Isherwood: The Berlin Years* (London: Macmillan, 1998); Peter Firchow, *Strange Meetings: Anglo-German Literary Encounters, 1910–1960* (Washington, DC: Catholic University of America Press, 2008); and Peter Parker, *Isherwood: A Life* (London: Picador, 2004).

17. For a useful recent study of Weimar Berlin sexual politics, see Laurie Marhoefer, *Sex and the Weimar Republic: German Homosexual Emancipation and the Rise of the Nazis* (Toronto: University of Toronto Press, 2015); see also *Gay Men and the Sexual History of the Political Left*, ed. by Gert Hekma et al. (New York: Harrington Press, 1995).

18. W. H. Auden, 'To a Writer on His Birthday', *New Verse*, 17 (October–November 1935), p. 9.

19. Ibid., p. 7.

20. W. H. Auden, Notebook Entry, 1964–65, in *'In Solitude, For Company': W.H. Auden After 1940, Unpublished Prose and Recent Criticism*, ed. by Katherine Bucknell and Nicholas Jenkins (Oxford: Clarendon Press, 1995), p. 53.

21. For an influential early essay tracing Brecht's influence on Auden and Isherwood, see Martin Esslin, 'Brecht and the English Theater', *Tulane Drama Review*, 11.2 (1966), 63–70; Esslin's position has, however, been opposed: see Ronald Gray, *Brecht The Dramatist* (Cambridge: Cambridge University Press, 1976), p. 191.

22. John Henry Mackay, *The Hustler: The Story of a Nameless Love from Friedrich Street*, trans. Hubert Kennedy (Boston: Alyson Publications, 1985), back cover.

23. Isherwood, *Christopher and His Kind*, p. 3.

24. Ibid., pp. 15–35.

25. See, for instance, Jonathan Fryer, 'Sexuality in Isherwood', *Twentieth Century Literature*, 22.3 (1976), 343–53; and Jamie Carr, *Queer Times: Christopher Isherwood's Modernity* (London: Routledge, 2006).

26. For a critique of this position and a fuller discussion of Isherwood's blend of leftist and queer writing in Berlin, see Glyn Salton-Cox, 'Boy Meets Camera: Christopher Isherwood, Sergei Tretiakov, and the Queer Potential of the First Five-Year Plan', *MLQ*, 76.4 (2015), 465–90.

27. Andrew O'Hagan, 'From Soup to Fish', review of Matthew Spender, *A House in St John's Wood: In Search of My Parents, London Review of Books*, 37.2 (17 December 2015), p. 9. For a wry look back at Spender and his circle, see also T. C. Worsley's fictionalised 1971 memoir *Fellow Travellers* (London: Gay Modern Classics, 1984).

28. Stephen Spender, *World Within World: The Autobiography of Stephen Spender* (London: Faber and Faber, 1977), pp. 211–12, 250–5, inter alia; and *The God That Failed*, ed. by Richard Crossman (New York: Bantam Books, 1966), pp. 208–48.

29. See, respectively, John Sutherland, *Stephen Spender: The Authorized Biography* (London: Penguin, 2005), p. 439; and James Smith, *British Writers and MI5 Surveillance, 1930–1960* (Cambridge: Cambridge University Press, 2013), pp. 73–9.

30. Janet Montefiore has been a major voice in this recuperative project: see her *Men and Women Writers of the 1930s: The Dangerous Flood of History* (London: Routledge, 1996) and Terry Castle, *The Apparitional Lesbian: Female Homosexuality and Modern Culture* (New York: Columbia University Press, 1993).

31. Elizabeth English, *Lesbian Modernism: Censorship, Sexuality, and Genre Fiction* (Edinburgh: Edinburgh University Press, 2015), p. 17.

32. See Glyn Salton-Cox, *Queer Communism and the Ministry of Love: Sexual Revolution in British Writing of the 1930s* (Edinburgh: Edinburgh University Press, 2018), pp. 3–4.

33. Claire Harman's edition of Sylvia Townsend Warner's diaries and her biography redact much radical material: see *The Diaries of Sylvia Townsend Warner*, ed. by Claire Harman (London: Virago, 1994), and Harman, *Sylvia Townsend Warner: A Biography* (London: Chatto and Windus, 1989). For a much fuller picture, see Wendy Mulford, *This Narrow Place: Sylvia Townsend Warner and Valentine Ackland: Life, Letters and Politics, 1930–1951* (London: Pandora, 1988); see also Arnold Rattenbury, 'Literature, Lying and Sober Truth: Attitudes to the Work of Patrick Hamilton and Sylvia Townsend Warner', in *Writing and Radicalism*, ed. by John Lucas (London and New York: Longman, 1996), pp. 201–44 (pp. 201–35).

34. See, inter alia, Gay Wachman, *Lesbian Empire: Radical Crosswriting in the Twenties* (New Brunswick, NJ and London: Rutgers University Press, 2001), pp. 71–102; Castle, *The Apparitional Lesbian*, pp. 74–91; Heather Love, *Feeling Backward: Loss and the Politics of Queer History* (Cambridge, MA: Harvard University Press), pp. 129–45; and Melanie Micir, '"Living in two tenses": On the Intimate Archives of Sylvia Townsend Warner', *Journal of Modern Literature*, 36.1 (2012), 119–31.

35. Evelyn Waugh, *Put Out More Flags*, in *Decline and Fall, Black Mischief, A Handful of Dust, Scoop, Put Out More Flags, and Brideshead Revisited* (London: Heineman, 1977), pp. 535–664 (p. 556).

36. Waugh, *Brideshead Revisited*, in Ibid., pp. 665–864 (p. 787).
37. Alan Sinfield, *Literature, Politics and Culture in Postwar Britain* (London: Continuum, 2004), pp. 68–9.
38. See Matthew Houlbrook, *Queer London: Pleasures and Perils in the Sexual Metropolis* (Chicago: University of Chicago Press, 2006).

CHAPTER 12

Remembering and Imagining War

Phyllis Lassner

Although the First and Second World Wars were fought a generation apart, their historical, ethical, and political meanings continue to be debated. The terms concern whether both wars should be regarded as constituting a continuous battle for political and cultural supremacy or as distinct events, as either one battle bleeding into another with a brief interruption or as the Second World War erupting from unresolved, conflicting ideologies and interests carried over from the First. Squeezed between these perspectives is the decade of the 1930s in which memories of the 1914–18 war and anxieties about another conflagration were troubled further by the economic and social consequences of the Great Depression that devastated people's lives on both sides of the divide. The 1930s in Britain was a war between, in which political, social, and cultural debates served as the only available weapons of defence against pervasive doubts about both the unstable present and the possibility of a stable future. Traumatic memories, the alienations of the present, and fears of a Second World War could be said to coalesce in Britain as a literature of posttraumatic, unsettling narrative forms – and it is this literature that this chapter will seek to address. I borrow the term 'posttraumatic' from Joshua Hirsch, who applies it to post-Holocaust films. The term is also productive for discussion of 1930s First World War memoirs because they also adopt 'modernist forms of narration that formally repeat the traumatic structure of the experience of witnessing the events themselves'.[1]

As Victoria Stewart has proffered, in its 'structural and thematic functions', dramatising 'remembering, mis-remembering, and forgetting', memory played several important roles in interwar writing, including disrupting divisions between literary or modernist fiction and middlebrow and popular fiction and their representations of subjectivity.[2] By the 1930s, Virginia Woolf had already made memory her subject, revising the conventions of realist characterisation and linear temporality to create narratives of interiority where the present tangles with the past and each impinges on the other as determinants of subjectivity. This entanglement offered creative opportunities to reimagine a narrative's chronological development as multidirectional and across the spectrum of literary and popular writing, with memory driving the consciousness and structures of the writing self and of fictional characters and plots.

Janet Montefiore asserts that 'Any useful account of the 1930s must begin with politics'.[3] The writers considered in this chapter would agree, especially because they saw politics as integral to both domestic and public spheres and relationships. As Storm Jameson illustrated in her 1932 novel *That Was Yesterday* and in her 1933 memoir *No Time Like the Present*, marriage and women's everyday life at home or at work were deeply affected by men's mouldering psychological and physical scars from the First World War. In his discussion of Jameson's 1930s writing, Charles Andrews concludes that the war affected Jameson, her family, and community so deeply 'that every memory is lacerated by violence'.[4] In these texts, the past is not remembered in isolation from the present but rather, as Victoria Stewart notes, engages 'with the process by which the past is revisited or recovered'.[5] A telling example of fictionalising this process is Storm Jameson's *Mirror in Darkness* trilogy, consisting of *Company Parade* (1934), *Love in Winter* (1935), and *None Turn Back* (1936). Its 1920s setting embeds conditions and responses to the political, social, and economic crises of the 1930s so that the two decades become coterminous, with the 1930s still bearing the scars of the Great War. This posttraumatic fiction is all the more affecting for its abiding sense that the Great War created a crisis relationship between the nation's citizens and the enclaves of industry, public media, and the government. The overlapping historical sites of the trilogy also suggest that the 1930s does not stand alone in British cultural history but rather represents a multifaceted nexus of commingled and disjunctive relations comprising memory, foretelling, and their shaping of the present.

Whereas Wilfred Owen's wartime poems express the anguish of his ambivalence towards battle as he grappled with it, a decade had to pass before the experiences of the First World War would crystallise into writing that mediated between the immediacy and self-questioning memory of men's posttraumatic ambivalence. The publication in 1928 of Siegfried Sassoon's *Memoirs of a Foxhunting Man*, R. C. Sherriff's play *Journey's End*, and Edmund Blunden's *Undertones of War* was followed in 1929 by Robert Graves's *Goodbye to All That* and Richard Aldington's *Death of a Hero*. Filtered through different genres and sites of action and remembering, the role of memory and its interplay with the present are crucial to the constructions of narrators' distinct voices. The past is inter-woven into writing in the present to register the physical and psychological impact of the ill-conceived strategies, punitive conditions, and horrific casualties of trench warfare on the memoirists' consciousness of the stulti-fying and shifting aftermath. Read together, this memory work coalesces in an epic rendering of the nation's collective aesthetic and moral conscience, tethering its readers and future writers to the humanity of the otherwise 'unknown soldier'. Written on the cusp of an unsettling decade, memoirs of the First World War carry forward an imperative to enter the tremulous spaces of a cataclysmic history and in its most searing challenge, to translate its responsibilities into the cultural production of Britain's 1930s.

Fragments of Memory

A double backward glance informs the Great War memoirs of Guy Chapman, publisher, historian, author, and husband of Storm Jameson. A veteran of the trenches, he published his memoir of fighting in France with the British New Army, *A Passionate Prodigality*, in 1933, but in a preface to the first American edition in 1966 he confessed to understanding the impact of his wartime experience only as a result of looking back at his earlier recorded memory. As a result of this re-remembering and rereading, he discovered that he 'hated war, was often terrified, but [he] was irrevocably bonded with those in the trenches, and like others of his kind, loathed the times behind the lines for their triviality and *lack* of reality'.[6] Neither Chapman's memoir nor his 1966 preface traces a process of healing or working through but rather the intensifying sense of loss of 'an attachment, the sentiment of belonging to a living entity and, of course its death'.[7] The memoir's subtitle, *Fragments of Autobiography*, suggests links to other Great War memoirs that became models of modernist narrative imperatives. If one could refer to lessons from the trenches, they would include the rejection of imparting coherent psychological or ethical meaning to the deaths of bodies and spirit. The very idea of forming holistic responses was destroyed in the mud and mess of body parts and shell shock. What one could grasp and narrate were the broken, unresolved paradoxes of felt experience that Chapman later interpreted as 'illuminat[ing] the enormous fascination of war, the repulsion and attraction, the sharpening of awareness, and as one became familiar with one's surroundings an apprehension which was not fear – a quickening rather'.[8]

Over the course of stalled and catastrophic battles, coherence for Chapman emerges with 'the touchstone of experience, the necessary touch of pride' that creates a 'tradition we had made for ourselves', and that 'was welded into a homogeneous unit'.[9] That this battleground bonding motivated the men to keep fighting, there is no doubt, as so many combatants then and now have attested. The experience also alienated them from nostalgic memories of pre-war optimism and assumptions about the comforts of home and family, as Storm Jameson has recorded in her own two-volume autobiography *Journey From the North* (1969). Chapman ponders the disjunction between feeling at home with his comrades and estrangement from home in England:

> It was – I think it still is – impossible to make those who had no experience of this war understand it, as it must be understood, through all the senses. Sitting in a shelter of sandbags and corrugated iron, shivering with cold, [. . .] hearing the sky rent by explosions and hammered by gun-fire, smelling the hundred stenches [. . .] fixed in the mud, tasting a tongue sour with perpetual tobacco smoke, I let my mind retreat further and further from thoughts of home. I could find nothing to say in letters. All communication was as 'dissed' as though the lines had been broken by a shell.[10]

Returning to London, Chapman feels 'foreign' and 'hostility growing up between the soldiers abroad and the civilians and soldiers at home'.[11] War profiteering 'tainted civilian life', undermining the unequivocal patriotism and sense of belonging that combatants had pledged to the nation. But instead of disabling the creative and critical imaginations of the war's participants, disenchantment and alterity cohered as the muse of interwar writing.

Inspired by the profusion of men's war memoirs, Vera Brittain decided to write her own story of a woman's war. Compiling and editing her diaries and letters, she began writing *Testament of Youth* at the end of 1929, publishing it in 1933. Her memoir differs from Chapman's and other male-authored war stories in interlacing her pre-war personal life and her work nursing wounded and traumatised men with a sturdy sense of purpose. By contrast, Chapman's writing is infused with a destabilising tension between his unsteady subjectivity, meticulous observations, and loss of purpose. The only resolution he offers is recognition that the ghostly presence of the battleground shadows his post-war sense of self and relationships, including his marriage to Storm Jameson. Vera Brittain's memoir strains to achieve equilibrium between public and private impera-tives, but shows that whatever her domestic challenges, including her second pregnancy and difficult marriage, the loss of her brother and fiancé and nursing experiences dominate her post-war outlook, life, and goals. The result is paradoxical: she commits herself to pacifism while endowing the combatants with mythical stature and meaning.[12] As Victoria Stewart argues, because Brittain needed 'to believe that the loved ones she had lost in 1914–18 had not died in vain', she heroicised the military actions of her brother and his friends while at the same time 'condemning the patriotic militarism' that led to their deaths.[13] Even if unintended, this disequilibrium mirrors the struggle to extract meaning from the horrors of the war.

Testament of Youth is a feminist pacifist war chronicle that inserted a woman's experience and voice into a genre that had been dominated by men's perspectives. As Bella Brodzki and Celeste Schenck theorise, 'a woman autobiographer [. . .] uses displacement strategically'.[14] Brittain published an article in November 1929 that can be viewed as an acknowledgement of such displacement in its response to Richard Aldington's 'misogyny in *Death of a Hero*'. She excoriates Aldington's writing for pouring a 'cynical fury of scorn' on the wartime suffering of women.[15] *Testament of Youth* is written with the intention of incorporating a woman's war work and its effects into the historical account and therefore 'to write history in terms of personal life'.[16] Although Brittain here refers to women's domestic lives, this focus would omit men's experiences in the trenches, which even as she heroicised the soldier at arms, she either ignored or misunderstood. Key to this misunderstanding is Chapman's testimony that the trenches would become the domestic sphere of the fighting men, complete with deeply interdependent personal relationships and building what would be a succession of home spaces for the combatants. Yet, for Brittain, the personal does not stand alone but rather broadens the perspective of war memoirs by creating a synthesis of subjective response and historical documentation. As a result, the memoir is suffused with research she gleaned at the British Museum and the British Red Cross headquarters and with the analytical methods provided by her Oxford education in history and international relations.

Despite the memoir's wealth of historical documentation, Brittain was also very aware that it might call attention to an inherent limitation. Whatever suffering her memoir evoked, she knew that a woman's experience could not begin to approach the horrors of the trenches which had become the iconic representation of the war. Yet, as Deborah Gorham observes, Brittain's feminist approach led her to replace the irony, despair, and acceptance that shaped men's memoirs with critical analysis of the war's causes and, perhaps most distinctively, 'how to prevent a future war'.[17] Brittain's narrative method self-consciously diverges from the restrictive points of view that reflected men's claustrophobic experience and splintered understanding of what was happening to them. Instead of the dissonances that characterised their non-linear, disjunctive representations, *Testament of Youth* constructs coherence by merging Brittain's immediate and analytical responses to her liminal position as a non-combatant nurse on the home front. Brittain's war memoir became a bestseller, fulfilling middlebrow narrative expectations with its accessible language and form and unambiguous moral conclusions. Yet, as recent studies of the middlebrow demonstrate, popularity and accessibility do not preclude audacious narrative experiment.[18] The graphic realism and narrative progression of *Testament of Youth* are conveyed in a feminist voice and perspective that assert the presence of women in war stories as expanding and complicating the traditional terrain of battle memoirs.

Transferred from the home-front nursing experience to the brutal edges of the battleground, Helen Zenna Smith's 1930 novel *Not So Quiet: Stepdaughters of War* dramatises the marginalised memories of women ambulance drivers on the Western Front. A feminist response to Erich Maria Remarque's novel *All Quiet on the Western Front*, which was published the previous year, Smith's novel also differs radically from the accounts of Vera Brittain and Guy Chapman. *Not So Quiet* fictionalises the war diary of Winifred Constance Young by interpreting the diary's present tense as posttraumatic fiction, recounting the traumatising experience of transporting combatants' mangled bodies as never-ending, as though experience and memory are indistinguishable. Smith's representation of her pacifism also differs from Brittain's in its monotonal, unequivocal ferocity. As Elizabeth Maslen observes of *Not So Quiet*: 'Raw emotion is expressed throughout, loss of faith in things human and divine.'[19] The novel's disjointed sentences evoke the women's unrelieved desperation, demonstrating the urgency of their work, their tense, sometimes antipathetic relations with each other, and breathless, choking attempts to overcome their lack of viable outlets in the past and present. Their grunting expletives become metonyms of their experiences and memories of the horrors they faced.

Situating the women as perennial outsiders, the novel presents these horrors as coterminous with deeply affecting class conflicts and the character of a lesbian whose psychological and social disaffections mirror the chaos of the battleground. Reading men's battleground memoirs alongside women's responses offers a comprehensive perspective in which women's memories no longer speak from the margins of war but intervene to take an equally significant place in the discourses of Great War memory and British cultural production of the 1930s.

Debating a New Danger: The Growing Shadow

Inscribing memories of the Great War produced new interpretations of the war's experiences but did not offer healing from its traumas. Instead, the losses haunted survivors, producing a sense of the past that overwhelmed the nation's ability to move forward. An example of this ghostliness is the 1936 novel by Agatha Christie, *Murder in Mesopotamia*, where a First World War combatant unsettles the narrative's chronology and produces terror.[20] Although he is assumed lost in battle, he is also suspected of living in disguise and threatening a traumatised coterie of archaeologists. With metaphorical resonance, the archaeological efforts to unearth an ancient civilisation are stalled by the overpowering presence of the First World War. As the 1930s wore on, this presence shadowed debates about responding to the rise of fascism in Europe and in Britain. For Vera Brittain, Virginia Woolf, and other writers, fascism's threats were both overwhelmed and exacerbated by fears that another world war would produce an intractable militarist culture in Britain and greater numbers of human losses. In 1934, Brittain published an essay, 'Can the Women of the World Stop War?', that acknowledged 'international crises in every part of this earth'. But instead of turning to established international groups for guidance or intervention, she argued that 'women might play [a part] in the prevention of war', representing 'a new element in politics'.[21] For others, including Rebecca West and George Orwell, the loss of national sovereignty, cultural integrity, and individual freedoms demanded the defeat of fascism. The question of how the international community could resist or defeat this growing threat and support cooperative efforts to sustain or build democratic institutions was addressed in a 1934 collection of essays edited by Storm Jameson, *Challenge to Death*. Fifteen contributors, including Vera Brittain, her husband, political scientist George Catlin, Guy Chapman, the evolutionary scientist Julian Huxley, and writer J. B. Priestley, represented a wide range of views and proposals. Rebecca West's essay took into account the emotional tug of nationalist identification, but argued that 'The test of real and valuable nationalism is to avail oneself of the tradition of one's country; and it happens that internationalism is one of the most ancient and firmly established elements in our [British] tradition.'[22]

Resistance to fascism began with the emergence of the British Union of Fascists (BUF) on British soil. Led by the charismatic Member of Parliament Oswald Mosley, the BUF began to organise rallies and marches in 1934 that proclaimed renewed power for Britain at home and on the world stage. Mosley threatened Britain's democratic stability by drawing on the supremacist, racist, and antisemitic edicts of Nazi Germany and Fascist Italy as a nationalist goal. As Mia Spiro's chapter in this volume addresses in detail, this rise of fascism challenged and provoked British writers in numerous ways, ranging from debates over the forms and contents of literature to the practical steps authors could take in the anti-fascist struggle. In this chapter, I am interested in how this resistance played out in certain modes of self-reflexive writing on conflict, and how this became part of the decade's corpus of posttraumatic war writing.

The decade saw a succession of dystopias concerned about the lure of fascism, initiated by Naomi Mitchison in her 1935 novel *We Have Been Warned*. Demonstrating the narrative fluidity of the genre, these dystopias predicted Britain's fate if fascism gained complete control of the government and the lives of its citizens. Offering a different perspective from that of Brittain, Orwell, and Woolf, Mitchison, who identified herself as a socialist, emphasised the dangerous attraction to power by both men and women whose social and economic conditions had marginalised them within British society. *We Have Been Warned* is shaped by the competing voices of men and women who envision self-determination and political equality as a contest between pacifism and militarism but who reconcile when their political desires are overwhelmed by a fascist counter-revolution.[23] The novel's prescience derives from its analysis of interwar tensions in British political culture that Mitchison relates to European fascism, which she had witnessed first-hand in her travels to Vienna in 1934, recounted in her *Vienna Diary* (1934). In 1938, Mitchison published her theory that economic equity was necessary to create a just society in *The Moral Basis of Politics*.[24]

Eschewing British exceptionalism, Mitchison's dystopia dramatises the weaknesses of British political ideologies and parties as deriving from endless parliamentary debates that diffuse the nation's sense of purpose and lose touch with its history of enlightened and humane progress. With no end in sight to this political devolution, *We Have Been Warned* imagines dire consequences – the inability of the government to withstand the more powerful attractions of fascism. Like other dystopias of the decade, including Storm Jameson's 1936 *In the Second Year* and Katharine Burdekin's 1937 *Swastika Night*, *We Have Been Warned* experiments narratively with points of view expressing simultaneous cooperation and conflict. Deploying and revising realist conventions, these writers offer graphic and polemical arguments that gender and economic inequalities threaten a turn to fascism whose rhetoric promised national unity and order. Their dystopias express yearning for political and moral progressivism in the face of the government's continuing unresolved concerns about intervention in Britain's social and economic instability and Europe's fascist turmoil. But rather than participate in policy-driven debates, these writers address the relationship between British and fascist political and social ideologies by envisioning the failure of parliamentary democracy to prevail.

For other writers, the outbreak of the Spanish Civil War in 1936, with Germany aiding General Franco's fascist takeover and the Soviet Union intervening on behalf of the Republicans, became the testing ground for these disparate responses to the growing instability and threat of a new world war. In his epic poem *Autumn Journal*, Louis MacNeice declared that the concerns of the 1930s climaxed in the 'frontier on the Spanish front' (Section VI), and it is the writing of George Orwell that came to most prominently echo and reconfigure this complex and shifting ground of debate. Even today, as Antony Shuttleworth shows, claims are made for and against Orwell's critical writing, concerning whether his investigations into the era's economic, social, and geopolitical conflicts produce conservative or progressive insights.[25] In the 1930s, however, Orwell's concern with the often-subliminal persuasive power of language and rhetoric became an instrument of political critique, applied incisively to propaganda and military threats to British and European democracies. Published in 1938, Orwell's self-reflective reportage of the Spanish Civil War, *Homage to Catalonia*, dissects 'the shifting barrier between mythic and reliable representations of conflict [as] a casualty of war'.[26] A key insight that applies to the multilayered and agonised vacillations of anti-fascist debates is that this war is being fought on ideological grounds. All sides engaged in the war zones and in writing argue their cases as though fascism and democracy are definitive terms and systems that are transparent in intended meaning and understanding. Yet this transparency turns out to be another rhetorical device, and one that critics apply to Orwell's exposition, which is complicated by his dual positions as reporter and combatant. Orwell, however, writes self-consciously about the impossibility of holding an objective, neutral position as a combatant: 'It is difficult to be certain about anything except what you have seen with your own eyes, and consciously or unconsciously everyone writes as a partisan.'[27] His own position solidified when he and his wife, Eileen O'Shaughnessy, barely

escaped Barcelona during the communist purges and he thereafter identified himself as a socialist opposed to Stalinist communism.

Homage to Catalonia was rejected by Orwell's publisher, Victor
Gollancz, who believed 'as did many people on the Left, that everything
should be sacrificed in order to preserve a common front against the rise of
Fascism'.[28] The internal debates in Orwell's writing represented the splintered responses within the left, evidenced in the solidified anti-war position
of the Peace Pledge Union led by Dick Sheppard and the interventionist
stances of some writers. For example, Phyllis Bottome and Storm Jameson,
who had both witnessed Nazi Germany's persecution of its deemed undesirables and its expansionist takeovers, felt compelled by empathy for
Hitler's victims to abandon their pacifism. In 1937, Bottome published
her anti-Nazi novel *The Mortal Storm*, which used a family melodrama to
depict the Nazis' persecution of the Jews and, in effect, called for the
Western democracies to rally to their cause and defeat Nazism.[29] That
same year, Eric Ambler published his first spy thriller, *Background to
Danger*, set in Central Europe, depicting the brutal actions of fascist
henchmen, the victimisation of Jews, and the reluctance to believe their
stories. In response, Ambler's novel represents the voices of various witnesses to argue for the defeat of fascism and Nazism and, in so doing,
reimagines conventions of the spy thriller as political critique.[30]

For such British writers as Orwell, E. M. Forster, and Virginia Woolf,
resistance to fascism was not a unified or free-standing issue but intertwined with such social concerns as patriotism and the meanings of
citizenship and belonging, women's place, roles, and rights in British
society, and the nation's ethical and political relationship to the fate of
Europe. Woolf's 1938 polemical treatise *Three Guineas,* written in agonised
response to the developing tragedy of the Spanish Civil War, locates fascist
power in an elongated history of patriarchal domination and the silencing
of women's voices. Although she sympathised with the Spanish
Republican efforts to fight for an equitable political and social culture,
her nephew's death in the war reinforced her pacifism that had responded
to the losses of the First World War and remained a searing memory.
Woolf's vision of a militarist male-dominated society extended from
Britain throughout Europe, arguing that fascism was encouraged by social
and cultural traditions that 'shut out and shut up' those who were outsiders
to the dominant male 'advance guard'.[31] That same year, E. M. Forster
published 'What I Believe', a confessional essay that argued that interper-
sonal relations were the testing ground for a democratic society based on
mutual sympathy and tolerance. Even when force was used by the State to

defend itself, he insisted that individual liberties must not be sacrificed. He would broadcast these views on BBC radio in 1940 once Britain was at war.

Historian Eric Hobsbawm argues that situating the Spanish Civil War as key to understanding 'the anti-fascist era, we have to bear in mind two things: the failure actually to resist fascism and the disproportionate success of anti-fascist mobilisation among Europe's intellectuals'.[32] Among British writers in the 1930s, many of those who expressed impassioned anti-fascism had their eyes on the fate of those already condemned by Nazi Germany to persecution, expulsion, and murder. Their writing would appear in letters to newspapers and magazines, to each other, in radio broadcasts, and popular and literary fiction.

Imagining the Second World War

In her essay 'Writing in the Margin: 1939', Storm Jameson argued that Britain's fate in the struggle against fascism and Nazism was intertwined with that of Europe:

> [The Writer] cannot think in terms of destroying Hitlerism in one country, but only of saving the Europe of which England is a part [. . .]. He must not, in conscience, be turned from pursuing his imagination of this Europe to its bounds, and from thrusting it on people's notice. Even the griefs of the war must not turn him from this, which is half of his clear task. The rest is to experience despair as a stage in courage, pain as inescapable but a source of strength, the thought of defeat as a reminder that no Dark Age has outlasted, or can outlast, the unquenchable energy and curiosity of the mind.[33]

While such celebrated writers as W. H. Auden and Christopher Isherwood fled the encroachment of war to settle in the United States, Storm Jameson used her office as President of British PEN to rally, as did Rebecca West, on behalf of Hitler's targeted victims. Others used their writing to imagine Europe's fate as necessary to Britain's moral consciousness. In 1937, Katharine Burdekin's dystopia *Swastika Night* imagined a world 700 years in the future decimated and dominated by the Third Reich. Yet the German setting exposes the self-destructiveness of Nazi ideology and practice. Caged as breeders, disallowed all forms of self-determination, women's bodies have rebelled and can no longer produce male warriors. Only at the end, when an English worker frees his sexual partner, are possibilities for individual and collective freedom envisioned.

Rex Warner's 1937 political fable *The Wild Goose Chase* represents disquiet about the desire for domestic reform and the search for a unified British cultural identity and sense of purpose as a response to the rise of European and British fascism. Warner creates three brothers whose mythic travels across a continent interweave revolutionary politics of public and private relations. Their encounters with kings and philosophers, artists and soldiers question British ideologies of pragmatism and conservatism as bulwarks against fascism. Suggesting a fractured Europe, Warner's imaginary continent questions whether pacifism is a viable alternative to aggression in an anti-fascist struggle. Warner also delved into this question in his 1938 novel *The Professor* and, once most of Europe was Nazi occupied, he anticipated a British fascist regime in his 1941 novel *The Aerodrome*. Unlike the anti-utopias of Mitchison and Burdekin, Warner does not engage gender relations in his political critique. Instead, *The Wild Goose Chase* reinscribes women's traditional roles as subordinate to men's political consciousness. By contrast, Stevie Smith's 1938 surrealist spy fiction *Over the Frontier* features a woman protagonist whose transformation into a warrior questions conventional dichotomies between masculine aggression and feminine compliance.[34] Androgynously named, Pompey travels into Germany, where it is impossible to avoid the totalising militarism of a fascist state. Donning military gear, she crosses a desolate battleground that recalls the devastations of the trenches and anticipates the annihilations perpetrated by the Third Reich. Traversing a defamiliarising landscape, a place devoid of welcoming landmarks, the legitimacy of belonging is lacerated. Nonetheless, even as she represents a call to defeat the Axis powers, her transformation calls attention to the unstoppable momentum of militarism as ideology and action.

The ambivalence of Stevie Smith's rallying cry to defeat fascism and anxiety about an indomitable militarism is mirrored in the divisions among other writers. Memories of the Great War's human losses jostled with recognition that, by 1938, the racialist laws enforced by the Third Reich were in full swing, targeting innocent adults and children throughout Central Europe for deportation, incarceration, and murder. The political and ethical relationship between Britain and Europe became a grave concern for those writers confronting British xenophobia and antisemitism as well as the racialist ideologies, policies, and practices of fascist Europe. From the heart of Nazi Europe, Christopher Isherwood's 1939 story collection *Goodbye to Berlin* offers a first-hand account of witnessing Jewish friends disappearing into the hands of the Gestapo. His is also one of the only accounts of Nazi persecution of homosexuals who, like himself, had enjoyed a vibrant culture in interwar Berlin. Standing helplessly aside, Isherwood's narrator raises questions about the role of bystanders or onlookers, from individual to national responsibility.[35]

Clashes between Britain's social stability, individual political responsibility, and the fate of Nazism's Jewish victims propel the plots of Pamela Frankau's 1939 novel *The Devil We Know* and Elizabeth Bowen's 1935 *House in Paris*. Frankau's novel features a young Jewish filmmaker, Philip Meyer, who emigrated to Britain as a child and, despite his later professional success, suffers the debilitating effects of having internalised the social and cultural antisemitism that not only engulfed Europe but also afflicted his host nation.[36] Frankau's confrontation with British antisemitism relates to Elizabeth Bowen's 1935 novel *The House in Paris* where a European refugee, Max Ebhart, suffers a fractured sense of self in being unwanted everywhere. Half-French and half-Jewish, but with no claim to any national belonging and protection, Max discovers only rejection in Britain and France. Depicting a range of transnational antisemitic sites, in various narrative styles, from the British drawing room to a gothic house in Paris, this novel, like Frankau's *The Devil We Know*, is prescient in depicting the lethal internalisation of psychological and social persecution. With no place to thrive, Bowen's wandering Jew is entrapped by displacement and commits suicide. From an alternative perspective, Frankau's novel ends with an act that frees her Jewish protagonist while risking his life. He decides to return to Germany to attempt to rescue his disabled brother who would be targeted for extermination by Hitler's T4 programme to rid the nation of its subhuman, unproductive undesirables. The awakening of Meyers's political ethics is a call to reject xenophobic insularity and embrace empathy for the imperilled European Other.

In letters to editors, reportage, public speaking, and in aiding the rescue of the unwanted, Rebecca West, Phyllis Bottome, Storm Jameson, and Rose Macaulay publicly disavowed the British government's policies that disregarded the tragedies already taking place on the Continent. Like Vera Brittain, Rose Macaulay was a sponsor of the Peace Pledge Union, but, as atrocity stories from Nazi Germany escalated, she organised a public meeting, 'Writers declare against Fascism', explaining that 'The idea of this meeting is to protest against the fantastic & horrible suppressions of liberty of thought & expression tht [sic] Fascism entails, & to emphasise tht freedom is the only soil out of which any decent life, thought, or art, is likely to grow'.[37] Other writers expressed conflicted responses that rejected any form of state violence and fears of invasion and destruction. Such conflicted views appear in an exchange of letters between Rebecca West and Naomi Mitchison in the feminist periodical *Time and Tide* between

November 1939 and 6 January 1940. Although war against Germany had been declared on 3 September 1939, this was the period of anxious waiting, the 'phony war', until the Battle of Britain and the Blitz began in September 1940.[38] Whereas Mitchison worried that Britain's 'privileged classes' controlled 'our present war machine', West felt that 'this is a war fought by all concerned "for some freedom and against Fascism"'.[39] West agreed with Mitchison that Chamberlain's government served the interests of capitalist power and not ordinary citizens, but critiques her correspondent's neglect of Nazism's greater danger. The women of Glasgow were indeed victims of capitalist exploitation but, for West, it would be more tragic to 'pretend that a Glasgow working woman would not notice the difference if Hitler and Goering and Himmler were governing her life. Are concentration camps and Jew-baiting then nothing?'[40]

It was not long, however, before both writers, alongside others, recognised that, to activate their empathy for Britain's citizens as well as Germany's targeted victims, they needed to support the Allies' war effort. This support, however, did not end debates about the ethics of embarking on a global war. Once war was declared, British periodicals, newspapers, and the radio were filled with deep concerns about the nation's political and cultural relationship to Europe, the internment of refugees, and state security measures. The issues shifted along with the war's shifting sites, including the bombing of Britain, but the political and ethical engagement of the nation's writers and artists only intensified.

Notes

1. Joshua Hirsch, *Afterimage: Film, Trauma, and the Holocaust* (Philadelphia: Temple University Press, 2004), p. 3.
2. Victoria Stewart, *Narratives of Memory: British Writing of the 1940s* (Basingstoke: Palgrave Macmillan, 2007), pp. 1, 3.
3. Janet Montefiore, *Men and Women Writers of the 1930s: The Dangerous Flood of History* (London: Routledge, 1996), pp. 7–8.
4. Charles Andrews, *Writing Against War: Literature, Activism, and the British Peace Movement* (Evanston, IL: Northwestern University Press, 2017), p. 2.
5. Stewart, *Narratives of Memory*, p. 5.
6. Elizabeth Maslen, *Life in the Writings of Storm Jameson: A Biography* (Evanston, IL: Northwestern University Press, 2014), p. 117.
7. Guy Chapman, Preface to *A Passionate Prodigality: Fragments of Autobiography* (New York: Holt, Rinehart and Winston, 1966), n.p.
8. Ibid.
9. Ibid., p. 119.

10. Ibid, p. 138.

11. Ibid.

12. In 1918, Brittain published a group of elegiac poems, *Verses of a V.A.D.*, written in a patriotic-heroic register that was typical of the war years. See Claire Buck, 'First World War English Elegy and the Disavowal of Women's Sentimental Poetics', *English Literature in Transition 1880–1920*, 53.4 (2010), 431–50 (p. 432).

13. Stewart, *Narratives of Memory*, p. 45.

14. *Life/Lines: Theorizing Women's Autobiography*, ed. by Bella Brodzki and Celeste Schenck (Ithaca, NY: Cornell University Press, 1988), p. 11.

15. Deborah Gorham, *Vera Brittain: A Feminist Life* (Oxford: Blackwell, 1997), p. 224.

16. Ibid., p. 9.

17. Ibid., p. 233.

18. See, for example, the special journal issues of *Modernist Cultures*, 'Modernism and the Middlebrow', 6.1 (2011), ed. by Andrzej Gasiorek, Deborah Longworth, and Michael Valdez Moses; and *The Space Between: Literature and Culture 1914–1945*, 'Reading Sideways: Middlebrow and Modernism', 9.1 (2013), ed. by Phyllis Lassner, Ann Rea, and Genevieve Brassard.

19. Elizabeth Maslen, *Political and Social Issues in British Women's Fiction, 1928–1968* (Basingstoke: Palgrave Macmillan, 2001), p. 68.

20. I discuss this and other Christie novels of the 1930s in 'The Mysterious New Empire: Agatha Christie's Colonial Murders', in *At Home and Abroad in the Empire: British Women Write the 1930s*, ed. by Robin Hackett, Freda Hauser, and Gay Wachman (Newark: University of Delaware Press, 2009), pp. 31–50.

21. Vera Brittain, 'Can the Women of the World Stop War?', in *History in Our Hands*, ed. by Patrick Deane (London: Leicester University Press, 1998), pp. 69–73 (p. 70).

22. Rebecca West, 'The Necessity and Grandeur of the International Idea', in *Challenge to Death*, ed. by Storm Jameson (London: Constable, 1934), pp. 240–60 (p. 242).

23. Mitchison's memoir of 1920–1940, *You May Well Ask: A Memoir 1920–1940* (London: Fontana, 1986), expresses her desire to see 'economic liberation' produce 'a fairer world', in which people of all classes would live together equitably, but she opposed a socialist revolution that would confine her children while necessary change was implemented.

24. Mitchison's analysis in *The Moral Basis of Politics* suggests a critical approach to Virginia Woolf's *Three Guineas*, written a year earlier. See also Storm Jameson's essay 'New Documents', in her *Civil Journey* (London: Cassell, 1939), pp. 261–274, which argues for realistic accounts of working-poor women.

25. Antony Shuttleworth, 'The Real George Orwell', in *And in Our Time: Vision, Revision, and British Writing of the 1930s*, ed. by Antony Shuttleworth (Lewisburg: Bucknell University Press, 2003), pp. 204–20.

26. Ibid., p. 206.

27. George Orwell, *Homage to Catalonia* (New York: Harcourt, 1938), pp. 230–31. See Kristin Bluemel's incisive discussion of Orwell's intermodern, contested position as a man of British letters, his rhetorical strategies, and literary relations to British women writers of the 1930s, *George Orwell and the Radical Eccentrics: Intermodernism in Literary London* (Basingstoke: Palgrave Macmillan, 2004).

28. Quoted in Eric Hobsbawm, 'Intellectuals and the Spanish Civil War' (2007). http://theorwellprize.co.uk/george-orwell/about-orwell/eric-hobsbawm-intellec tuals-and-the-spanish-civil-war/ accessed 22 February 2018).

29. Scholarship on Bottome's anti-fascist writing includes Pam Hirsch, *The Constant Liberal: The Life and Work of Phyllis Bottome* (London: Quartet, 2010); Alexis Pogorelskin, 'Phyllis Bottome's *The Mortal Storm*: Film and Controversy', *The Space Between*, 6.1 (2010), 39–58; Phyllis Lassner, *British Women Writers of World War II* (Basingstoke: Palgrave Macmillan, 1998); and Judy Suh, *Fascism and Antifascism in Twentieth-Century British Fiction* (Basingstoke: Palgrave, 2009).

30. For further discussion of Ambler's anti-fascist fiction, see my *Espionage and Exile: Fascism and Anti-Fascism in British Spy Fiction and Film* (Edinburgh: Edinburgh University Press, 2016).

31. Virginia Woolf, *Three Guineas* (New York: Harcourt Brace, 1938), p. 103.

32. Hobsbawm, 'Intellectuals and the Spanish Civil War'.

33. Storm Jameson, 'Writing in the Margin: 1939', in *The Writer's Situation* (London: Macmillan, 1950), pp. 189–200 (p. 200).

34. I discuss Burdekin and Smith more fully in *British Women Writers of World War II.*

35. For analysis of anti-Nazi writing by Isherwood, Djuna Barnes, and Virginia Woolf, see Mia Spiro, *Anti-Nazi Modernism: The Challenges of Resistance in 1930s Fiction* (Evanston, IL: Northwestern University Press, 2013).

36. I discuss Frankau's novel extensively in *Espionage and Exile*. Betty Miller's 1941 novel *Farewell Leicester Square* also treats the subject of a British Jewish film-maker who after unsuccessfully attempting a non-Jewish life, embraces his Jewish family. Kristin Bluemel analyses the liminal position of the Jew in 1930s British culture, 'The Urban Geography of English Antisemitism and Assimilation: A Case Study', in *Antisemitism and Philosemitism in the Twentieth and Twenty-first Centuries*, ed. by Phyllis Lassner and Lara Trubowitz (Newark: University of Delaware Press, 2008), pp. 175–95.

37. Quoted in Sarah LeFanu, *Rose Macaulay* (London: Virago, 2003), p. 205.

38. See Kristine Miller's *British Literature of the Blitz* (Basingstoke: Palgrave Macmillan, 2009) for astute analysis.

39. Naomi Mitchison and Rebecca West, 'War Aims', in *Time and Tide*, 2 December 1939, p. 1520.

40. Ibid.

CHAPTER 13

Fascism and Anti-Fascism

Mia Spiro

In his remarks to the Congress of American Writers in 1937, Ernest Hemingway addressed the audience with the bold declaration that 'There is only one form of government that cannot produce good writers, and that system is fascism. [. . .] [F]ascism is a lie told by bullies. A writer who will not lie cannot live or work under fascism.'[1] Fighting fascism in the 1930s, for many of the world's most influential writers, was not simply a political or ideological battle – it was a symbolic struggle for integrity, freedom, and liberty under threat of intellectual enslavement. Hemingway was not alone in believing that writers were obliged to be 'good' through an active critique of fascist ideologies. In Britain, writers and artists were front-row spectators to the growing appeal of fascism in Europe and the threat it posed to liberal values. As they observed the conditions of economic collapse in the United States and Germany, the rise of dictators such as Mussolini and Hitler, and mounting support for the British Union of Fascists (BUF) at home, many literary figures used their skill and influence to respond to the increasingly menacing political climate. Among the many 1930s authors discussed in this volume, Stephen Spender, Aldous Huxley, Virginia Woolf, George Orwell, W. H. Auden, E. M. Forster, Christopher Isherwood, Margaret Storm Jameson, and Sylvia Townsend Warner are but a few examples of those who employed a wide range of strategies to respond to their times. Arguably, no other period since has so galvanised intellectuals and literary figures to become politically active. Rarely has the belief that artists and writers *could* influence politics been stronger than it was in the 1930s.[2]

This chapter will provide an overview of key historical and political events that influenced many of the writers in Britain during the 1930s, and the various methods they employed to respond to the rise of fascism in the 1930s within the larger political sphere. As we will see in what follows, British writers were far more perceptive of political and social theories regarding fascism, and far more concerned with the nuances of international politics, than many historians credit them for. Throughout the decade, writers played decisive roles in the fight against fascism, as both social and political critics, as well as committed activists in organisations spanning a wide range of political platforms, from the far left to more conventional liberal views. Although disillusionment set in for many following the events of the Spanish Civil War, the Munich Agreement, and the Hitler–Stalin pact, for a short while, belief that a cultural revolution could solve the political turmoil seemed reasonable. By outlining the historical context of fascism and anti-fascism in Britain and key writers involved in political writing, we can better understand how history and politics influenced 1930s literary culture.

The Context of Fascism and Anti-fascism in Britain

Although a small group of intellectual elite on the right believed that fascism held possibilities for the rebirth of a 'natural order' that would revive a more authentic form of art and culture (Ezra Pound being one example) – or refused to take a stand one way or another (like T. S. Eliot) – most prominent British writers of the 1930s opposed fascism. For some, such as George Orwell, Margaret Storm Jameson, or Naomi Mitchison, political engagement took the form of polemical works, journalistic essays, public talks, or even reportage and military action in conflict zones. Others, like Virginia Woolf, used both essays and experimental fiction to encourage individuals to think critically about the social issues that had contributed to the allure of fascism, such as the interconnectedness of group thinking, nationalism, war, and patriarchy. And some, like Christopher Isherwood, embedded anti-fascist themes more obliquely, in documentary-like observations of their times. Whichever method they chose, clearly by the mid-1930s British writers were increasingly drawn into debates about how to respond to the emerging political crises. If reading about fascism could inspire individuals to think critically, at the very least, the writer had an opportunity to persuade readers to become less passive in their political choices. The question for many politically concerned writers of the 1930s, therefore, was not *whether* their writing could effect change in the tumultuous political climate but *how*.

Subsequent history has revealed that both questions – whether and how to effect political change – were not simple at all. Looking back on the period in her essay 'The Writer's Situation' (1947), Storm Jameson observes, 'the question of our age seemed to be almost simple. Fascism or democracy? Slavery or Freedom? Tyranny or liberal humanism?'[3] In the political climate of the 1930s these types of simplistic left/right dichotomies, at least for some, appeared necessary to gather enough momentum and garner public support. In its crudest understanding, the two sides were easy to identify: on the left, socialism, headed by the Russian experiment after 1917; on the right, fascism, promoted by dictators and conservatives. In actual fact, the spectrum of ideologies that fell along those dividing lines, the reasons that individuals supported left- or right-wing philosophies – as well as the specific features of these ideologies that drew public support – are more complex. Nonetheless, in most constitutional governments in the West, the main parties were indeed divided along those lines, becoming more polarised at each end of the spectrum as the political future of their countries became more uncertain.[4] Arguably, both socialist and fascist philosophies stemmed from the desire to provide radical, and often utopian, solutions to what appeared to be the failure of democracies to evade war and economic depression or maintain social order. Marxism in particular appealed to British intellectuals who felt that democracies had been ineffectual in solving the unemployment crisis their country faced and in stopping the rise of dictatorships abroad. In the Marxist view of history, social and political upheaval was the rational and inevitable outcome of the masses' disillusionment with capitalism. As Marx posits in the oft-quoted line from the Preface to *A Contribution to the Critique of Political Economy*, when 'the material productive forces of society come in conflict with the existing relations of production', so 'begins an epoch of social revolution'.[5] It was only through massive social change and revolution that freedom, equality, and liberty – the conditions that writers need to create – would be secure. At the same time, Marxist propaganda of the 1930s often portrayed fascism in 'the apotheosis of unreason', a gruesome alter ego growing out of a natural reaction to imperialist, corporate mass manipulation.[6]

Needless to say, the more insightful of those writers of the period understood that the mass attraction to fascism and Nazism could not simply be explained as a product of irrationality or an inevitable outcome of capitalism. Fascism, as many recognised, was menacing because it was attractive. If nothing else, the establishment of Mussolini's fascist dictatorship in Italy in 1922 proved this in successfully gaining support by exploiting the public desire for harmony, unity, and order. By the time Adolf Hitler became Chancellor of Germany in 1933, firmly establishing the Nazi Party's monopoly over the German government, it seemed that all constitutional states were vulnerable to the growing appeal of fascism. Even in Britain, Sir Oswald Mosley's BUF, founded in 1932, was acquiring more adherents; by 1934, at its most popular, the BUF boasted an estimated membership of 40,000 to 50,000.[7] When the Spanish Civil War began in 1936, with Hitler and Mussolini supporting the Spanish Nationalists to topple the democratically elected Republican government, fascism was already a serious concern for British writers, rousing a sense of foreboding in much of the writing of the era. It also inspired many writers in the early 1930s to not only fight with their pens but join anti-fascist organisations, sign manifestos, write propaganda, and raise money for refugees and to support volunteers in the war effort.

What did the term 'Fascism' mean to British writers at the time? In 1944, Orwell acknowledged the difficulty in defining fascism when he remarked that people 'recklessly fling the word "Fascist" in every direction' when what they actually mean is a 'bully'.[8] Even in today's politics, delineating what might be considered 'fascist' is highly contested. Common facets are acknowledged as extreme nationalism, anti-communism (or, rather, a preference for corporatist solutions to economic problems), emphasis on charismatic leadership and authoritarianism, advanced propaganda techniques, an emphasis on youth and military prowess, and a tendency toward political violence.[9] Few British writers of the time differentiated among types of fascism – Italian fascism, Nazism, Action Française, and the BUF all had distinct qualities. Nevertheless, core elements of what Umberto Eco later termed 'Ur-fascism' were being highlighted and critiqued in works from across the 1930s.[10]

The first was the danger of nationalism, especially in the form of home-grown fascist movements. The BUF was not the only, or the first, British fascist movement but it was of grave concern to anti-fascist writers in the early 1930s. Founded in response to Britain's economic crisis (and what was perceived as an ineffectual Labour government response), the BUF promised to rekindle trade and production through radical capitalism, based in the philosophy of economist John Maynard Keynes (i.e. demand-side economics). It also introduced specifically fascist themes based on ideas of a 'Greater Britain' as an autocratic Corporate State, which appealed to many conservatives.[11] The second element of fascism important in galvanising British writers' opposition was their recognition that elitism and racism were not incidental to fascism but rather integral to fascist – and especially Nazi – ideology. Nazi racism in particular posed an immediate and imminent threat to Jews, Roma, and Sinti. For British writers, knowledge of the persecution of Jews was available early on. In 1933, the English translation of Hitler's *Mein Kampf* was in print and widely available, making Hitler's attitudes clear; by 1935, the Nuremburg race laws were also in effect, stripping Jews of their citizenship and rights.

Many writers recognised that not only in Europe but also in Britain Jews were being used as scapegoats for the current state of economic and political turmoil. The third element of fascism to which British writers responded strongly could be called the psychological or cultural dimensions of fascism. Writers of the period analysed the psychology of fascism, observing the draw of charismatic dictators and especially the creation of the fascist spectacle. The allure of fascism, as writers of the time began to discern, was in its ability to reinforce an image of unity and illusion of harmony among the masses through rallies and mass meetings. It was the image of the masses as beautiful, virile, and noble in their pursuit of supremacy that was, according to many theorists, fascism's greatest appeal.[12] This made fascist ideology the greatest risk to philosophical liberalism, which relied on individual thinking and critique. It also posed the greatest personal threat to all outsiders who did not fit into the harmonious image of the Nation, whether they be political opponents, Jews, homosexuals, liberated women, mentally and physically disabled, Jehovah's Witnesses, or otherwise 'asocial'.

If the majority of influential British writers were convinced that the public's passive acceptance of the fascist spectacle would eventually lead to an abrogation of their freedom, there were nevertheless those for whom fascism had a modicum of appeal. Mosley's New Party, the precursor to the BUF, attracted intellectuals like Harold Nicolson, John Strachey, and Aldous Huxley. Other fascist movements – including Action Française and Italian Fascism – also held sway for cultural elites. Ezra Pound's support of Italian Fascism, for example, as well as his antisemitism, originated in a profound dissatisfaction with capitalism and liberal government, as did Wyndham Lewis's support of fascism (although he never joined a fascist party).[13] T. S. Eliot too 'hovered ambiguously on the periphery' of fascist movements and was an admirer of Charles Maurras, the political theorist and founder of France's Action Française fascist party.[14] As a revolutionary movement, fascism provided a more palatable alternative to Marxism for middle- and upper-class sectors of society dissatisfied with the current economic and political climate. Fascism respected capital and property and, moreover, appealed to those threatened by modern social developments, such as women's rights, perceived sexual 'decadence', and increased migration, by stressing traditional 'family values', national unity, and community. What is more, fascism prescribed a cultural revolution that had spiritual aspects. Especially in Britain, the BUF presented itself as a movement of energetic and philosophical vitalism.[15] The virility and spirit projected by fascist parties did not appeal to male followers only: the BUF promoted powerful images of modern women, even as it relegated their roles to the domestic sphere. The BUF women's division was created not long after the establishment of the party, headed by Mary Richardson, a former suffragette; by 1934, it had multiple branches around the country.[16]

By the mid-1930s, many British intellectuals who had early on been attracted to the BUF distanced themselves from their associations with Mosley. Controversy surrounding Mosley's increasingly vitriolic, antisemitic attacks on 'international finance' run by Jews, violent exchanges at BUF rallies, and fear that Mosley was aligning too closely with Hitler caused many to withdraw their support. John Strachey, who had at first edited Mosley's New Party's *Action* magazine, parted ways with Mosley in 1932, the same year when Mosley established the BUF. It was apparent that Mosley was supporting Hitlerism, a movement Strachey unequivocally opposed. Strachey soon after published his widely read Marxist anti-fascist polemic *The Menace of Fascism* (1933), which warns that German fascism's purpose is to drive the masses 'back to the unquestioning acceptance of lives of unrelieved drudgery'.[17] Huxley, too, who had been impressed by Mosley's 'political vigour' and 'radical proposal for national renewal', did an about-face once Hitler became Chancellor and reports of book burnings and Jewish boycotts reached Britain.[18] Following a BUF rally in Olympia in 1934, where anti-fascists were beaten badly by Mosley's blackshirts, and the infamous 'Cable Street Battle' in the East End of London in 1936, membership dropped from an estimated 40,000 to fewer than 8,000.[19] Huxley, among the many who attended the rally, shortly afterwards posited that it was modern despair that drove people 'to seek consolation and a vicarious triumph in the religion of nationalism' and to succumb to the desire to worship 'gods that can be actually seen and heard' – i.e. dictators.[20]

1930s Anti-fascist Writing

If it appeared that modern despair drove people to dictatorships, the question remained: how to prod the public out of their complacency and 'desire to worship'? In his influential study of 1930s literature, Samuel Hynes identifies one of the main concerns among writers of that generation articulating their central question: could a writer 'respond to the immediate crises of this time, and yet remain true to his art?'[21] And what was the best way to respond? Imagined scenarios that would warn the public of impending catastrophe? Realist prose? Experimental works which encourage thinking and questioning to critique the times? Or should writers use their skills and notoriety for a more direct expression of political opinions in essays and public talks? If not all writers responded to these questions in the same way, many of them did self-consciously reflect on the place of politics in art, and the role of artist in politics. Looking back on the 1930s in his essay 'Why I Write' (1946), George Orwell states that even the 'opinion that art should have nothing to do with politics is itself a political attitude'. His goal was 'to make political writing into an art'.[22] For Aldous Huxley, books had the potential to be politically influential, but it was the quality of the reader that determined the impact. As he remarks in 'Writers and Readers' (1936): 'It is possible to argue that the really influential book is not that which converts ten millions of casual readers, but rather that which converts the very few who, at any given moment, succeed in seizing power.'[23] In yet another approach, Stephen Spender divides the 'art' self and the 'political' self, identifying his generation of anti-fascist writers as 'extremely non-political with half themselves and extremely political with the other half'.[24] More decisively, in 1947 Margaret Storm Jameson retrospectively critiques her generation of writers, asserting that in the 1930s writers were far too busy seeking answers to easy 'pro or anti' political questions. In considering the events that happened in the Second World War she determines that the writer's more important role is to 'find out the questions' or to at least have the courage 'to penetrate the darkness closing round us'.[25]

Perhaps one of the most influential writers to grapple with 'the questions' posed to writers in the 1930s was Virginia Woolf. Woolf is widely acknowledged by recent critics for her anti-fascist strategies, and especially for linking gender politics with war and fascism. In her political treatise *Three Guineas* (1938), for example, Woolf conveys an underlying message that fascist thinking 'mak[es] distinctions [...] between the sexes', and its categorisation of 'normal' and 'abnormal' leads to oppression of all types of difference.[26] As Woolf explains to her readers: 'The whole iniquity of dictatorship, whether in Oxford or Cambridge, in Whitehall or Downing Street, against Jews or against women, in England or in Germany, in Italy or in Spain is now apparent to you.'[27] In her fiction of the 1930s, Woolf develops her critique of fascism both thematically and stylistically. While much political writing of the time employed realist prose to introduce a clear, resounding political message, in her fiction Woolf deliberately uses experimental strategies, such as non-linear plots, shifts in time and points of view, and unreliable narration as a purposeful political strategy. If fascist propaganda promoted communal harmony,

Woolf's writing instead encourages readers to think critically – as individuals. She also highlights the subjective experiences of those she would deem part of the 'Outsider's Society' described in *Three Guineas* – and the threat fascism poses to them. Both *The Waves* (1931) and *Flush* (1933), for example, have been interpreted as early warnings of fascist ideology.[28] Even more prominently, *The Years* (1937) highlights BUF graffiti chalked on East End London doors immediately preceding Sara Pargiter's tirade about her Jewish neighbour Abrahamson, 'the Jew in the Bath', who snorts as he sponges himself and leaves a 'line of grease round the bath'.[29] Several critics interpret this scene as Woolf's exposure of British casual antisemitic attitudes of the period, albeit exceedingly problematic in its stereotyping.[30]

This idea of public passivity in response to fascist oppression is reinforced in a number of other works of the era. Christopher Isherwood's semi-autobiographical *Goodbye to Berlin* (1939), for example, uses a documentary style of writing to show snapshots of individuals who passively succumb to Hitler's growing appeal in Germany. A close analysis of *Goodbye to Berlin* reveals how a nation loses its sense of reality when the illusion of unity and harmony has completely replaced reason. In one scene, for example, a Nazi, patrolling a street to watch for 'anti-Nordic' activity, tries to stop two young Jewish men in a car from picking up a couple of German women. A small crowd of spectators gather to watch but do nothing. 'Very few of them sided openly with the Nazi', the narrator comments, 'several supported the Jews; but the majority confined themselves to shaking their heads dubiously and murmuring: "*Allerhand!* [of all the things]."'[31] Likewise, casual antisemitic remarks by otherwise sympathetic characters appear ominous as the novel progresses, such as Frau Nowak who 'would sometimes say: "When Hitler comes, he'll show these Jews a thing or two. They won't be so cheeky then."' Yet, when the narrator points out that Hitler intends to get rid of Jews completely, she takes it back: '"Oh, I shouldn't like that to happen."'[32] By the end of the novel, the support of Nazism that passively allows Jews to be terrorised, the narrator observes, is one of the many signs of doom facing a nation that could be 'made to believe in anybody or anything'.[33]

At the same time that Woolf and Isherwood portray antisemitism from an 'Outsider's' perspective, British Jewish writers were also responding to the terrifying threat of Nazism and continuous verbal attacks of BUF anti-Jewish propaganda. Simon Blumenfeld, in *Jew Boy* (1935), was but one author who challenged the stereotyping Jews faced not only in Germany but at home in London. Alec, the Marxist protagonist of *Jew Boy*, hears antisemitic and anti-communist whispers from the sidelines of a political march in London. In a criticism of both fascists, liberals, and British 'philosemites', Alec responds with an internal counter-voice: 'Jews wouldn't be lumped together as financiers and Bolsheviks. Nor would they be pointed out like tame zoological specimens by tolerantly superior Anglo-Saxons. "See here – these are our Jews. [. . .] they're quite different, but they can't help it."'[34] At the same time, Blumenfeld draws attention to the dissenting voices *within* the Jewish community, using multivoiced dialogue in crowd scenes of synagogues and social clubs, reflecting the wide range and diversity of Jewish viewpoints. Likewise, well-known Jewish political thinkers such as Leonard Woolf wrote treatises against fascism, and publishers like Victor Gollancz supported socialist and anti-fascist authors by promoting and marketing their works.

And yet, anti-fascist affiliations were complicated for many Jews. Clearly, it would have been difficult to find a British Jewish writer at the time who was not against fascism. The Jewish Bureau of the Communist Party of Great Britain (CPGB), established in 1936, mobilised Jews to support the Party, so that Stepney in the Jewish East End became one of CPGB's leading branches.[35] Nevertheless, while scholars agree that a disproportionate number of Jews were members of the CPBG, officially, mainstream Jewish leaders were wary of supporting communist causes, cautious not to contribute to the stereotype that Jews were 'radicals' or in some way unpatriotic as British citizens.[36] By the latter half of the 1930s, the Communist International was also taking an increasingly hostile stance towards 'Jewish cosmopolitan activities' and Jewish intellectuals were often perceived as 'enemies' within the Party.[37] Among others, a great number of Jewish writers in the Soviet Union had been targeted during Stalin's Great Purges (1936–8). Likewise, left-leaning Jewish writers were among the first to be critical of Stalin. Most prominently, Arthur Koestler in *Darkness at Noon* (first published in 1940) produced one of the most famous criticisms of totalitarian regimes, when the protagonist, as he is about to die, becomes confused, unsure if a portrait staring down at him is that of Hitler or Stalin. Koestler, who left the Communist Party in 1938, in this way articulates a sense of disillusionment that was common to many works by Jewish authors, especially as the horror of the Second World War drew near.[38]

The Writer as Activist

If, by 1938, authors like Arthur Koestler were in doubt that the Party could provide a solution to the political crisis of the time, in the early and mid-

1930s a great many authors used both their prominence and their pens to support anti-fascist organisations affiliated with the Communist International. Political activism took a variety of forms: signing pledges, joining the CPGB, supporting affiliated organs and anti-war movements, raising money to help refugees, and even simply publishing in left-wing journals. A number of British writers joined organisations such as the International Union of Revolutionary Writers (IURW, commonly referred to as Writer's International, founded in Russia in 1925). This was followed by other international organisations of progressive writers, such as the International Congress of Writers in Defense of Culture (Paris, 1935), backed by the Communist International. At the Communist International's Seventh World Congress in 1935, plans were laid for a united front against fascism, or the 'Popular Front' (also known as the People's Front Against Fascism and War). The Popular Front aligned a wide spectrum of left-wing, communist, and anti-fascist groups together with the aim of isolating fascist dictatorships.[39] British intellectuals were seen as having a key role to play and were immediately mobilised to help support the Popular Front and use their influence in public campaigns.[40] As Peter Mark's chapter in the present volume discusses in further detail, the *Left Review* (1934–8), the magazine of the British Section of the Writer's International, became a crucial venue for the Popular Front. It published Marxist literary theory but, in line with the Popular Front's goals, reviewed a wide spectrum of literary works. At different points during its four years of production, Auden, Jameson, Mitchison, John Lehmann, Stephen Spender, Winifred Holtby, Nancy Cunard, and Sylvia Townsend Warner, among others, all wrote for the *Left Review*.[41] Later came John Lehmann's *New Writing*, which not only published Auden's poems and Isherwood's sketches about pre-Hitler Berlin but gave space for refugee writers like Anna Seghers and exposed British readers to Spanish, French, and Soviet authors.[42] The Left Book Club, established by Victor Gollancz in 1936, also provided an outlet for anti-fascist and communist writers by endorsing books to its members (estimated at more than 50,000 by 1937) that addressed the moral questions of the period, and included works by John Strachey, Koestler, and Katharine Burdekin (under the pseudonym Murray Constantine).[43]

Other writers who were not part of CPGB-affiliated organisations found ways to lend their support as well. Storm Jameson and Naomi Mitchison, for example, were involved in PEN (now known as PEN International, the association of 'Poets, Playwrights, Editors, Essayists, and Novelists'), which, founded in London in 1921, played a key role in helping Jewish writers find refuge in England. Huxley, a committed pacifist, became the first president of 'For Intellectual Liberty', an anti-fascist organisation 'uniting British intellectuals against tyranny and oppression both at home and abroad'.[44] Along with Jameson, Vera Brittain, Rose Macaulay, and Siegfried Sassoon, Huxley signed the pacifist Peace Pledge Union, refusing to support any kind of military violence, although some were to change their views after 1938, when military intervention to protect victims of Nazism appeared to be the lesser of evils.

Conflict in Spain

When war broke out in Spain, in July 1936, politically active writers were already organised and coordinated, and many were ready to take action against fascism. They were also convinced that their own government was not able – or willing – to prevent the spread of fascism. Since its first democratic election in 1931, Spain had been swinging between left-wing and right-wing governments. When elections in 1936 resulted in a government coalition of left-wing parties (Republicans, Socialists, and Communists), a right-wing military revolt against the democratically elected government began, supported by Hitler and Mussolini. European countries, including Britain and France, felt that the best way to avoid another world war was not to intervene, while the Soviet Union provided support to the Republican side.

Britain's refusal to help the Republican government motivated many anti-fascist writers to take action. In June 1937, Nancy Cunard organised a special issue of the *Left Review, Authors Take Sides on the Spanish War*, with a survey of 150 writers with the question: 'Are you for, or against, the legal Government and the People of Republican Spain? Are you for, or against, Franco and Fascism?'[45] Unsurprisingly, 127 answered 'for' the Republican government. There were those who were more sceptical of the role of the writer in politics. Notably, T. S. Eliot refused to answer the survey, responding: 'While I am naturally sympathetic, I still feel convinced that it is best that at least a few men of letters should remain isolated, and take no part in these collective activities.'[46] Despite the few doubters, the Spanish conflict, to quote Valentine Cunningham, 'became the Spanish War of words and images' as a number of the most influential writers in the world rallied to the Republican cause, producing some of the era's most significant works, including Hemingway's *For Whom the Bell Tolls* (1940), Auden's 'Spain 1937', Pablo Neruda's *Spain in the Heart*

(1938), Orwell's *Homage to Catalonia* (1938), and works by Garcia Lorca, Thomas Mann, and Albert Camus.[47]

British writers not only used their pens to raise both public awareness and money (proceeds from sales of much anti-fascist writing went to help refugees) – a significant number also went to Spain to cover the conflict for media outlets or fight with the International Brigades, which included some 35,000 volunteers from more than fifty countries (2,500 from Britain, Ireland, and the Commonwealth).[48] Among them, Virginia Woolf's nephew, Julian Bell, who served as an ambulance driver; W. H. Auden, who spent seven weeks in Spain broadcasting propaganda; and George Orwell, who was part of the Workers' Party of Marxist Unification (POUM) militia rather than the International Brigades. Many, like Julian Bell, along with writers Ralph Fox, John Cornford, and Christopher Caudwell, were part of the 500 British volunteers who died in the battles.[49] The Spanish conflict was a bloody fight; it was also a dispiriting one that left many of the idealistic volunteers changed forever. On 20 July 1937, Woolf writes of 'incredible suffering' on receiving news of her nephew's death in the war in Spain.[50] Orwell was shot and badly wounded in 1937, and on returning to England wrote a scathing criticism of the Communists and especially the May 1937 revolution in Barcelona. In *Homage to Catalonia* and a news article entitled 'Spilling the Spanish Beans', Orwell presents a first-person account of the arrests, slander, and murder the Communists used to eliminate opponents on the left.[51] When invited to answer the survey in *Authors Take Sides*, Orwell answered that the whole survey was 'bloody rubbish'.[52] W. H. Auden, too, was distraught to find Republican forces burning churches in Barcelona. In his famous poem 'Spain 1937' (the proceeds of which went to the Spanish Medical Aid Committee), Auden describes both the contrition and culpability of the fighters – and the revolutionary movement as a whole – in the famous (and most controversial) lines: 'To-day the deliberate increase in the chances of death, / The conscious acceptance of guilt in the necessary murder.'[53] But there were also many other perspectives. As Janet Montefiore's chapter in this volume suggests, authors such as Cunard and Warner wrote pieces on the war that were long overlooked by critics, and which offer important counterpoints to the writing offered by the Auden circle.

If the beginning of the 1930s began as one of the most idealistic periods for leftist writers who believed that literature could make some difference in their chaotic, unstable, and volatile world, by the end of the Spanish Civil War, in April 1939, with Franco victorious, they held no such illusions. As Albert Camus wrote: 'It was in Spain that [my generation] learned that one can be right and yet be beaten, that force can vanquish spirit, that there are times when courage is not its own recompense. It is this, doubtless, which explains why so many, the world over, feel the Spanish drama as a personal tragedy.'[54] Fascism had won major battlefields in Europe, which added to the disillusionment of September 1938 and the Munich Agreement, in which Britain signed an appeasement treaty with Germany, France, and Italy, an act that allowed Nazi Germany to annex parts of Czechoslovakia, in effect strengthening its position to invade Europe and spread its reign of tyranny. And, for many anti-fascist writers, the Molotov–Ribbentrop Pact signalled a further betrayal when it was signed between Nazi Germany and the Soviet Union in August 1939. After years of fighting against Nazi fascism, in the non-aggression treaty, the Soviet Union promised to support Nazi Germany and not to aid their enemies. In September 1939, Nazi Germany and the Soviet Union invaded Poland and the Second World War began. The Popular Front came to an end.

For many writers on the left, 1939 spelled the end of an era. As Europe was launched into another world war, many writers felt betrayed by the communist movement, and some also feared for their lives as it became feasible that Britain could lose the war against Hitler's forces. Aldous Huxley, whose pacifism instigated him to move to California in 1937, remained a staunch pacifist. Likewise, in January 1939, Christopher Isherwood, along with W. H. Auden, left Europe for America with the admission 'it just doesn't mean anything to me anymore [...] the anti-fascist struggle'.[55] Virginia Woolf was both disturbed and personally affected by the threat of a Nazi invasion, to the point of planning to commit suicide with Leonard if Hitler invaded.[56] After completing *Between the Acts* in 1941, a novel in which planes drone overhead, newspapers report disasters from Germany, and people whisper about war, she committed suicide by drowning herself in the river Ouse.

Even still, writers like Storm Jameson, Orwell, and Arthur Koestler continued to write and critique politics throughout the war and beyond. Indeed, as chapters in this *Companion* such as Kohlmann's suggest, postwar developments such as the welfare state can trace their lineage back to the energies and debates of this earlier era. As Jameson urges other writers in 1939: 'No one must despair, not even those who believe that civilisation cannot survive this war' as 'There is too much to do.'[57] If the early 1930s was occupied with the question of 'Left or Right?' then, by 1939, British writers had other kinds of dilemmas to ask of their writing, namely what role must the writer now play in the catastrophe of war that was to come.

Granted, none of the writers at the time could anticipate that by the end of the Second World War and the Holocaust more than sixty million people would be dead, and close to 70 per cent of Europe's Jews systematically murdered (approximately six million). Yet British writers and artists still had an important role to play, whether by contributing to the war effort against the Nazis or by shaping debates about the radical impact of the war on British society. Jameson's 1939 essay perhaps summed it up best: 'We cannot afford to be blabbers, but we cannot afford to be silenced, either.'[58]

Notes

1. Ernest Hemingway, 'The Writer and War', in *The Writer in a Changing World*, ed. by Henry Hart (London: Lawrence & Wishart, 1937), pp. 69–73 (p. 69).
2. Peter Monteath, *Writing the Good Fight: Political Commitment in the International Literature of the Spanish Civil War* (Westport, CT and London: Greenwood Press, 1994), p. xii.
3. Margaret Storm Jameson, 'The Writer's Situation', in *The Writer's Situation and Other Essays* (London: Macmillan, 1950), p. 2.
4. George Watson, *Politics and Literature in Modern Britain* (London: Macmillan, 1977), p. 40.
5. Karl Marx, 'Introduction', to *A Contribution to the Critique of Political Economy*, trans. N. I. Stone (Chicago: Charles Kerr and Co., 1904), p. 12.
6. Frederick R. Benson, *Writers in Arms: The Literary Impact of the Spanish Civil War* (London: University of London Press, 1968), p. 33.
7. Thomas Linehan, *British Fascism 1918–39: Parties, Ideology and Culture* (Manchester: Manchester University Press, 2000), pp. 160–1.
8. George Orwell, 'What is Fascism?', in *The Collected Essays, Journalism and Letters of George Orwell, Volume Three*, ed. by Sonia Orwell and Ian Angus (London: Secker & Warburg, 1968), p. 114.
9. See, for example, Ernst Nolte, *Three Faces of Fascism: Action Française, Italian Fascism, National Socialism*, trans. by L. Vennewitz (New York: Holt, Rinehart & Winston, 1966); Zeev Sternhell, *Neither Right nor Left: Fascist Ideology in France*, trans. by D. Maisel (Princeton: Princeton University Press, 1995); Robert O. Paxton, *The Anatomy of Fascism* (New York: Knopf, 2004); and Stanley G. Payne, *A History of Fascism, 1914–1945* (New York: Routledge, 1996).
10. Umberto Eco, 'Eternal Fascism: Fourteen Ways of Looking at a Blackshirt', *New York Review of Books*, 22 June 1995. www.nybooks.com/articles/1995/06/22/ur-fascism/ (accessed 22 February 2018).
11. Linehan, *British Fascism*, pp. 85–9; Richard C. Thurlow, *Fascism in Britain: From Oswald Mosley's Blackshirts to the National Front* (New York: Palgrave Macmillan, 1998), p. 140.

12. See, for example, Susan Sontag's well-known description of Nazi aesthetics in 'Fascinating Fascism' as 'choreography' that 'rehearses the very unity of the polity'. *Under the Sign of Saturn* (New York: Farrar, Straus & Giroux, 1980), pp. 91–2.

13. Lewis's notoriously hateful comments about Jews and homosexuals show an affinity for fascist xenophobia, but his defence of fascism was economic. See Wyndham Lewis, *Hitler* (New York: Gordon Press, 1972).

14. Paul Morrison, *The Poetics of Fascism* (Oxford: Oxford University Press, 1996), p. 10.

15. Gary Love, '"What's the Big Idea?": Oswald Mosley, the British Union of Fascists and Generic Fascism', *Journal of Contemporary History*, 42.3 (2007), 447–68.

16. Among the prominent women who supported fascism were two notorious British socialites, the Mitford sisters Diana (married to Oswald Mosley) and Unity. See Julie Gottlieb, *Feminine Fascism: Women in Britain's Fascist Movement* (London: I. B. Tauris, 2003).

17. John Strachey, *The Menace of Fascism* (New York: Covici-Friede, 1933), p. 41.

18. David Bradshaw, 'Introduction', in *The Hidden Huxley, Contempt and Compassion for the Masses*, ed. by Bradshaw (London: Faber and Faber, 1994), pp. vii–xxvi (p. xviii).

19. Linehan, *British Fascism*, p. 161.

20. Aldous Huxley, 'Writers and Readers', in *The Olive Tree and Other Essays* (London: Chatto & Windus, 1936), p. 11.

21. Samuel Hynes, *The Auden Generation: Literature and Politics in England in the 1930s* (Princeton: Princeton University Press, 1982), p. 207.

22. George Orwell, 'Why I Write,' in *The Collected Essays, Journalism and Letters of George Orwell, Volume One*, ed. by Sonia Orwell and Ian Angus (London: Secker and Warburg, 1968), pp. 4, 6.

23. Huxley, 'Writers and Readers', p. 14.

24. Stephen Spender, *The Thirties and After: Poetry, Politics, People (1933–75)* (London: Macmillan, 1978), p. 13.

25. Storm Jameson, 'The Writer's Situation', p. 2.

26. Virginia Woolf, *Three Guineas* (London: Hogarth, 1991), p. 118.

27. Ibid.

28. See Jessica Berman, 'Of Oceans and Opposition: *The Waves*, Oswald Mosley, and the New Party', *in Virginia Woolf and Fascism: Resisting the Dictator's Seduction*, ed. by Merry M. Pawlowski (New York: Palgrave Macmillan, 2001), pp. 105–21; and Anna Snaith, 'Of Fanciers, Footnotes, and Fascism: Virginia Woolf's *Flush*', *Modern Fiction Studies*, 48.3 (2002), 614–36.

29. Woolf, *The Years*, p. 323.

30. Scholars such as Phyllis Lassner, Jane Marcus, David Bradshaw, Anna Snaith, Maren Linett, and Leena Kore Schröder have all interpreted this scene from both positive and negative stances.

31. Christopher Isherwood, *Goodbye to Berlin* (London: Minerva, 1989), p. 236.
32. Ibid., p. 148.
33. Ibid., p. 235.
34. Simon Blumenfeld, *Jew Boy* (London: London Books, 2011), p. 48. See also Phyllis Lassner and Mia Spiro, 'A Tale of Two Cities: Virginia Woolf's Imagined Jewish Spaces and London's East End Jewish Culture', *Woolf Studies Annual*, 19 (2013), 58–82.
35. Dave Renton, *Fascism and Anti-Fascism in Britain in the 1940s* (London: Macmillan, 2000), p. 88.
36. Henry Srebrnik, *London Jews and British Communism 1935–1945* (London: Vallentine Mitchell, 1995), p. 71.
37. Cathy Gelbin, 'Rootless Cosmopolitans: German-Jewish Writers Confront the Stalinist and National Socialist Atrocities', *European Review of History: Revue européenne d'histoire*, 23.5–6 (2016), 863–79 (pp. 863–4).
38. Ibid., p. 873.
39. See Nigel Copsey, *Anti-fascism in Britain* (New York: Routledge, 2017), pp. 43–4.
40. Margot Heinemann, 'The People's Front and the Intellectuals', in *Britain, Fascism and the Popular Front*, ed. by Jim Fyrth (London: Lawrence and Wishart, 1985), pp. 157–86.
41. David Margolies, *Writing the Revolution: Cultural Criticism from* Left Review (London and Chicago: Pluto Press, 1998), p. 1.
42. Heinemann, 'The People's Front', p. 166.
43. Jim Fyrth, 'Introduction', in *Britain, Fascism and the Popular Front*, ed. by Fyrth, pp. 9–29 (p. 19).
44. Bradshaw, *Hidden Huxley*, p. xxi.
45. *Authors Take Sides on the Spanish War* (London: Left Review, 1937).
46. T. S. Eliot, in *Authors Take Sides*, n.p.
47. Cunningham, 'The Spanish Civil War', in *The Cambridge Companion to War Writing*, ed. by Kate McLoughlin (Cambridge: Cambridge University Press, 2009), p. 187.
48. Richard Baxell, *Unlikely Warriors* (London: Aurum Press, 2014), p. 6.
49. Ibid., pp. 6–7.
50. Virginia Woolf, *The Diary of Virginia Woolf, Volume Five*, ed. by Anne Olivier Bell (New York: Harcourt Brace Janovich, 1985), p. 104.
51. On his return to England, some left-wing venues such as Left Book Club refused to publish his work, which they felt did not support the Popular Front. John Newsinger, *Orwell's Politics* (London: Macmillan, 1999), pp. 55–6.
52. Newsinger, *Orwell*, p. 55.
53. W. H. Auden, 'Spain 1937', in *The Penguin Book of Spanish Civil War Verse*, ed. by Valentine Cunningham (rev ed., Harmondsworth: Penguin, 1996), p. 99. The original poem was simply called 'Spain'. Auden edited the lines in 1939 and, in 1950, refused to republish the poem in his selected works.
54. Albert Camus, Preface to *L'Espagne Libre* (Paris: Calmann-Levy, 1945). Cited in Benson, *Writers in Arms*, p. 302.

55. Christopher Isherwood, *Christopher and His Kind: 1929–1939* (New York: Farrar, Strauss and Giroux, 1976), p. 248.
56. In a diary entry, Woolf records that she and Leonard 'discussed suicide if Hitler land[ed]', in *Diaries: Five*, p. 284.
57. Jameson, 'Writing in the Margin: 1939', in *The Writer's Situation*, p. 193.
58. Ibid., p. 194.

CHAPTER 14

Fashioning the 1930s

Benjamin Kohlmann

Periodisation, Eric Hayot has observed, 'is the untheorized ground of the possibility of literary scholarship'.[1] Few decades testify more powerfully to the claim that periodisation provides the basis for literary scholarship – by lending support to scholars' critical habits and to tacit assumptions about literary value – than the 1930s. By turns championed and reviled for the attempt to harness art to radical (left-wing or right-wing) politics, the 1930s can seem 'the most self-contained decade in the literary history of the last century'.[2] When the literary culture of the 1930s is described in this way, as a self-sufficient literary-historical unit, it is often implied that the period was bookended by a surge of *marxisant* writing early in the decade and by disillusionment with literary-political commitment after 1939.

Many critics have claimed that the literature of the 1930s can be subsumed under two complementary 'myths': while the first, originating early in the decade, asserts literature's ability to promote political agendas, the other, crystallising towards its end, insists on the essential incongruity of art and politics. These two master narratives offer contrary assessments of the period's literary politics, yet neither fundamentally challenges the idea that the decade constitutes a largely self-contained unit. Indeed, both accounts periodise the decade in ways that naturalise dominant assumptions about literary value. In order to make these assumptions explicit, we need to address two related sets of questions: first, why the decade came to be thought of as a distinct literary-historical entity and how this view continues to influence current scholarship on the period; and, second, how we might periodise it differently.

The Two 1930s: Anti-Modernism vs. Late Modernism

The codification of the 1930s as a period of politicised art was well underway in the decade itself, and it frequently took the form of an opposition to the

Thanks to Matthew Taunton for discussing an earlier version of this chapter with me.

perceived apoliticalness of 1920s high modernism. 'James Joyce, Mrs. Woolf, T. S. Eliot', the young communist intellectual A. L. Rowse wrote disparagingly in 1931, 'are caviar to the bourgeois and academic public'.[3] Rowse's comment suggests that the young authors of the 1930s viewed their writing not as a continuation of but as an attack on modernism. Many other writers chimed in, insisting that the period of artistic experimentation had proved sterile and that a new art – popular, realist, politically committed – was required in response to the pressing social and political problems of the day. Writing in the 1970s, Stephen Spender recalled:

> Politics, when it overtook our generation, meant for us the partial abrogation of a passive, receptive, analytic poetry – attitudes present [. . . in] the impersonality of Eliot – in favour of a poetry of will and the directed analytic intellect. We were aware of having renounced values which we continued nevertheless to consider aesthetically superior, in Joyce, Yeats, Eliot, Lawrence and Virginia Woolf.[4]

Spender indicates that the young generation's attempt to cut itself loose from a notional 'high' phase of modernism continued to exist in a complex dialectical relationship *with* modernism. His remarks register a break between modernism and the politicised literature of the 1930s, but they do so on terms which clearly privilege the artistic quality of the modernism of Joyce, Yeats, Eliot, Lawrence, and Woolf. The contrast implied by Spender – between the committed writing of the 1930s, on the one hand, and an 'aesthetically superior' modernism apparently untainted by politics, on the other – involves a periodising gesture which has been central to the conventional view of the 1930s as a self-contained literary-historical unit. By conflating periodisation with questions of literary value, this move has helped to enforce a logic of canonisation that relegates the decade's politicised 'poetry of will' to the margins of literary historiography.

On or about September 1939, the myth of the 1930s as a period of politicised art began to harden into literary-historical orthodoxy. The most famous dismissal of the decade's political aspirations came in W. H. Auden's assault on that 'low dishonest decade' in his poem 'September 1, 1939'. Written on the occasion of the outbreak of the Second World War, Auden's line has often been taken to epitomise the disillusionment which many writers felt as a result of the Soviet purges, the debacle of Britain's appeasement policy, and the increasing ideological orthodoxy of the Popular Front. In his book *The Thirties and After* Spender recorded another iconic moment of political recantation. According to Spender's account, Auden visited Cyril Connolly after the war and, seeing a first edition of his Spanish Civil War poem 'Spain' on Connolly's bookshelf, opened the volume and crossed out a number of lines, writing under them: 'This is a lie.' This kind of symbolic self-castigation by former left-wing writers became an integral part of the 1930s' mythical status as a Red Decade, and it effectively served to draw a literary-historical cordon sanitaire around the period.

The most damning retrospective account of the decade's leftist political passions is *The God That Failed* (1949), the book that brought together autobiographical testimonies by former communist fellow travellers including Spender, Arthur Koestler, Richard Wright, and André Gide. *The God That Failed* contributed to the Cold War subgenre of communist recantation which pitted Western liberalism – and its quintessential aesthetic expression, modernism – against the communist East. *The God That Failed* featured stern reproaches made by older authors to their younger selves and it helped to set the picture of the 1930s as a literary-historical anomaly. This view was further cemented by the spate of auto-biographies written by former leftists after 1940, including Louis MacNeice's *The Strings are False* (written 1941, published 1965), Spender's *World Within World* (1951), and Claud Cockburn's *The Devil's Decade* (1973). The anti-communist narrative established by these accounts left little room for alternative views of the decade and its cultural legacy. Among the works habitually ignored by literary historians are post-war autobiographies which refused to let anti-communist triumphalism colour their accounts of 1930s radical culture, such as Douglas Hyde's *I Believed: The Autobiography of a Former British Communist* (1950), Cecil Day-Lewis's *The Buried Day* (1960), and Edward Upward's autobiographical novel trilogy *The Spiral Ascent* (1962–77). The dominant post-war narrative of ideological apostasy also set the tone of what are still the most important scholarly studies of 1930s literature, Samuel Hynes's *The Auden Generation: Literature and Politics in England in the 1930s* (1976) and Valentine Cunningham's landmark *British Writers of the Thirties* (1988). Both studies tell the narrative of the 1930s in terms of a movement from high political ambition to disillusionment. This is not to deny Hynes's and Cunningham's major achievements: Cunningham's study in particular paved the way for revisionist accounts of the decade by drawing attention to the vast field of cultural production that had been eclipsed by the cliquish (and exclusively left-wing) myth of the Auden Generation.

The end of the 1930s afforded many literary figures – self-styled mod-erates like George Orwell and members of the 1920s modernist establish-ment like Woolf – an opportunity to reassert their credentials. In her essay

'The Leaning Tower' (1940), Virginia Woolf complained that the young authors of the 1930s had failed to write poetry which 'we listen to [...] when we are alone': their writings were too 'full of discord and bitterness', too intently focussed on the present, to measure up to modernism's high artistic standards.[5] George Orwell agreed in his essay 'Inside the Whale' (1940), claiming that '[o]n the whole the literary history of the thirties seems to justify the opinion that a writer does well to keep out of politics'. To support his disparaging view of the decade's 'orthodoxy-sniffers', Orwell quoted a few lines from Auden's poem 'Spain' which mused on 'The conscious acceptance of guilt in the necessary murder' during wartime. 'Notice the phrase "necessary murder"', Orwell writes in his famous gloss on this passage: 'It could only be written by a person to whom murder is at most a *word*. Personally I would not speak so lightly of murder.'[6] The politicised writing of the decade, on Orwell's account, was not just formally conservative; even more damagingly, its rhetoric was morally complicit in the armed destruction that was about to be unleashed on the world. Malcolm Muggeridge, in his hostile period-survey *The Thirties* (1940), gloated that 'strangely, sadly and rather foolishly, the thirties drew to a close'.[7] The age of political quietism and middle-class hegemony anticipated by Orwell and Muggeridge had little going for it, but at least it seemed to avoid the ideological extremism of the preceding decade.

The spectacular ideological volte-faces by former communists, including the confessions and recantations collected in *The God That Failed*, have attracted much popular attention. Of similar consequence, though arguably less well recognised, is the degree to which this anti-communism was bound up with the hope that literature after 1939 would return to the modernist gold standard of writing. Orwell's 'Inside the Whale' offered an early articulation of the hope that the passing of the 1930s would enable the re-emergence of a version of modernism. Cyril Connolly's literary magazine *Horizon* (1940–50) likewise propagated the idea that modernism was once more on the rise. In his first *Horizon* editorial, Connolly opined that '[s]ince the Marxist attack ten years ago' good writing 'has been lost sight of, and it is our duty gradually to reeducate the peppery palates of our detractors to an appreciation of delicate poetry and fine prose'.[8] Many former communist sympathisers, including the likes of Spender and Day-Lewis, shared Connolly's assessment. In *The Creative Element* (1953), a book-length rejection of the cultural pessimism expressed in his left-wing classic *The Destructive Element* (1935), Spender aimed to cleanse post-war literature of the 'fatigued disillusionment' which was 'the result of the feeling of artists in every field that their preoccupation with society, and society's preoccupation with them, saps their vision'. The book called for art's retreat from immediate social concerns and for a celebration of 'the creative energy of the individual'.[9]

Connolly's anticipation of a modernist revival seems exaggerated given the success story of post-war social realism and the anti-modernist outlook of literary groups such as The Movement. Even so, the post-war critical reaction against engagé writing has become deeply ingrained in our own periodising habits as well as in our notions of aesthetic value. For example, the American New Criticism emerged in part from a conservative resistance to the politicised writing of the 1930s. Like Woolf and Orwell, the New Critics measured the quality of literary writing according to its ability to resist the immediate pressures of history and politics. One of Cleanth Brooks's central New Criticist essays begins by attacking 'the propaganda art' advocated by 'the Marxist critics of the thirties'. Arguing against the 1930s' perceived preoccupation with politics, Brooks asserts that poetry deals in universal experiences: literature inhabits the realm of 'slow time' – what Brooks memorably calls 'history without footnotes' – rather than the busy sphere of day-to-day *Realpolitik*. William K. Wimsatt, Brooks's fellow New Critic at Yale, likewise sought to disengage poetry from politics by arguing that the quality of a poem is the effect of a complex internal dialectic of 'parts' and 'whole' rather than the result of an instrumental logic of (artistic) 'means' and (extra-artistic) 'ends'.[10]

The attempt to make poetry immune to the vagaries of history is closely connected to the New Critics' anti-communist credentials – a conservative agenda that is already evident in the subtitle ('A Tract Against Communism') which Allen Tate and Robert Penn Warren had considered for their early manifesto *I'll Take My Stand* (1930).[11] The association of modernist literature with the transcendence of historical particularity became a key tenet of literary anti-communism on both sides of the Atlantic, and Spender's decision to dedicate *The Creative Element* to Allen Tate is only one (albeit a particularly instructive) instantiation of this wider trend. Central to this endeavour were the pedagogical protocols of close reading advocated by the New Criticism: echoing Connolly's attempt to 'reeducate' the 'peppery palates' spoiled by the preceding decade, close reading enshrined assumptions about literary value which could be used to consolidate the canon of 'good' modernist writing. The practice of close reading became central to the disciplinary identity of English Literature as an academic field after the end of the Second World War and it served to naturalise the opposition to politicised writing. It also helped to entrench particular periodising habits: the carefully constructed myth of the 1930s as a self-contained literary period became a way of containing the unruly literary-political energies of that troublesome decade.

The evaluative standards embedded in post-war literary criticism have continued to cast a long shadow on more recent accounts of 1930s literature. This is even true of current work in modernist studies which breaks open the perceived self-containment of the 1930s by pointing to the persistence in it of certain strands of modernist writing. The newly expanded remit of modernist studies has fostered a more complex understanding of modernism as a literary-cultural phenomenon and it has given us a range of new periodising labels such as 'intermodernism' and 'late modernism'.[12] By shifting attention to the end points of modernism, these new labels have done important critical work in decentring older literary-historical accounts which traditionally focussed on the question of modernism's origins and emergence. Just as importantly, however, the popularity of terms such as 'late modernism' and 'intermodernism' illustrates how difficult it has been for scholars of interwar literature to move away from the institutional prestige of the 'modernism' label in the first place.

While the narrative of the 1930s as a self-contained decade of politicised art relied on two absolute literary-historical breaks (separating the 1930s from the modernism of the 1920s as well as from the post-war culture of the 1940s and 1950s), more recent accounts have presented late modernism as a tertium quid that links modernism to an emergent postmodernism. This emphasis on the long life of modernism has generated exciting new research, but it has also led to the sidelining of literature which does not fit the modernist mould, including a large segment of 1930s politicised writing. These developments have given rise to a paradoxical situation in which two starkly different accounts of the 1930s exist side by side: while one literary-historical narrative identifies the decade as a period of overtly politicised writing, the other places it in an elongated history of modernism. These two accounts tend to support their periodising claims through recourse to two largely distinct canons of writers. For example, Tyrus Miller's field-defining study of late modernism drew attention to hitherto neglected authors such as Mina Loy and Djuna Barnes, whose writing had helped to extend the modernist paradigm of formal experimentation into the 1930s and to adapt it to the needs of a new generation of writers. By contrast, scholarship that explores the decade's politicised literature usually invokes a different set of authors (e.g. the communist writers John Sommerfield, James Barke, Jack Lindsay, and Edward Upward), genres (e.g. proletarian writing, the historical novel, and the Living Newspaper), and institutions (e.g. the Left Book Club and *Left Review*).

The coexistence of these distinct literary-historical narratives suggests that Orwell's judgement regarding the Spanish Civil War – that the war's 'true history' cannot be written because any account of it will inevitably be a 'partisan history' – can be applied with some justification to the literary history of the 1930s as a whole.[13] How might we move beyond this impasse? In a remarkable passage, one of the period's more sympathetic critics, the poet Roy Fuller, describes a symposium in 1972 which brought together several protagonists of the decade, including the writers John Lehmann, Jack Lindsay, Stephen Spender, and Julian Symons. Recording his surprise at the large size of the audience, Fuller writes:

> I think the main interest [in the Thirties] is ideological, though there is also a technical one. Perhaps neither is ever very clearly felt or expressed. [. . .] The ideological interest has elements of nostalgia. The Thirties were a period when the brotherhood of man was not only believed in but seemed capable of practical achievement. The labour movement, despite its weaknesses, divisions and confusions, couldn't be regarded as other than international in scope.[14]

The passage presents the continued significance of the 1930s not as a matter of academic debate but as born of a popular need: the audience, Fuller claims, is joined by a yearning for the socialist 'brotherhood of man'. This 'nostalgi[c]' attachment to the 1930s offers a different understanding of the period, one that is difficult to comprehend in terms of existing literary-historical categories. Propelled by a desire to recover the vitality of an earlier (and now seemingly lost) ideological cause, Fuller's account indicates that one way to reinvigorate critical debate about the 1930s is by thinking about the decade not as a self-contained period of politicised art or as the end point of an elongated modernism but as a historical moment whose hopes and anxieties are intimately connected to our own present.

The Long 1930s

The curious coexistence of two largely distinct critical narratives about the 1930s – one foregrounding the decade's politics and the other singling out its specifically literary, or modernist, dimensions – raises the question of what a more comprehensive account of the decade would look like. The form which a more inclusive account of the 1930s might take has remained elusive. The encyclopaedic approach adopted in Cunningham's *British Writers of the*

Thirties – with its professed refusal to establish value hierarchies between different genres, texts, and authors – has come closest to offering a total view of the decade. Cunningham himself indicates that the openness of his account, which marshals the literature of the period under loose rubrics such as 'Going Over', 'Seedy Margins', and 'High Failure', is dictated by the fragmentedness of the decade's literary field: 'The '30s do not comprise just a single generation', Cunningham points out, 'they contain at least three literary generations', with the younger writers sandwiched 'somewhere in the middle' between 'a most distinguished older generation, in it the heroes and heroines of British Modernism', and 'the [even] younger brothers: [...] the Roy Fullers and Bernard Spencers, the [John] Cornfords and the [Kenneth] Allotts, the [Charles] Madges and [Gavin] Ewarts'.[15] This observation suggests that a predominantly descriptive mode which mandates maximal inclusiveness is most suited to mapping the 1930s' fragmented literary-cultural terrain.

Literary historians who seek an alternative to the encyclopaedic mode championed by Cunningham might take their cue from Fredric Jameson's article 'Periodizing the 60s' (1984). Jameson's essay engages in the cultural periodisation of a single decade and attempts to portray it in its totality without claiming 'some massive kinship and homogeneity or identity' within the period as whole:

> Here, in any case, the 'period' in question is understood not as some omnipresent and uniform shared style or way of thinking and acting, but rather as the sharing of a common objective situation, to which a whole range of varied responses and creative innovations is then possible, but always within that situation's structural limits.[16]

Jameson proposes that we treat the 1960s as a long decade, making it the focal point from which new analyses of capitalism's crises and cultural transformations in the twentieth century will be able to proceed. Elongating the 1960s in this way, Jameson suggests, can help us interrogate habitual assumptions about the self-containment of literary-historical units by producing a geographically and temporally expansive 'theory of the 60s': 'the discovery of a single process at work in first and third worlds, in global economy and in consciousness and culture, a properly dialectical process, in which "liberation" and domination are inextricably combined'.[17] By way of an analogous operation, literary historians working on the 1930s might attempt a 'characterization of the period as a whole' by making the decade the focal point for an exploration of the economic, political, and cultural dynamics of the mid-century. Such a procedure would defamiliarise existing accounts of the interwar period and the mid-century by treating the 1920s and 1940s as an extension of the 1930s, instead of using those two decades to frame, contain, or subsume the literary field of the 1930s. The task that is involved in this reperiodisation is not simply to make the decade 'longer': after all, most standard accounts of the 1930s (including the books by Cunningham, Hynes, Miller, and Frank Kermode) have already paid attention to the decade's surrounding – literary, social, and political – contexts.[18] Instead, the aim is to identify the specific literary and cultural questions that were raised within the 'structural limits' of the 1930s and to use them as reference points for a new periodisation of the mid-century.

This reperiodisation of the 1930s as a long decade can proceed along a number of different routes. For example, recent scholarship has produced important insights into the development of new cultural institutions (e.g. radio broadcasting, television, the publication of paperback books), emerging artistic genres (e.g. documentary film, mass-produced poetry), and new geopolitical constellations (e.g. the postcolonial) during the decade. A more local, and more specifically literary, instance of these continuities is the Spring 1941 issue of John Lehmann's *Folios of New Writing*, which assembled responses to Virginia Woolf's 'The Leaning Tower' essay by the communist writer Edward Upward, the proletarian author B. L. Coombes, and the poet Louis MacNeice. In contrast to the received view of Woolf's essay, the pieces published in the Spring 1941 issue indicate that critics have been wrong to treat 'The Leaning Tower' (published in an earlier number of *New Writing*) as a conclusive verdict on the 1930s. When it is read in light of the responses by Upward, Coombes, and MacNeice, Woolf's essay is best described as a complex opening move in an ongoing debate about the value of politicised writing that extended well into the post-war years.

Coombes's contribution ('Below the Tower'), for example, notes that Woolf's writings gesture towards a genuinely democratic aesthetic, but it also points out that this aesthetic invariably comes up against the material limits of Woolf's class affiliation:

> Now, I am sure that if Virginia Woolf should visit this mining area in which I live, she would be taken into the parlour – if the family was fortunate to have one – and the behaviour of the adults as well as the play of the children would be restrained to the soberness of a Sunday afternoon; but if I went to that same house I would be invited into the kitchen where the play of the children or the discussion of problems concerning work and living would continue without any pause[.][19]

Woolf's class position imposes strict limits on what she can know, and these limitations explain why 'The Leaning Tower' roundly dismisses 'the stories of working-class writers' as 'grim' and conveying 'either a perpetual snarl or a whine'. As Coombes observes, Woolf's writing is 'not true to life': 'for even in the hardest conditions and heaviest work there is always humour flashing out'.[20] From the reactionary perspective of the bourgeoisie, it appears that the socialists' desire for radical change must inevitably give way to a sense of political futility and limitation. Woolf's essay, Coombes claims, misses the fundamentally future-directed quality of the workers' struggle as well as their unbroken optimism in the face of socialism's failures.

MacNeice's essay ('The Tower That Once') also remarks on Woolf's aesthetic attempt to represent 'a classless society' in which the minds of individuals are 'no longer crippled, evasive, divided'.[21] Like Coombes, MacNeice is attuned to the limitations of this artistic enterprise, and he points out that Woolf is all too willing to buy into the myth of political disillusionment that started to take root at the end of the 1930s. Looking ahead to the genre of ideological recantation popularised by *The God That Failed*, MacNeice complains that '[r]ecantation is becoming too fashionable; I am sorry to see so much self-flagellation, so many *Peccavis*, going on on the literary Left. We may not have done all we could in the Thirties, but we did do something.'[22] Taken together, Coombes's and MacNeice's essays offer a critique of modernism that points towards a revisionist historiography of the 1930s. This alternative account describes the writing of the decade not as a form of late modernism but as a corrective to the class limitations of modernist writing itself. Resisting the 'propagandist use of the notion of failure' which seeks to discredit socialism by pointing to its historical crises, this account also offers a rebuttal of the view that 1939 marked the demise of the 'low dishonest' decade's political hopes.[23]

Of course, the question of classlessness raised so urgently during the 1930s was never simply a matter of aesthetics. Its social and political dimensions came to the fore again in early debates about the welfare state, following Labour's victory in the 1945 General Election. Cyril Connolly, for example, argued against the belief that the socialist energies of the 1930s had simply evaporated in 1939. Pointing out that these energies persisted into the post-war period, Connolly claimed that a socialist reconstruction of Britain's political institutions was possible: 'The Election result', Connolly wrote in September 1945, 'is a blow struck against the religion of money. It has given us a Government of reasonable people, people like ourselves who are "we", not "they", and who are unlikely to be overcome by power.'[24] While some critics have described the establishment of the welfare state in Britain as the consolidation of the capitalist status quo and as the continuation of wartime social patriotism, Connolly's comment indicates that it has also been possible to describe it as the deferred outcome of the collectivist aspirations of the preceding decade, as the co-optation of the radicalised lower middle class into a collectivist post-war politics.

The long 1930s also bequeathed to the post-war decades a distinct form of heterodox left-wing politics. Several key works of post-war cultural criticism – ranging from Richard Hoggart's *The Uses of Literacy* (1957) and Raymond Williams's *Culture and Society* (1958) to E. P. Thompson's *The Making of the English Working Class* (1963) – belong to this tradition. Thompson's publications from the 1960s and 1970s, in particular, amount to a sustained attempt to restore to view the radical culture of the 1930s and the domestic tradition of Marxist thought which he associated with the later interwar period. Thompson's essays on Randall Swingler, Edgell Rickword, Christopher Caudwell, and others seek to establish that '[l]ong before "1956"', that is, the year of the Soviet invasion of Hungary which turned many Western intellectuals against communism, 'there were centres of "premature revisionism" among Communist intellectuals and others, who resisted the didactic methods of the Party's officers, the wooden economism of its policies, and the correct pabulum offered as "Marxism"'.[25] On this account, Thompson's *The New Reasoner* (1957–9), the journal of dissident communism that was the precursor of the *New Left Review* (founded in 1960), can be understood as the rearticulation of a distinctly British brand of communism represented in the 1930s by *Left Review* and other publications.

Thompson was not the only intellectual who made claims for the British post-war left's substantial continuity with the socialism of the 1930s. Jack Lindsay, the Marxist novelist and erstwhile contributor to *Left Review*, for example, pointed out in his book *The Crisis in Marxism* (1981) that his own literary and critical work of the period had arrived at conclusions strikingly similar to those expressed in the oeuvre of the interwar Italian Marxist Antonio Gramsci. Gramsci's work, which only began to be published in English translation in the 1950s, demonstrated that ideological consent in Western societies was being manufactured through 'hegemonic' cultural forms rather than through overt Soviet-style state control. Gramsci's work is widely recognised as a central influence on the emergence of British cultural studies in the 1960s and 1970s, but Lindsay's remarks in *The Crisis in Marxism* and elsewhere highlight that the British version of cultural studies was able to draw on a domestic tradition of Marxist theorising. The persistence of 1930s socialism into the post-war decades was also noted by prominent figures in the emerging field of cultural studies, including Richard Hoggart and Stuart Hall, the first directors of the Centre for Contemporary Cultural Studies (CCCS) at Birmingham (founded in 1964). Hall's essay 'The Social Eye of Picture Post' (1972) pointed to the revolutionary energies of the 1930s as central both to the formation of the post-war British welfare state and to the egalitarian understanding of culture that lay at the heart of the CCCS's own work. Similar claims can be made for the oeuvre of Raymond Williams. In his autobiographical novel *Border Country* (1960), Williams movingly recorded his personal debt to the values of comradeship and solidarity which he associated with the radical culture of the 1930s. And some decades later, in the essay 'The Future of Cultural Studies' (1989), Williams looked back once more at the 1930s, pointing out that British cultural studies had its roots in the WEA (Workers' Education Association), which had flourished during the decade.

Equally important to the historiography of the long 1930s are the sustained reflections on literary-political 'commitment' which were passed down from the decade and which form a neglected current of post-war conversations about literary value. Thompson's 'Outside the Whale' (1960) targeted Orwell's 1940 essay, blasting the 'ideology of apathy' – a 'capitulation to the *status quo*, [...] an abdication of intellectual responsibility in the face of all social experience' – that had paralysed Western literary culture since 1939.[26] One particularly influential contribution to post-war debates about the politics of writing, T. W. Adorno's essay 'Commitment' (1962), had altogether avoided considering the question of literature's social agency in terms of propaganda and *Tendenzpoesie* by locating literature's commitments at the deep level of moral attitudes rather than on the plane of explicit political content. By contrast, most British contributions to this conversation – ranging from John Mander's *The Writer and Commitment* (1961) to Raymond Williams's 'The Writer: Commitment and Alignment' (1980) and Thompson's 'Commitment in Poetry' (1979) – specifically explored the category of commitment with the aim of unsettling assumptions about good writing. Thompson's 'Commitment in Poetry', for instance, implicitly rejected the Adornian dialectical manoeuvre that identified (modernist) art's apparent apoliticalness as the very precondition of its critique of commodity culture. Instead, Thompson contended that the left's defeatist negation of poetry's ability to intervene in social reality was itself the symptom of a '*déraciné* "Left"' that had lost its radical orientation.[27] Thompson's line of inquiry in this essay has more in common with debates about literature's political usefulness that were conducted during the 1930s – in venues such as *Left Review*, the Left Book Club, and the Communist Party of Great Britain's Ralph Fox Writers' Group – than with the forms of modernist autonomy influentially celebrated by the German philosopher Adorno in the 1960s.

Bracketing conventional periodisations in favour of an elongated 1930s can also help us develop critical methods capable of registering the sense of extreme urgency with which committed writing explores the social and political topics of its day. Modernist scholars have long been interested in the relationship between politics and literature in the interwar years, but much of their work has tended to reflect the assumption, paradigmatically formulated in Fredric Jameson's *The Political Unconscious* (1981), that literary works displace politics to the level of form. On this account, formally complex texts offer particularly rich evidence for the existence of an imperfectly repressed political unconscious. This still-dominant view of the interaction between literature and politics returns us to a point made earlier: that the extension of modernism into the 1930s has eclipsed a certain understanding of the ways in which committed writing engages with history and politics. Similar to the practice of close reading championed by the New Critics, the Jamesonian model fetishises formal complexity while depriving politics of its historical specificity. Finding politics encoded in literary form rather than locating it in extra-literary events, Jameson gives us a formalism by other means: the political unconscious, like Cleanth Brooks's concept of 'slow time', does not require us to pay detailed attention to the unfolding of historical events in order to decode the formal composition of any given work.

Reperiodising the 1930s as a long decade makes it possible to trace cultural genealogies that extend well into the post-war period, but it can also help us interrogate conventional assumptions about the politics of writing. It specifically foregrounds the significance of the ephemeral genres and media of 1930s writing – such as the Living Newspaper, the Mass Observer report, the strike pamphlet, or the mass declamation – which were conceived as artistic responses to the unpredictable shocks of contemporary politics. It is hard to think of these artistic forms primarily in terms of a political unconscious because politics is precisely what these works are so centrally and self-consciously about. The focus on types of occasional, ephemeral, and politically active art can prompt a more fine-grained, microhistorical account of the 1930s' politics of writing which reconstructs the decade's literary history as it unfolded day by day, week by week, in response to political events. Such a literary-historical account may well turn out to be another kind of 'partisan history', but it has the advantage of heeding the literary-historical imperative advanced in Jameson's 'Periodizing the 60s', namely that our own historiographical practice must take into account the '*concept* of history' – and the sense of political urgency – which underpins the literary culture of the period under investigation.[28] No matter what form future attempts to reframe and reperiodise the 1930s will take, it seems certain that they will continue to challenge the critical categories that inform – and constrain – the ways in which we make sense of the literary history of the twentieth century.

Notes

1. Eric Hayot, 'Against Periodization; or, on Institutional Time', *New Literary History*, 42.4 (2011), 739–56 (p. 744).
2. Rod Mengham, 'The Thirties: Politics, Authority, Perspective', in *The Cambridge History of Twentieth-Century Literature*, ed. by Laura Marcus and Peter Nicholls (Cambridge: Cambridge University Press, 2004), pp. 359–78 (p. 359).
3. A. L. Rowse, *Politics and the Younger Generation* (London: Faber and Faber, 1931), p. 182.
4. Stephen Spender, *The Thirties and After: Poetry, Politics, People* (London: Macmillan, 1978), p. 17.
5. Virginia Woolf, 'The Leaning Tower', in *The Moment, and Other Essays* (New York: Harcourt Brace, 1948), pp. 128–54 (p. 142).
6. George Orwell, 'Inside the Whale', *in The Collected Essays, Journalism and Letters: Volume One*, ed. by Sonia Orwell and Ian Angus (London: Secker and Warburg, 1968), pp. 518, 516 (emphasis in original).
7. Malcom Muggeridge, *The Thirties: 1930–1940 in Britain* (London: Hamilton, 1940), p. 318.
8. Cyril Connolly, 'Comment', *Horizon*, 1 (January 1940), p. 70.
9. Stephen Spender, *The Creative Element* (London: Hamilton, 1953), p. 13.
10. Cleanth Brooks, *The Well Wrought Urn: Studies in the Structure of Poetry* (London: Methuen, 1947), p. 124; William K. Wimsatt, *The Verbal Icon* (Lexington: University of Kentucky Press, 1954), p. 243.
11. See Barbara Foley, *Radical Representations: Politics and Form in U.S. Proletarian Fiction, 1929–41* (Durham, NC: Duke University Press, 1993), p. 4.
12. See, e.g., Tyrus Miller, *Late Modernism: Politics, Fiction, and the Arts between the World Wars* (Berkeley: University of California Press, 1999); *Intermodernism: Literary Culture in Mid-Twentieth-Century Britain*, ed. by Kristin Bluemel (Edinburgh: Edinburgh University Press, 2009). For the wider resonance of these studies, see the titles of period surveys such as Chris Baldick's *The Modern Movement, 1910–1940* (Oxford: Oxford

University Press, 2004), John Smart's *Modernism and After: English Literature 1910–1939* (Cambridge: Cambridge University Press, 2008), and Christopher Wilk's *Modernism: Designing a New World, 1914–1939* (London: V&A Publications, 2006).

13. George Orwell, 'Looking Back on the Spanish Civil War', in *The Collected Essays, Journalism and Letters: Volume Two*, ed. by Sonia Orwell and Ian Angus (London: Secker and Warburg, 1968), p. 258.

14. Roy Fuller, *Professors and Gods: Last Oxford Lectures on Poetry* (London: Deutsch, 1973), p. 136.

15. Valentine Cunningham, *British Writers of the Thirties* (Oxford: Oxford University Press, 1988), pp. 21–2.

16. Fredric Jameson, 'Periodizing the 60s', in *Social Text*, 9–10 (1984), 178–209 (p. 178).

17. Jameson, 'Periodizing the 60s', 207.

18. For Kermode's account of the decade, see *History and Value* (Oxford: Clarendon Press, 1988). For a recent account of the long 1930s, see *A History of 1930s British Literature*, ed. by Benjamin Kohlmann and Matthew Taunton (Cambridge: Cambridge University Press, 2019); see also the special issue of *Critical Quarterly*, 57.3 (2015), ed. by Leo Mellor and Glyn Salton-Cox.

19. B. L. Coombes, 'Below the Tower', in *Folios of New Writing* (Spring 1941), pp. 30–6 (p. 31).

20. Coombes, 'Below the Tower', p. 35.

21. Louis MacNeice, 'The Tower That Once', in *Folios of New Writing* (Spring 1941), pp. 37–41 (p. 37).

22. MacNeice, 'The Tower That Once', p. 41.

23. On the 'propagandist use' of failure, see Alain Badiou, *The Communist Hypothesis* (London: Verso, 2010), p. 8.

24. Cyril Connolly, 'Comment', *Horizon*, 69 (September 1945), pp. 148–55 (p. 149).

25. E. P. Thompson, 'Edgell Rickword', in *Persons and Polemics* (London: Merlin Press, 1994), p. 239. First published 1979.

26. E. P. Thompson, 'Outside the Whale', in *The Poverty of Theory* (London: Merlin, 1979), pp. 1–33 (p. 3).

27. E. P. Thompson, 'Commitment in Poetry', in *Persons and Polemics*, p. 240.

28. Jameson, 'Periodizing the 60s', 180 (emphasis in original).

Index

AUTHORS

Edward Albee edited by Stephen J. Bottoms
Margaret Atwood edited by Coral Ann Howells
W. H. Auden edited by Stan Smith
Jane Austen edited by Edward Copeland and Juliet McMaster (second edition)
Balzac edited by Owen Heathcote and Andrew Watts
Beckett edited by John Pilling
Bede edited by Scott DeGregorio
Aphra Behn edited by Derek Hughes and Janet Todd
Walter Benjamin edited by David S. Ferris
William Blake edited by Morris Eaves
Boccaccio edited by Guyda Armstrong, Rhiannon Daniels, and Stephen J. Milner
Jorge Luis Borges edited by Edwin Williamson
Brecht edited by Peter Thomson and Glendyr Sacks (second edition)
The Brontës edited by Heather Glen
Bunyan edited by Anne Dunan-Page
Frances Burney edited by Peter Sabor
Byron edited by Drummond Bone
Albert Camus edited by Edward J. Hughes
Willa Cather edited by Marilee Lindemann
Cervantes edited by Anthony J. Cascardi
Chaucer edited by Piero Boitani and Jill Mann (second edition)
Chekhov edited by Vera Gottlieb and Paul Allain
Kate Chopin edited by Janet Beer
Caryl Churchill edited by Elaine Aston and Elin Diamond
Cicero edited by Catherine Steel
J. M. Coetzee edited by Jarad Zimbler
Coleridge edited by Lucy Newlyn
Wilkie Collins edited by Jenny Bourne Taylor
Joseph Conrad edited by J. H. Stape
H. D. edited by Nephie J. Christodoulides and Polina Mackay
Dante edited by Rachel Jacoff (second edition)
Daniel Defoe edited by John Richetti
Don DeLillo edited by John N. Duvall
Charles Dickens edited by John O. Jordan
Emily Dickinson edited by Wendy Martin
John Donne edited by Achsah Guibbory
Dostoevskii edited by W. J. Leatherbarrow
Theodore Dreiser edited by Leonard Cassuto and Claire Virginia Eby
John Dryden edited by Steven N. Zwicker
W. E. B. Du Bois edited by Shamoon Zamir

George Eliot edited by George Levine and Nancy Henry (second edition)
T. S. Eliot edited by A. David Moody
Ralph Ellison edited by Ross Posnock
Ralph Waldo Emerson edited by Joel Porte and Saundra Morris
William Faulkner edited by Philip M. Weinstein
Henry Fielding edited by Claude Rawson
F. Scott Fitzgerald edited by Ruth Prigozy
Flaubert edited by Timothy Unwin
E. M. Forster edited by David Bradshaw
Benjamin Franklin edited by Carla Mulford
Brian Friel edited by Anthony Roche
Robert Frost edited by Robert Faggen
Gabriel García Márquez edited by Philip Swanson
Elizabeth Gaskell edited by Jill L. Matus
Edward Gibbon edited by Karen O'Brien and Brian Young
Goethe edited by Lesley Sharpe
Günter Grass edited by Stuart Taberner
Thomas Hardy edited by Dale Kramer
David Hare edited by Richard Boon
Nathaniel Hawthorne edited by Richard Millington
Seamus Heaney edited by Bernard O'Donoghue
Ernest Hemingway edited by Scott Donaldson
Homer edited by Robert Fowler
Horace edited by Stephen Harrison
Ted Hughes edited by Terry Gifford
Ibsen edited by James McFarlane
Henry James edited by Jonathan Freedman
Samuel Johnson edited by Greg Clingham
Ben Jonson edited by Richard Harp and Stanley Stewart
James Joyce edited by Derek Attridge (second edition)
Kafka edited by Julian Preece
Keats edited by Susan J. Wolfson
Rudyard Kipling edited by Howard J. Booth
Lacan edited by Jean-Michel Rabaté
D. H. Lawrence edited by Anne Fernihough
Primo Levi edited by Robert Gordon
Lucretius edited by Stuart Gillespie and Philip Hardie
Machiavelli edited by John M. Najemy
David Mamet edited by Christopher Bigsby
Thomas Mann edited by Ritchie Robertson
Christopher Marlowe edited by Patrick Cheney
Andrew Marvell edited by Derek Hirst and Steven N. Zwicker
Ian McEwan edited by Dominic Head
Herman Melville edited by Robert S. Levine
Arthur Miller edited by Christopher Bigsby (second edition)

TOPICS